RACE AND ETHNIC RELATIONS

GARLAND BIBLIOGRAPHIES IN SOCIOLOGY
(VOL. 3)

GARLAND REFERENCE LIBRARY
OF SOCIAL SCIENCE
(VOL. 226)

GARLAND BIBLIOGRAPHIES IN SOCIOLOGY

General Editor: Dan A. Chekki

1. *Conflict and Conflict Resolution: A Historical Bibliography*
   by Jack Nusan Porter

2. *Sociology of Sciences: An Annotated Bibliography of Invisible Colleges, 1972–1981*
   by Daryl E. Chubin

3. *Race and Ethnic Relations: An Annotated Bibliography*
   by Graham C. Kinloch

RACE AND ETHNIC RELATIONS
An Annotated Bibliography

Graham C. Kinloch

GARLAND PUBLISHING, INC. • NEW YORK & LONDON
1984

Library of Congress Cataloging in Publication Data

Kinloch, Graham Charles.
  Race and ethnic relations.

  (Garland bibliographies in sociology ; vol. 3)
(Garland reference library of social science ; vol. 226)
  Includes indexes.
  1. United States—Race relations—Bibliography.
2. United States—Ethnic relations—Bibliography.
3. Race relations—Bibliography.   4. Ethnic relations—
Bibliography.   I.Title.   II. Series: Garland
bibliographies in sociology ; v. 3.   III. Series:
Garland reference library of social science ; v. 226.
Z1361.E4K54   1984   016.3058'00973   83-49297
[E184.A1]
ISBN 0-8240-8971-5 (alk. paper)

Printed on acid-free, 250-year-life paper
Manufactured in the United States of America

CONTENTS

PREFACE OF THE GENERAL EDITOR

Forty years ago Gunnar Myrdal's *An American Dilemma* was a watershed in the history of the study of race relations. This classic work attempted to present the problem of race relations in America in all its manifest forms and analyzed the dynamics of social change affecting the problem. Since then numerous studies on race and ethnic relations have been published. However, there are, it seems, more opportunities to study various aspects of race and ethnic relations in the United States and elsewhere today than there are social scientists studying them.

Most, if not all, contemporary societies are pluralistic in the sense that they contain a multiplicity of racial and ethnic groups. Much of our daily life is concerned with intergroup behavior. We do not just react to people solely as other human beings. Our behavior towards others is often influenced by the fact that they are of a particular race, sex, social class, religion and language, etc. Negative attitudes based on beliefs, prejudices, stereotypes and discriminatory practices prevent, especially for visible minorities, equal opportunity in education, employment, power, and status and maintain the status quo within a nation.

Diversity of race, language, religion and values has, in different nations, contributed to harmony and cohesiveness as well as tension and conflict. The size, composition, geographic concentration, and resources of racial and ethnic groups constitute an important base from which majority-minority group relations tend to emerge. Moreover, the roots of racial and ethnic conflict create pervasive political problems. In recent decades "racism" and ethnic relations have become issues of great concern. These problems are often complex, controversial, and sensitive, frequently arousing strong emotions. Moreover, there seems to be little agreement over the causes and solutions.

The Civil Rights Movement was manifested by mass protests, demonstrations, confrontations, civil disobedience, and violence. It produced judicial and legislative actions. These actions played a major role in reducing institutional barriers to the access, by minority groups, to those resources which were hitherto restricted to them. During the past two decades, raised consciousness and collective action have helped blacks and other minorities to make limited advances in their socio-economic and political conditions. Nevertheless, such questions as: "Is affirmative action in its various forms an effective means toward equality of opportunity and condition?" have been raised. The thesis that "social habits and prejudices are so deeply rooted that they are extremely difficult to change" still persists. Even today it comes as no surprise to find discrimination against minorities in schools, at the workplace, in the media, and in the administration of justice.

Sociologists, more than any other social scientists, have been exploring the complex issues of race and ethnic relations and have tried to link sociological theories with specific empirical inquiries. Many studies in the past twenty years reported the emergence of a new sense of racial and ethnic consciousness, identity, and pride leading to the creation of numerous cultural organizations and strengthening ethnic loyalty. The traditional "melting pot" image of America was seriously challenged. Canada, especially since the early 1970's, has been increasingly acknowledged as an "ethnic mosaic."

As researchers, a significant number of sociologists in recent years have not remained value-neutral objective observers and analysts of race and ethnic relations phenomena. Influenced by early socialization, their racial and ethnic background, and subcultural values, many sociologists have, consciously or unconsciously, used ideologically derived approaches. These, in turn, have their impact on the interpretation of their findings, conclusions, and suggested policy directions.

This volume is probably the first of its kind in providing a fairly comprehensive overview of the most important and representative social science research on race and ethnic relations during the 1960s and 1970s. Professor Graham Kinloch of Florida State University is a specialist in this subfield of sociology, and he has published several books and articles on various dimensions of this subject. Moreover, he has firsthand experience of living and working in different multiracial and multiethnic societies such as New Zealand, Rhodesia (now Zimbabwe), South Africa, and Hawaii.

This reference work attempts a thorough coverage of race and ethnic relations in America and throughout the world based on published social science literature during the 1960s and 1970s. In addition to focusing on developments in theory and research methods, a major segment of the book is devoted to intergroup dynamics in the United States. Social scientists interested in comparative analysis will find studies on intergroup relations in Africa, Asia, Australasia, Europe, the Middle East, Central and South America very useful.

This book, besides reporting the complexity and richness of events of the past two decades, presents a review of significant trends in social science research, general conclusions concerning race and ethnic relations, and major factors used to explain such relations. The analysis of the research literature by Kinloch identifies a shift from psychological to more structural factors, a concern with change, measurement problems, and minority rather than majority perspectives of the problem.

Like other sociological subfields, that of race and ethnic relations probably will grow vigorously by internal dialectics. It is in this context that we can observe that while it is voluminous, the research is particularly scanty when it comes to reducing prejudice and discrimination effectively. Sociological research on race and ethnic relations, like much of sociology, appears to follow recent events and concentrate on "relevant" topics of the day rather than focus on this crucial social problem in its long-term context of inequality, exploitation, oppression, and injustice.

Different sociological researches often lead to different results and, thus, inconsistent and sometimes even contradictory generalizations. This branch of sociology is no exception. There is a need to explore further the causes, consequences, and patterns of intergroup rivalry and conflict and, more importantly, the cure and prevention of racial and ethnic group hatred, violence, and resulting loss of life and property. At the present stage, when much of the literature on race and ethnic relations is long on fact and short on theory, it is necessary to undertake more intra- and international comparative analyses. This would go a long way in building theory and in designing appropriate strategies to deal with the problem. Furthermore, it should be emphasized that since most research continues to be carried out by majority whites, more research needs to be undertaken by minority social scientists to provide an "insider's view" of the problem.

Outbreaks of racial violence and frequent ethnic tensions and conflicts in many parts of the world constantly remind us of the need to understand the problem and suggest policy alternatives in an attempt to contribute to the resolution of what is potentially an important national and international concern. This volume, I hope, would serve as an important aid toward an attempt to achieve this goal.

Dan A. Chekki
University of Winnipeg

FOREWORD

Race and ethnic relations have long been a central concern of the social sciences. Recent decades are particularly relevant to an understanding of the dynamics of such intergroup relations given the striking events and the pace of social change during the 1960s and 1970s. Accordingly, this bibliography aims at a thorough coverage of these intergroup relations both in America and the world as reflected in the major social science literature published during these two decades.

Approximately 120 social science journals along with a wide range of relevant texts and books were consulted and annotated for the period in question, producing a total of 1,068 entries. These were then sorted into major categories which emerged from the literature rather than being predefined. Chapter topics developed as follows: Chapter 1 focuses on general bibliographies and analyses of research trends in race and ethnic relations. Chapter 2 contains articles on theories and methodologies used to explain such relations, including discussions of the sociology of race and ethnic relations, methodological issues involved in analyzing these intergroup dynamics, the history of race and ethnic relations, theories focusing on socioeconomic and power factors underlying such relations, explanations concerned with the long-term effects of intergroup contact, deprivation theory, labeling theory, theories concerned with demographic factors, structure-functional and system theories, typologies of race and ethnic relations and types of intergroup relations. Chapter 3, representing the bulk of the bibliography, centers on race and ethnic relations in the United States. Its major subsections deal with general and comparative intergroup relations, whites such as Southerners, ethnic immigrants, Jewish Americans, Italian and Latin Americans, and a large section on black Americans focusing on their attitudes, identity, economic and occupational conditions, education, characteristics of the black ghetto, black history, the relationship between blacks and the law, and emerging black politics. Other racial groups in the society include Asian Americans, intergroup relations in Hawaii, Indian Americans, Mexican Americans, and Puerto Ricans. The next subsection summarizes studies dealing with racial attitudes and stereotypes, minority group identity, prejudice, social distance, and factors influencing attitudinal change. Discrimination and segregation are then dealt with, including social and attitudinal discrimination, economic and occupational discrimination, residential segregation, and other forms of discrimination including the negative experiences of minorities in the military and public transportation. Racial and ethnic conflict in the society are concentrated on next, including social movements, the dynamics of conflict and protest, as well as factors underlying riots and disturbances. The final section on American intergroup relations deals with ongoing social change, desegregation, assimilation, and integration.

Chapter 4 turns to literature which analyzes intergroup relations in other societies. This begins with comparative studies of race and ethnic relations worldwide, moving to intergroup relations in Africa generally, articles dealing with the Mid-East, including Israel, and studies of other areas of Africa, including Zimbabwe and South Africa. Europe is also covered, highlighting Great Britain, Ireland, France, Belgium, West Germany, Switzerland, Italy, Turkey, and the U.S.S.R. The final section of this chapter focuses on a number of other areas of the world including Canada, Mexico, the Caribbean, South America, Australasia, the Pacific, and Asia. The bibliography ends with a list of major journals and their addresses.

The introductory chapter that follows this Foreword focuses on major trends in this bibliography as a whole, general conclusions with respect to its central topics, factors used to analyze them, and an analysis of predominant journals in the field. Finally, it should be noted that articles were annotated in accordance with the racial terminology used by their authors (e.g., "Negroes," "blacks," "Afro-Americans") rather than the compiler.

THE CHANGING STUDY OF
RACE AND ETHNIC RELATIONS:
AN INTRODUCTION

The 1960s and 1970s were of crucial significance to race and ethnic relations in American society: the assassinations, civil rights movements and riots of the 1960s, combined with attempts at desegregation, equality of opportunity and integration, the bitterness of the Vietnam War, and the economic recession of the 1970s make these decades fascinating periods of analysis. This bibliography attempts to cover the complexity and richness of these events by analyzing the major literature developed by social scientists concerned with them. In this introductory discussion we shall examine the major trends in this literature over time, general conclusions concerning race and ethnic relations, major factors used to explain such relations, and the major publishing outlets used to disseminate their work.

I

The distribution of major research topics by period of publication is presented in Table 1. While not assuming that these data completely represent all race and ethnic relations literature published during these two decades, it appears reasonable to assume that the trends reflected in them are useful indicators of particular research interests over time. As can be clearly seen, the early 1960s involved an emphasis on research bibliographies, white Americans, racial and ethnic attitudes, and change in intergroup relations. However, this emphasis began to shift in the latter part of the decade to a concern with intergroup conflict, black Americans, and other minorities in the society, reflecting

Table 1. Distribution of Major Topics by Publication Period

TOPICS

PUBLICATION PERIOD	Bibliographies Research Trends %	Theories %	General/ Comparative %	U.S. Whites %	Blacks %	Other Minorities %	Attitudes %	Discrim./ Segregation %	Conflict %	Change %	Other Societies/ Comparative %	Africa %	Europe %	Other Societies %
1960-1964	55.1	16.2	8.8	38.2	22.3	15.6	31.8	18.2	27.2	30.0	6.1	26.5	21.2	38.6
1965-1969	11.1	15.6	10.5	5.9	23.3	20.3	18.9	11.4	25.9	17.4	9.1	16.9	18.2	13.6
1970-1974	22.2	31.8	38.6	26.5	27.2	35.9	26.5	14.8	37.0	15.3	42.4	24.1	27.3	6.8
1975 +	11.1	36.4	42.1	29.4	27.2	28.1	22.7	55.7	9.9	37.5	42.4	32.5	33.3	41.0
N:	18	154	57	34	103	64	132	88	81	144	33	83	33	44

the emerging racial conflict of the times. The early 1970s, on the other hand, were concerned with comparative race and ethnic relations and an emphasis on theoretical attempts to understand such relations generally along with a continuing interest in conflict. The later 1970s continued to reflect a concern with comparative understanding, theoretical attempts to explain race and ethnic relations, as well as a focus on whites and other racial minorities within the society. A distinct difference, however, was the major concern with discrimination and segregation, indicating a clear shift away from an attitudinal view of this social problem. Such trends suggest a movement away from the psychological towards a more structural understanding of the problem, understood in theoretical and comparative contexts, thereby elevating the understanding of race and ethnic relations to a more general level.

Examining these trends in terms of major subtopics not reflected in these tabular data, there is a clear emphasis on general bibliographies and research trends in the early 1960s rather than later periods. Concern with the sociology of race and ethnic relations as well as methodological issues, the history of these relations, socioeconomic and power-oriented theories, and theories focusing on deprivation, demographic factors, systemic elements and typologies of intergroup relations all tend to emerge in the 1970s, indicating a shift toward more theoretical, methodological, and historical concerns.

American race and ethnic relations reveal a comparative emphasis during the 1970s also, along with an interest in the society's white majority. Literature on blacks indicates a concern with attitudes and identity during the 1960s, with negative socioeconomic and ghetto conditions a central focus in the late 1970s. Black history is also a concern in the 1970s as is a research interest in other minorities such as Asian Americans, Hawaiians, American Indians, and Mexican Americans.

Attitudes and stereotypes are central issues throughout both decades although research on prejudice reached its peak during the early 1960s. Social distance was also an early interest while concern with attitudinal change tended to emerge later. Negative social conditions reflected in discrimination and segregation, however, were clearly highlighted during the late 1970s.

It would be reasonable to expect that concern with intergroup conflict such as social movements, protest, and riots would be highest during the years in which they occurred. The research literature clearly reflects this in the emphasis on riots during the 1960s, social movements during the early 1970s, and protests during the initial years of both decades. A fairly accurate reflection of historical events appears evident here.

The trends with respect to changing race and ethnic relations are not as clear: interest in social change, desegregation, and integration is reflected throughout both decades, although assimilation appears to be a more recent concern during the late 1970s. Attempts to deal with race and ethnic relations in terms of ongoing change, desegregation, integration, and assimilation are clearly reflected in the research literature.

We turn finally to race and ethnic relations in other societies. As indicated earlier, a general concern with comparative intergroup relations emerged primarily in the 1970s. Interest in Africa generally and South Africa in particular was highest during this period, as was the case with intergroup relations in Great Britain, Canada, Australasia and the Pacific, while South America and Asia were analyzed primarily in earlier periods. It should be stressed, however, that in many cases the number of non-U.S. research articles covered is too small to permit accurate generalizations.

To summarize, the race and ethnic relations literature tended to focus on bibliographies, whites, attitudes, and change during the early 1960s, moving to a concern with blacks, other minorities, and conflict in the latter portion of the decade. The early 1970s involved more comparative and theoretical analyses of intergroup relations, a concern with conflict and white reactions to it, while the late 1970s reflected increased interest in the problems of discrimination and segregation. Historical events and a shift towards the more comparative and structural appear to be reflected here.

II

What general conclusions is it possible to draw from this large body of literature? We shall attempt to summarize them as follows:

1. General bibliographies highlight a declining emphasis on prejudice combined with increased concern over discrimination, nationalism, and attempts to broaden the concept of minority status.

2. Analyses of research trends indicate increasing concern with change, structural factors, and critiques of majority social scientists as ethnocentric.

3. Those concerned with the sociology of race and ethnic relations emphasize that such a topic is part of general sociological theory.

4. Methodological concerns reflect increased interest in the historical context of intergroup relations, measurement problems, ambiguous definitions of key concepts, the difficulties posed by ethnocentrism and the changing roles of social scientists.

5. The history of race and ethnic relations reveals increasing concern with the development of the notion of race, changes in intergroup relations, and the viability of minority institutions (e.g., the family and press) under negative conditions (i.e., slavery) in contrast to negative white attitudes, particularly racial supremacy.

6. Socioeconomic-oriented theories underline factors such as power struggles, intergroup competition, resource mobilization, intergroup threat, class approaches, conflict-oriented explanations, demographic factors and the colonial model in an attempt to understand these relationships.

7. Other theories delineate the positive and negative effects of different types of contact.

8. Deprivation theory highlights the importance of voluntary organizations to minority political efficacy.

9. Labeling theory explains elite prejudice in terms of projections and "blaming the victim."

10. Demographic theories highlight rural-urban differences, North-South contrasts, the effects of migration, and tipping point in minority-majority relations.

11. System-oriented theories critique structure-functionalism for its inability to deal with conflict and change.

12. Those concerned with developing typologies of race and ethnic relations delineate different types of ethnic groups and minority goals.

13. Those concerned with different types of intergroup situations underline the effects of intergroup interaction and situational definitions of situations on intergroup relations in particular contexts.

Turning specifically to race and ethnic relations in the United States, we can make these observations.

14. On the general and comparative level, minority group profiles of educational, occupational, economic, and demographic characteristics are developed, combined with a major emphasis on racial discrimination, the historical emergence of racial hierarchies, the effects of urbanization, and a wide range of texts dealing primarily with prejudice and discrimination.

15. With respect to whites, their ethnocentrism, Protestantism, resentment against migrating minorities, inconsistent attitudes, and community organizations are highlighted.

16. Turning to Jewish Americans, the literature emphasizes their self-segregation, low levels of assimilation, and generally high social status.

17. Italian Americans are depicted primarily in terms of the negative conditions surrounding their migration into the society.

18. Latin Americans are also portrayed negatively with respect to the conflict and discrimination they have experienced in the society.

19. Blacks are depicted in terms of their negative attitudes, rage and frustration, negative class effects, the continuing socioeconomic gap between themselves and whites, the degree to which they continue to experience educational and professional discrimination, the academic barriers experienced within educational institutions, the strengths of their community structures, the history of anti-black prejudice, increasing residential segregation, disproportionate subjection to the draft, and emergence of nationalist/liberationist political orientations over time in the context of socioeconomic change.

20. Asians, in contrast, are viewed as high in cultural and educational achievement and defined as one of the society's most successful minorities.

21. Hawaiian intergroup relations are viewed as class-based with high levels of prejudice among Asian Americans.

22. American Indians are depicted in terms of their trib-

alism, poverty, cultural differences, isolation from the larger society, and reserve-urban differences.

23. Mexican Americans are noted for their low social status, political participation, self-esteem, negative socioeconomic conditions and colonial-type domination.

24. Puerto Ricans are similarly viewed in terms of their low status and lack of community organization.

With respect to intergroup attitudes and prejudice, the literature indicates that:

25. Racial and ethnic attitudes tend to reveal declining support for integration, high levels of institutionalized racism, parent-child attitudinal similarities, the effects of background factors such as education, race, religion, and class on prejudice, attitudes towards desegregation and the effects of integration.

26. Minority group identity reveals the strength of ingroup loyalty as well as increasing ethnic consciousness.

27. Prejudice reflects background factors, family structure, religion, authoritarianism, self-centeredness, frustration, and political conservatism.

28. Social distance is also influenced by factors such as sex, age, region, and type of society, and appears to be declining over time but is reinforced by segregation.

29. Changing attitudes are related to integration, education, socioeconomic status, urban residence, reference groups, age, and positive interaction.

Turning to discrimination and segregation, it appears that:

30. Negative attitudes are a function of fear, conventionalism, and conservative political background.

31. Economic and occupational discrimination reflect high levels of segregation, racial exclusion, the effects of regional differences, increasing interracial disparities, subcultural factors, racial competition, and high levels of minority layoffs.

32. Educational segregation tends to be maintained.

33. Educational discrimination in graduate school affects black as well as ethnic minorities.

34. Residential segregation is influenced by socioeconomic status, cultural background, demographic differences, and geographical region.

35. Other areas of discrimination reveal negative treatment

in the military, public transportation, sports, and the provision of family planning facilities.

In regard to intergroup conflict, the literature reveals that:

36. Minority social movements are part of a worldwide struggle, experience leadership problems, and have reduced their ties with white liberals.

37. Intergroup conflict is a function of partial minority assimilation and is part of the emergence of minority power.

38. Riots are explained in terms of social psychological as well as structural factors, the effects of deprivation and discrimination, reactions to police harassment, minority population size, are influenced by the urban context, and tend to spread.

Research on changing intergroup relations appears to indicate:

39. A need for planned change exists, minorities have gained certain advantages over time, legal rationality is crucial in maintaining positive change, attitudinal modification tends to be slow, affirmative action has increased rather than reduced some tensions, while industrialization and urbanization have effected the most significant economic changes.

40. Desegregation has met with mixed acceptance, reflects peer group pressure, requires government intervention and enforcement, and highlights the importance of role clarity in changing conditions.

41. Assimilation is reflected in declining ethnic endogamy, does not appear to be increasing, is reflected in structural rather than behavioral assimilation, while racial assimilation is particularly slow.

42. Finally, ongoing integration is viewed by minorities as too slow, tends to reduce conflict, appears to meet with increased acceptance, produces anxiety, reflects structural rather than social integration, tends to be resisted more by females, and highlights the importance of cooperative learning environments in the encouragement of intergroup friendships.

Finally, analyses of intergroup relations in other societies reveal that:

43. Comparative analyses emphasize economic and political factors, varying cultural values, the worldwide impact of white supremacy, potent effects of religion and conformity-oriented

attitudes, negative effects of economic development, and continuing relevance of class and ethnic factors.

44. Analyses of Africa as a whole highlight the reinforcement of stratification by modernization, low impact of colonialism in certain areas, and the potent effect of white urbanization.

45. Intergroup relations in the Mid-East highlight ethnic identity, prejudice against newcomers, and effects of religious background.

46. Intergroup relations in West, East, and Central Africa are defined by tribalism, elite size, and residential propinquity.

47. Intergroup relations in Zimbabwe involve ethnic change, changing attitudes, and the influence of demographic and economic factors on prejudice and racial conflict.

48. The South African situation illustrates the relevance of racial ideology, adaptation of the Afrikaner elite, marginality of the Coloreds, economic factors such as a split labor market, ongoing effects of economic change, and the continuation of white fear and racial prejudice.

49. In Europe, particularly Great Britain, intergroup relations are tied to the processes of immigration and urbanization, negative effects of religious background, competitive neighborhoods and comparatively low minority numbers. However, Ireland, France, and Belgium indicate the negative consequences of class stratification, regionalism, black immigration and ethnic conflict.

50. Finally, minority group relations in other areas of the world are analyzed in terms of ethnic dominance, unity, and status distinctions, while racial situations existing in Mexico, South America and the Pacific are conceptualized negatively with respect to elite control, subordination, and prejudice.

What do such statements indicate about the status of race and ethnic relations literature as a whole? We turn next to summarize the major factors used to conceptualize, portray, and explain such relations.

III

Looking at this literature as a whole, certain trends are clearly evident.

1. Studies of race and ethnic relations are increasing in structural emphasis, a concern with change, measurement problems, and minority rather than majority perspectives of the problem.
2. Theories have shifted from the psychological to the more structural, demographic, and social psychological.
3. Such relations in the United States are portrayed in terms of group profiles, whites are seen as ethnic and successful while other minorities are depicted in negative psychological and socioeconomic terms.
4. Negative attitudes are correlated with a wide range of background factors while change is conceptualized in terms of intergroup interaction and integration.
5. Discrimination and segregation are explained in terms of all major factors including the psychological, cultural, demographic, background characteristics, and intergroup competition.
6. Intergroup conflict is also accounted for in such terms but with specific emphasis on the effects of minority exclusion from the larger society.
7. Change in intergroup relations requires training and planning along with majority acceptance.
8. Intergroup relations in other societies are compared on the basis of structural, socioeconomic, and demographic factors rather than using psychological explanations, European situations are portrayed in ethnic terms, and other situations are seen as negative and primarily racial in nature.

To summarize, it is evident that the research literature has shifted from psychological to more structural factors, including demographic group profiles, delineation of minority group situations in structural, demographic, and cultural terms, with change dealt with in terms of training and majority acceptance, and non-European societies viewed in racial rather than ethnic terms, reflecting a general movement away from negative attitudes to an emphasis on discriminatory situations. Such perspectives and changes, of course, reflect the degree to which the field continues to be under the control of majority academics and their limited responses to historical, socioeconomic, demographic, and political change.

We turn finally to the literature's major publishing outlets.

IV

While a wide range of approximately 120 journals was consulted in compiling this bibliography, tabulation of the articles revealed the following concentration: *Social Forces* (72 articles), *Phylon* (62), *Race* (41), *Sociology and Social Research* (35), *Social Problems* (31), *American Journal of Sociology* (29), *American Sociological Review* (26), *The Annals of the American Academy of Political and Social Science* (26), *The Journal of Social Issues* (24), and *Social Science Quarterly* (23). The top ten journals thus tend to reflect sociology predominantly but also include interdisciplinary outlets with a wide range of editorial boards and authors. The journals cover the full spectrum of the social sciences.

Race and Ethnic Relations

CHAPTER I

GENERAL BIBLIOGRAPHIES AND RESEARCH TRENDS

GENERAL BIBLIOGRAPHIES

1. Barron, Milton L. "Recent Developments in Minority and Race Relations," ANNALS OF THE AMERICAN ACADEMY OF POLITICAL AND SOCIAL SCIENCE, 420 (1975), 125-176.

   An analysis of the years 1968-73, highlighting increased ethnic nationalism, ethnic consciousness, enlargement of the concept of minority status, changing demographic and status dynamics of minorities, emergence of black studies, and attempts to achieve integration.

2. Blumer, Herbert. "Recent Research on Racial Relations: United States of America," INTERNATIONAL SOCIAL SCIENCE BULLETIN, 10 (1958), 403-447.

   Reports studies dealing with racial minorities, types of discrimination, racial prejudice, critiques of prejudice research, and changes in prejudice.

3. Gordon, Milton M. "Recent Trends in the Study of Minority and Race Relations," ANNALS OF THE AMERICAN ACADEMY OF POLITICAL AND SOCIAL SCIENCE, 350 (1963), 148-156.

   Reviews research focusing on the scientific meaning of race, causes of prejudice, the issue of Negroes and discrimination, as well as ethnic and religious minorities.

4. Yinger, J. Milton. "Recent Developments in Minority and Race Relations," ANNALS OF THE AMERICAN ACADEMY OF POLITICAL AND SOCIAL SCIENCE, 378 (1968), 130-145

Summarizes studies dealing with demographic trends, theory and method, the social psychology of prejudice and discrimination, pluralism, the relationship between minorities and major institutions, the civil rights movement and Black Power.

RESEARCH TRENDS

5. Bahr, Howard M. "Influential Scholars and Works in the Sociology of Race and Minority Relations, 1944-1968," THE AMERICAN SOCIOLOGIST, 6 (1971), 296-298.

A study of the most cited authors in ten leading sociological journals for the period 1944-1968, highlighting E. Franklin Frazier, Robert E. Park, Gunnar Myrdal, J.G. Drake and Cayton, and T. Adorno.

6. Hannerz, Ulf. "Research in the Black Ghetto: A Review of the '60's," JOURNAL OF ASIAN AND AFRICAN STUDIES, 9 (1974), 139-159.

Reviews research using participant observation and argues for the need to take socioeconomic and mainstream cultural environments into account.

7. Harris, Marvin. "Race Relations Research: Auspices and Results in United States," SOCIAL SCIENCE INFORMATION, 1 (1962), 28-51.

A critique of literature focusing on intergroup relations, and advocates testing fundamental propositions regarding social and cultural change.

8. Lambert, John R. and Camilla Filkin. "Race Relations Research: Some Issues of Approach and Application," RACE, 12 (1971), 329-335.

A study of housing problems encountered by colored immigrants in Great Britain, emphasizing the relevance of system constraints rather than individual attitudes.

9. Long, Herman H. "Major Issues of Intergroup Relations of the'60's," JOURNAL OF INTERGROUP RELATIONS, 1 (1960), 5-11.

While race relations achievements in the 1950's are significant, remaining issues include housing quotas, federal intervention, and the clash between property and human rights.

10. Mead, Margaret. "The Student of Race Problems Can Say.....," RACE, 3 (1961), 3-9.

Highlights the scapegoating function of racism and argues that more change can be effected by emphasizing the economic waste caused by prejudice.

11. Michel, Andree. "New Trends in the Sociology of Race Relations," REVIEW FRANCAIS SOCIOLOGIE, 3 (1962), 181-190.

Examines the study of race relations in the U.S., England, and France, indicating a shift away from prejudice towards a concern with the social environment, action research, ecological perspectives, and power structures.

12. Montero, Darrel. "Research among Racial and Cultural Minorities: An Overview," THE JOURNAL OF SOCIAL ISSUES, 33 (1977), 1-10.

Deals with the problem of majority social scientists carrying out research dealing with minorities.

13. Richmond, Anthony H. "Research on Racial
    Relations: Britain," INTERNATIONAL SOCIAL
    SCIENCE BULLETIN, 10 (1958), 344-372.

    Surveys research on racial attitudes, colored commun-
    ities, colored colonial workers, colonial students,
    and Jews.

14. Rossi, Peter H. "New Directions for Race Relations
    Research in the '60's," REVIEW OF RELIGIOUS
    RESEARCH, 5 (1964), 125-132.

    Emphasizes the need for research on social changes in
    race relations, the politics involved in such changes,
    as well as understanding religious and ethnic
    minorities.

15. Sodhi, Kripal S. "Recent Research on Racial Relations:
    Federal Republic of Germany," INTERNATIONAL SOCIAL
    SCIENCE BULLETIN, 10 (1958), 387-403.

    Summarizes empirical studies of racial prejudice in
    Western Germany and outlines a long-range project
    focusing on intergroup stereotypes and perception.

16. Tumin, Melvin M. "Some Social Consequences of
    Research and Racial Relations," AMERICAN SOCIOL-
    OGIST, 3 (1968), 117-123.

    Discusses the findings of basic and applied research-
    ers and reactions to them, highlighting the relevance
    of such studies to peaceful change.

17. Vander Zanden, James W. "The Sociological Study of
    American Blacks," SOCIOLOGICAL QUARTERLY,14 (1973)
    32-52.

    Advocates the use of concepts such as network and
    field in understanding black disadvantages, racist
    ideas, and discrimination.

18. Ward, Barbara E. "Recent Research on Racial Relations: Africa," INTERNATIONAL SOCIAL SCIENCE BULLETIN, 10 (1958), 372-380.

Summarizes major research to date which is seen as focusing on colonial prejudice and stratification, ethnocentrism, and the effects of economic development.

CHAPTER II

THEORY AND METHODOLOGY

SOCIOLOGY OF RACE AND ETHNIC RELATIONS

19. Armstrong, Edward G. "Black Sociology and Phenom-
    enological Sociology," SOCIOLOGICAL QUARTERLY,
    20 (1979), 387-397.

    A comparative analysis of black sociology and
    phenomenological sociology, emphasizing their
    complementarity with respect to aims, critique,
    and methods.

20. Banton, Michael. "Sociology and Race Relations,"
    RACE, 1 (1959), 3-14.

    Emphasizes that race relations possesses no specific
    theory of its own but focuses on the problem of
    social distance and associated factors.

21. Barth, Ernest A.T. and Donald L. Knoel. "Conceptual
    Frameworks for the Analysis of Race Relations:
    An Evaluation," SOCIAL FORCES, 50 (1972), 333-
    348.

    Evaluates the race cycle, consensus, inter-dependence,
    and conflict frameworks with respect to the most
    useful application of each.

22. Cohen, Percy S. "Need There Be a Sociology of
    Race Relations?" SOCIOLOGY, 6 (1972), 101-108.

    A review of three major books on race relations,
    highlighting the manner in which racial attitudes

in any society tend to be coherent and enduring.

23. Goldsby, Richard A. RACE AND RACES. New York:
    Macmillan, 1971.

    Deals with the concepts of "race" and "races" in
    terms of their biological significance, including
    their relationship to intelligence.

24. Hildebrand, Robert F. "Academicians and Race
    Relations," EDUCATION AND URBAN SOCIETY, 5
    (1972), 23-38.

    A questionnaire study of 182 academics in the mid-
    east indicating that the more active tended to be
    younger, involved in the social sciences, and less
    mobile than the norm.

25. Hughes, Everett C. "Race Relations and the Socio-
    logical Imagination," AMERICAN SOCIOLOGICAL
    REVIEW, 28 (1963), 879-890.

    Argues that race relations situations represent a
    laboratory for the study of social problems and
    change. French-English Canadian and Negro-white
    relations are discussed as case studies.

26. Katz, Irwin and Patricia Gurin, eds. RACE AND THE
    SOCIAL SCIENCES, New York: Basic Books, 1969.

    A book which summarizes major research on racial
    inequality with respect to aspects such as social
    psychology, education, politics, demographic factors,
    the labor market, and social change.

27. Kuper, Leo. "Continuities and Discontinuities in
    Race Relations: Evolutionary or Revolutionary
    Change?" CAHIERS D'ETUDES AFRICAINES, 10 (1970),
    361-383.

    A study which finds little utility in Durkheim's

model of social solidarity and evolutionary change when applied to racial and ethnic conflict.

28. Ladner, Joyce A., ed. THE DEATH OF WHITE SOCIOLOGY, New York: Vintage, 1973.

A set of essays dealing with the socialization of black sociologists, the victimization of blacks, black sociology, black psychology, black perspectives on social research, subjective research, and two cases in institutional racism.

29. Melvin, Bruce L. and Abdul J. Araim. "Sociology in International Relations," REV. MEXIC. SOCIOL. 18 (1956), 113-123.

Highlights the contribution sociologists can make to improving international relations through their research on social organization and value systems at the national level.

30. Mirande, Alfredo. "Chicano Sociology: A New Paradigm for Social Science," PACIFIC SOCIOLOGICAL REVIEW, 21 (1978), 293-312.

A paradigm based on Chicano cultural and familial values applied to this minority as a colonized group is outlined and discussed.

31. Osborne, Richard H., ed. THE BIOLOGICAL AND SOCIAL MEANING OF RACE. San Francisco: Freeman, 1971.

Deals with biological and social factors related to race, including diversity, disease, behavior, intelligence, and fertility.

32. Pettigrew, Thomas F. "Sociological Consulting in Race Relations," AMERICAN SOCIOLOGIST, 6 (1971), 44-47.

Argues that long-term and relatively equalitarian consultant-client relationships are important to effective consulting.

33. Rex, John. "The Concept of Housing Class and The Sociology of Race Relations," RACE, 12 (1971), 293-301.

Deals with the concept of housing classes as applied to race relations in Birmingham, England. The importance of residence to such relations is emphasized.

34. Rose, Peter I. THE SUBJECT IS RACE. New York: Oxford University Press, 1968.

An empirical survey of the focus and content of race relations courses in American colleges with regard to orientation, major focus, school, and area characteristics.

35. Schuman, Howard. "Sociological Racism," TRANSACTION, 7 (1969), 44-48.

Discusses the degree to which white Americans are unable to perceive the manner in which racism is a structural, institutional problem rather than an issue of minority deficiencies.

36. Turner, James. "The Founding Fathers of American Sociology: An Examination of their Sociological Theories of Race Relations," JOURNAL OF BLACK STUDIES, 9 (1978), 3-14.

A review of the ideas of Park, Sumner, Ward, Ross, Giddings, and Cooley highlights the prevalence of racial prejudice within early American social science.

37. Banton, Michael. "1960: A Turning Point in the Study of Race Relations," DAEDALUS, 103 (1974), 31-44.

   Argues that race relations should be studied historically, cross-culturally, and with value premises, using multivariate modes of analysis.

38. Bengston, Vern L., Eugene Grigsby, et al. "Relating Academic Research to Community Concerns: A Case Study in Collaborative Effort," THE JOURNAL OF SOCIAL ISSUES, 33 (1977), 75-92.

   Documents a five-year multidisciplinary research project in which minority community members became involved. Implications for future projects are discussed.

39. Cortese, Charles F., R. Frank Falk, et al. "Further Considerations on the Methodological Analysis of Segregation Indices," AMERICAN SOCIOLOGICAL REVIEW, 41 (1976), 630-637.

   Discusses problems involved in interpreting the Index of Dissimilarity and suggests methods for overcoming them.

40. Daniels, Douglas H. "Visual Documents and Race Relations," JOURNAL OF ETHNIC STUDIES, 7 (1980), 1-22.

   Graphic documents such as illustrations, cartoons, and photographs are viewed as valuable in analyzing the history of race relations.

41. Danzger, M. Herbert. "Validating Conflict Data," AMERICAN SOCIOLOGICAL REVIEW, 40 (1975), 570-584.

Discusses problems encountered in explaining causes
of racial conflict, in particular spurious
correlations.

42. Grimshaw, Allen D. "Some Problematic Aspects of
    Communication in Cross-Racial Research in the
    United States," SOCIOLOGICAL FOCUS, 3 (1969-70),
    67-85.

    Highlights the failure to take language and speech
    behavior into account in sociological research,
    particularly differences in speech and other types
    of communication.

43. Harris, Marvin. "Race Relations Research, Auspices
    and Results in the United States," SOCIAL SCIENCE
    INFORMATION, 1 (1962), 28-51.

    A critique of research organizations and literature
    dealing with race relations, particularly in regard
    to ambiguities concerning the notion of "race"
    itself.

44. Katz, Irwin and P. Gurin, eds. RACE AND THE SOCIAL
    SCIENCES. New York: Basic Books, 1969.

    A reader which attempts to formulate relevant
    research goals and strategies relevant to practical
    policy recommendations relating to race relations
    and deals with the fields of social psychology,
    education, political science, demography, economics,
    and social change.

45. Ledvinka, James. "The Intrusion of Race: Black
    Responses to the White Observer," SOCIAL SCIENCE
    QUARTERLY, 52 (1972), 907-920.

    Underlines the manner in which white researchers
    may reinforce negative majority views of blacks by
    forcing the latter to conform to their own expec-
    tations.

46. Levin, Jean N. "Some Concluding Remarks: Research among Racial and Cultural Minorities," THE JOURNAL OF SOCIAL ISSUES, 33 (1977), 175-178.

    Deals with methodological problems involved in surveying minorities, inappropriate projects, and uses made of resultant data.

47. Maykovich, Minako K. "The Difficulties of a Minority Researcher in Minority Communities," THE JOURNAL OF SOCIAL ISSUES, 33 (1977), 108-119.

    Highlights problems caused by fluctuating researcher-community social distance during a project.

48. McCarthy, John D. and William L. Yancey. "Uncle Tom and Mr. Charlie: Metaphysical Pathos in the Study of Racism and Personal Disorganization," AMERICAN JOURNAL OF SOCIOLOGY, 76 (1971), 648-672.

    Disputes the notion that Negro Americans experience crises of identity, self-hatred, and low self-esteem, attributing them to stereotypes.

49. McGee, D. Phillip. "White Conditioning of Black Dependency," JOURNAL OF SOCIAL ISSUES, 29 (1973), 53-56.

    Dependent and acquiescent behavior among blacks is explained by the conditioning techniques used by white researchers.

50. Norman, Charles M. "The Role of Sociologists in Race Relations," PHYLON, 32 (1971), 193-197.

    A survey of 20 sociologists involved in the study of race relations finds support for popularizing sociological findings and advising civil rights groups but little enthusiasm regarding their own participation in political action.

13

51. Obidinski, Eugene. "Methodological Considerations in
     the Definition of Ethnicity," ETHNICITY, 5 (1978),
     213-228.

     Argues that ethnicity should be observable, quanti-
     fiable, and subject to exact measurement if the term
     is to be meaningful.

52. Plax, Martin. "On Studying Ethnicity," PUBLIC
     OPINION QUARTERLY, 36 (1972), 99-104.

     Questions the assumption that ethnic identity always
     involves group commitment, highlighting other aspects
     and possibilities.

53. Rossi, Peter H. "New Directions for Race Relations
     Research in the Sixties," REVIEW OF RELIGIOUS
     RESEARCH, 5 (1964), 125-132.

     Underlines the importance of charting future inter-
     group relations, research on the politics of inte-
     gration, and long range research on religious and
     ethnic groupings.

54. Tillman, James A. and Mary Tillman. "Black Intell-
     ectuals, White Liberals, and Race Relations:
     An Analytical Overview," PHYLON, 33 (1972),
     54-66.

     Perceives existing views on race relations as
     distorted by fashions, fads, and the rhetoric of
     equality advocated by white liberals rather than
     an understanding of white racism.

55. Tsukashima, Ronald T. "Merging Fieldwork and Survey
     Research in the Study of a Minority Community,"
     JOURNAL OF SOCIAL ISSUES, 33 (1977), 133-143.

     A combination of fieldwork and survey research is
     used to explore black anti-Semitism.

56. Villemez, Wayne J. and Allan R. Rowe. "Black
    Economic Gains in the 60's: A Methodological
    Critique and reassessment," SOCIAL FORCES, 54
    (1975), 181-193.

    Critiques perceived black economic gains of the
    1960's as failing to take distributional changes
    into account and concludes that such gains have,
    in fact, been slight.

57. Vowles, Robert C. "Professional Research on Minority
    Economic Problems and its Effect on Academic
    Hiring," THE AMERICAN JOURNAL OF ECONOMICS AND
    SOCIOLOGY, 38 (1979), 61-72.

    A study of the effects of social and institutional
    variables on the academic hiring of economists,
    taking publishing and doctoral programs into account.

58. Warren, Donald I. "Some Observations for Post-Riot
    Detroit: The Role of the Social Researcher in
    Contemporary Racial Conflict," PHYLON, 34
    (1973), 171-186.

    Critiques much race relations research as outdated,
    oversimplified and biased by institutional interests.
    Concludes that protection from public criticism
    is needed to effect legitimate research for the
    minority concerned.

59. Weiss, Carol H. "Survey Researchers and Minority
    Communities," THE JOURNAL OF SOCIAL ISSUES, 33
    (1977), 20-35.

    Argues that most survey research has made little
    effort to benefit the poor and advocates involving
    them significantly in the research process in order
    to avoid "blaming the victim."

15

THE HISTORY OF RACE AND ETHNIC RELATIONS

60. Abbott, Carl. "Plural Society in Colorado: Ethnic
    Relations in the Twentieth Century," PHYLON,
    39 (1978), 250-260.

    Delineates the history of ethnic relations in modern
    Colorado (1900 through 1930), involving the changing
    three-way adjustment of Hispanic, black, and Anglo-
    American residents.

61. Banton, Michael. "What Do We Mean by Racism?"
    NEW SOCIETY, 13 (1969), 551-554.

    Examines contemporary defenses of ethnic inequality
    as opposed to previous racist views and emphasizes
    the importance of research into the general causes
    of hostility.

62. Boskin, Joseph. "Race Relations in Seventeenth
    Century America: The Problem of the Origins
    of Negro Slavery," SOCIOLOGY AND SOCIAL
    RESEARCH, 49 (1965), 446-455.

    A critique of recent works on the origins of Negro
    slavery with suggestions for future research.

63. Bruening, William H. "Racism: A Philosophical
    Analysis of a Concept," JOURNAL OF BLACK
    STUDIES, 5 (1974), 3-18.

    Analyzes racism in terms of its logical fallacies,
    psychological dimensions, ethical aspects, and
    ontological parameters.

64. Clarke, John H. "Race: An Evolving Issue in
    Western Social Thought," JOURNAL OF HUMAN
    RELATIONS, 18 (1970), 1040-1054.

    An historical analysis of racism in the context
    of the European slave trade and colonialism, the
    missionary effort, and emergence of the New World.

65. Dann, Martin E., ed. THE BLACK PRESS, 1827-1890.
    New York: Capricorn, 1971.

    A collection of excerpts from black newspapers
    published between 1827 and 1890, focusing on the
    role of the black press, the black view of American
    history, and black politics, labor, and community
    organization.

66. Davis, David B. THE PROBLEM OF SLAVERY IN WESTERN
    CULTURE. Ithaca: Cornell University Press,
    1966.

    An analysis of attitudes toward slavery among
    Greeks, Romans, early Christians, and early Americans
    as well as major sources of antislavery sentiment.

67. Degler, Carl N. "Slavery in the Genesis of American
    Race Prejudice," COMPARATIVE STUDIES IN
    SOCIOLOGY AND HISTORY, 2 (1959), 49-66.

    Discusses the early history of the American Negro,
    showing that he was viewed as inferior regardless
    of status - slave, servant, or free.

68. Deighton, H.S. "The History and the Study of Race
    Relations," RACE, 1 (1959), 15-25.

    Advocates studying white attitudes since the early
    days of colonial expansion in order to understand
    contemporary race relations.

69. Fredrickson, George M. THE BLACK IMAGE IN THE WHITE
    MIND. New York: Harper and Row, 1971.

    An historical analysis of racial concepts and
    theories involved in American debates over the
    character and destiny of blacks during the period
    1817-1914, highlighting the assumptions of white
    supremacy.

17

70. Gerber, David A. "A Politics of Limited Options:
     Northern Black Politics and the Problem of
     Change and Continuity in Race Relations
     Historiography," JOURNAL OF SOCIAL HISTORY, 14
     (1980), 235-255.

     Critiques the interpretation of civil rights
     legislation as an index of improved race relations
     in contrast to enforcement and black enfranchisement.
     In any case, all of these changes reflect only
     limited ameliorative trends.

71. Handlin, Oscar. "Historical Perspectives on the
     American Ethnic Group," DAEDALUS, 90 (1961),
     220-232.

     Accounts for the viability of American ethnic groups
     as a reaction to the heterogeneity and fluid
     structure of American society.

72. Gould, Stephen J. THE MISMEASURE OF MAN. New
     York: Norton, 1981.

     A critical examination of nineteenth-century cranio-
     metry (the measurement of skulls), highlighting
     its racist assumptions and applications.

73. Gutman, Herbert G. THE BLACK FAMILY IN SLAVERY
     AND FREEDOM, 1750-1925. New York: Pantheon,
     1976.

     A study which shows that enslavement did not destroy
     black family ties; rather, powerful familial and
     kin associations were maintained, despite the
     harshness of slavery.

74. Hershberg, Theodore. "Toward the Historical Study
     of Ethnicity," THE JOURNAL OF ETHNIC STUDIES,
     1 (1973), 1-5.

Outlines the Philadelphia Social History Project
which aims at the comparative study of blacks,
Germans, Irish, and natives in nineteenth century
Philadelphia.

75. Holden, Jr., Mathew. THE WHITE MAN'S BURDEN. New
York: Chandler, 1973.

An attempt to deal with racial conflict as a
republican crisis - reconciling two sociocultural
nations within the same polity - focusing on the
historical development of and possible solutions to
such a problem.

76. Jacobs, Paul and Saul Landau, eds. TO SERVE THE
DEVIL, vols. 1,2. New York: Vintage, 1971.

A set of historical documents dealing with the
position of American Indians, blacks, Chicanos,
Hawaiians, Chinese, Japanese, and Puerto Ricans as
racial minorities in American society.

77. Jones, Rhett S. "Race Relations in the Colonial
Americas: An Overview," HUMBOLDT JOURNAL OF
SOCIAL RELATIONS, 1 (1974), 73-82.

A summary of literature on comparative colonial
race relations in the New World, highlighting the
importance of religion, nationality, economics,
civilization, nonelites, women, demographic factors,
and kinship.

78. Jordan, Winthrop D. WHITE OVER BLACK. Chapel Hill:
University of North Carolina Press, 1968.

A detailed study of American attitudes toward the
Negro during the period 1550 through 1812, highlighting the dichotomy of "liberty and justice
for all" and "the white man's country."

19

79. Kren, George M. "Race and Ideology," PHYLON, 23 (1962), 167-176.

Delineates a number of historical stages in anti-semitism: religious prejudice in the Middle Ages, sixteenth century Protestant reformism, enlightenment rationalism, nationalistic exclusion, and nineteenth century racism.

80. Morgan, Edmund S. AMERICAN SLAVERY AMERICAN FREEDOM. New York: Norton, 1975.

An historical analysis of the simultaneous emergence of slavery and an emphasis on freedom in colonial Virginia.

81. Nye, William P. "The Emergent Idea of Race: A Civilization-Analytic Approach to Race and Racism in the United States," THEORY AND SOCIETY, 5 (1978), 345-372.

Analyzes American racism in terms of cultural ideas linking the self to skin color with consequent typification of others.

82. Osofsky, Gilbert. HARLEM: THE MAKING OF A GHETTO. New York: Harper, 1963.

A historical study of Negro New York and its changing development between 1890 and 1930.

83. Osofsky, Gilbert, ed. THE BURDEN OF RACE. New York: Harper, 1967.

A collection of historical documents dealing with Negro-white relations in America from slavery through the 1960's.

84. Polenberg, Richard. ONE NATION DIVISIBLE. New
    York: Viking, 1980.

    An historical analysis of the effects of class,
    race, and ethnicity in the United States since
    1938, focusing on World War II, the cold war,
    suburbia, the age of reform, and Vietnam.

85. Rabinowitz, Howard N. "From Exclusion to Segregation:
    Southern Race Relations, 1865-1890," JOURNAL OF
    AMERICAN HISTORY, 63 (1976), 325-350.

    Traces the shift from post Civil War exclusion of
    blacks to their segregation - a status more
    acceptable than the former and reinforced by black
    leadership and economic pressures.

86. Sarna, Jonathan D. "From Immigrants to Ethnics:
    Toward a New Theory of "Ethnicizitation,"
    ETHNICITY, 5 (1978), 370-378.

    A study of the immigrant press and organizations
    which concludes that the American "melting-pot"
    unified weak social aggregates into strong ethnic
    groups.

87. Stocking, George W. AMERICAN SOCIAL SCIENTIST AND
    RACE THEORY: 1890-1915. Diss. Univ. of
    Pennsylvania, 1960.

    A content analysis of 20 scholarly journals published
    in the U.S. between 1890 and 1915 reveals the
    shifting nature of the term "race," moving from the
    notion of types of groups, through destruction of
    the physiological approach by anthropologists, to
    theories of cultural determinism and relativism.

88. Takaki, Ronald T. IRON CAGES. New York: Knopf,
    1979.

A study of the history of race in nineteenth-century
American society with respect to the three "iron
cages" - the republican, corporate, and demonic -
reflecting the emergence of the United States as a
colonial empire.

89. Thompson, Edgar T. PLANTATION SOCIETIES, RACE
    RELATIONS, AND THE SOUTH: THE REGIMENTATION
    OF POPULATIONS. Durham: Duke University
    Press, 1975.

    A collection of essays focusing on the plantation,
    race as a "situational emergent," and the South
    as a "morally sensitive society."

90. Williams, Robin M. "Social Change and Social
    Conflict: Race Relations in the United States,
    1944-1964," SOCIOLOGICAL INQUIRY, 35 (1965),
    8-25.

    Discusses changing race relations in the United
    States between 1944 and 1964 with respect to changes
    in group structure and identities, social structure
    and prejudice, the bases of organized process, and
    conflict resolution.

SOCIOECONOMIC AND POWER-ORIENTED THEORIES OF RACE AND
ETHNIC RELATIONS

91. Bagley, Christopher. "Race Relations and Theories
    of Status Consistency," RACE, 11 (1970), 267-288.

    Examines the relevance of rank equilibrium theory to
    race relations, relating such equilibrium to
    stability in intergroup relations and disequilibrium
    to racial conflict.

92. Baker, Donald G. "Identity, Power, and Psycho-
    cultural Needs: White Responses to Nonwhites,"
    JOURNAL OF ETHNIC STUDIES, 1 (1974), 16-44.

White-nonwhite encounters in the U.S. and Canada
from colonial times through World War II are analyzed
in terms of identity factors, power relationships
and the psychocultural needs of white society.

93. Baker, Donald G. "Race, Power and White Siege
    Cultures," SOCIAL DYNAMICS, 1 (1975), 143-157.

    Argues that when a group's racial beliefs are
    threatened, it is transformed into a siege culture,
    as illustrated by white U.S. Southerners, South
    African Afrikaners, and white Rhodesians.

94. Baker, Donald G. "Race and Power: Comparative
    Approaches to the Analysis of Race Relations,"
    ETHNIC AND RACIAL STUDIES, 1 (1978), 316-335.

    Views race relations as power struggles involving
    resource mobilization and strategy, resulting in
    coercive structural and psychosocial dominance.
    South Africa and Rhodesia are used as case studies.

95. Blalock, H.M. "A Power Analysis of Racial
    Discrimination," SOCIAL FORCES, 39 (1960),
    53-59.

    Racial discrimination is analyzed in terms of the
    degree and efficiency of resource mobilization among
    majority groups.

96. Blalock, H.M. TOWARD A THEORY OF MINORITY GROUP
    RELATIONS. New York: Wiley, 1967.

    An analysis of minority group relations based on
    a general power framework, distinguishing between
    potential and actual resource mobilization.

97. Bonacich, Edna. "A Theory of Ethnic Antagonism:
    Split Labor Market," AMERICAN SOCIOLOGICAL
    REVIEW, 37 (1972), 547-559.

Views ethnic antagonism as based on a split labor
market - differential labor prices for the same
occupation - a system exploited by business elites.

98. Dickie-Clark, Hamish F. "Some Issues in the
    Sociology of Race Relations," RACE, 15 (1973),
    241-247.

    Advocates an approach to the understanding of inter-
    group conflict which involves the comparative,
    historical analysis of conflict situations.

99. Eitzen, D. Stanley. "A Conflict Model for the
    Analysis of Majority-Minority Relations,"
    KANSAS JOURNAL OF SOCIOLOGY, 8 (1967), 76-92.

    Conceptualizes majority-minority relations in terms
    of power, conflict, and struggle over resources and
    rewards.

100. Featherman, David L. "The Socioeconomic Achievement
     of White Religio-Ethnic Subgroups: Social and
     Psychological Explanations," AMERICAN
     SOCIOLOGICAL REVIEW, 36 (1971), 207-222.

     Compares the socioeconomic achievements of Jews and
     white Roman Catholics, concluding that education
     rather than religious, ethnic, or motivational
     factors is most crucial.

101. Flanagan, Robert J. "Segmented Market Theories and
     Racial Discrimination," INDUSTRIAL RELATIONS,
     12 (1972), 253-273.

     A study which reveals that accessibility to on-the-
     job training rather than residential segregation
     influences continuing education and entrance to
     the job market.

24

102. Forsythe, Dennis. "Race Relations from Liberal, Black, and Marxist Perspectives," RESEARCH IN RACE AND ETHNIC RELATIONS, 1 (1979), 65-85.

Argues that the Marxist perspective, in contrast to liberalism and black radicalism, is most useful in understanding institutional variation in racism and the historic problems of capitalism and colonialism.

103. Gabriel, John. "The Conceptualization of Race Relations in Sociological Theory," ETHNIC AND RACIAL STUDIES, 2 (1979), 190-212.

Attempts to improve conceptualizations of race relations using Weber's notion of common descent applied to ethnic differences, the relationship between race and class, and the concept of "race."

104. Geschwender, James A. "Status Discrepancy and Prejudice Reconsidered," AMERICAN JOURNAL OF SOCIOLOGY, 75 (1970), 863-865.

After correcting for previous methodological problems and errors, the data in this study reveal a relationship between status consistency and pro-integration views.

105. George, Hermon H. Jr. RACE RELATIONS THEORY: A REVIEW OF FOUR MODELS. Diss. Univ. California at Irvine, 1979.

An evaluation of the ethnic group, caste, colonial, and Marxist models of race relations, rejecting the first two and combining the latter two in a satisfactory synthesis.

106. Harris, Marvin. "Caste, Class, and Minority," SOCIAL FORCES, 37 (1959), 248-254.

Conceptualizes minorities and majorities in terms
of type of affiliation, endogamy versus exogamy, and
attitudes toward position in the social hierarchy.

107. Hawkins, Darnell F. "Social Structure as Metatheory:
Implications for Race Relations Theory and
Research," RESEARCH IN RACE AND ETHNIC RELATIONS,
2 (1980), 133-150.

Critiques the notion of "social structure" as
reflecting cultural deprivation ideology, arguing
instead for a more "skeptical" approach.

108. Henderson, Donald. "Minority Response and the
Conflict Model," PHYLON, 25 (1964), 18-26.

Analyzes Negro response to white constraints as
possibly involving racial adjustment, protest,
maintenance, and synthesis attempts. Accordingly,
conflict becomes regulated and institutionalized.

109. Himes, Joseph S. "A Theory of Racial Conflict,"
SOCIAL FORCES, 50 (1971), 53-60.

Views racial conflict resulting from group motivation, creation of power, power mobilization, and
the use of tactical devices. Under these circum-
stances, racial conflict is inevitable.

110. Hodge, Robert W. "Toward a Theory of Racial Differences in Employment," SOCIAL FORCES, 52 (1973),
16-31.

Group differences in employment are explained in
terms of determinants of employability, variability
in such determinants, economic depression, and group
size.

111. Howard, Dale R. AMERICAN RACE RELATIONS: A
STRUCTURAL ANALYSIS. Diss. Oklahoma State Univ.
1974.

An evaluation of the social pathology, assimilationist, vicious circle, culture of poverty, radical, and colonial models as applied to race relations, with extensive elaboration and application of the last of these to the U.S. situation.

112. Hurst, Charles E. "Race, Class and Consciousness," AMERICAN SOCIOLOGICAL REVIEW, 37 (1972), 658-670.

Argues that both race and occupational status influence attitudes regarding economic subjugation and emphasizes the need to clarify the roles of race, class, age, and size of birthplace in group consciousness.

113. Jackson, John D. "A Study of French-English Relations in an Ontario Community: Towards a Conflict Model for the Analysis of Ethnic Relations," CANADIAN REVIEW OF SOCIOLOGY AND ANTHROPOLOGY, 3 (1966), 117-131.

A model which uses variables such as institutionalization of conflict, consensus level, and conflict superimposition to explain intensity and militancy in ethnic relations.

114. Kinloch, Graham C. THE DYNAMICS OF RACE RELATIONS, A SOCIOLOGICAL ANALYSIS. New York: McGraw-Hill, 1974.

An attempt to develop a general theory of race relations which is applicable both within and between societies, based on the colonial model and applied to relations at the individual, group, and societal level.

115. Kinloch, Graham C. THE SOCIOLOGY OF MINORITY GROUP RELATIONS. Englewood Cliffs: Prentice-Hall, 1979.

A structural, demographic-economic theory of all
major types of minority group relations (physically-
defined, cultural, economic, and behavioral) which
focuses on their evolution and policy implications.

116. Kuper, Leo. "Theories of Revolution and Race
        Relations," COMPARATIVE STUDIES IN SOCIETY AND
        HISTORY, 13 (1972), 87-107.

     Highlights the relevance of race to revolutionary
     attacks in Zanzibar and Rwanda on groups who share
     similar class situations.

117. Labovitz, Sanford and Robert Hagedorn. "A Structural-
        Behavioral Theory of Intergroup Antagonism,"
        SOCIAL FORCES, 53 (1975), 444-448.

     Outlines a theory of intergroup antagonism based on
     social power, competition, labor force structure,
     and contact.

118. Leggon, Cheryl B. "Theoretical Perspectives on
        Race and Ethnic Relations: A Socio-Historical
        Approach," RESEARCH IN RACE AND ETHNIC RELATIONS,
        1 (1979), 1-15.

     Advocates an international approach to.the study of
     race and ethnic relations, using both conflict
     and order theories in understanding social change.

119. Mason, D. "Race Relations, Group Formation and
        Power - A Framework for Analysis," ETHNIC AND
        RACIAL STUDIES, 5 (1982), 421-439.

     Deals with the economic, political, and symbolic
     aspects of social and systemic integration in race
     relations and is illustrated in the case of South
     Africa.

120. Newman, William M. AMERICAN PLURALISM. New York: Harper and Row, 1973.

A theoretical discussion of the study of minority relations, American society, theories of social pluralism and conflict, prejudice and discrimination, and the concept of race.

121. Nikolinakos, Marios. "Notes on an Economic Theory of Racism," RACE, 14 (1973), 365-382.

An analysis of racism within the context of opposing economic interests, within which racial groups are defined by their relation to surplus value created by capitalism.

122. Redekop, Calvin and John A Hostetler. "Minority/ Majority Relations and Economic Interdependence," PHYLON, 27 (1966), 367-378.

Highlights the intention of the host society and minorities in understanding majority-minority relations, viewing the market place as crucial to minority assimilation.

123. Rex, John. RACE RELATIONS IN SOCIOLOGICAL THEORY. London: Weidenfeld and Nicolson, 1970.

Deals with the problem of race and racism with reference to colonial institutions, colonial stratification, metropolitan minorities, and discrimination in the context of sociological theory.

124. Rex, John. "The Right Lines for Race Research," NEW SOCIETY, 48 (1979), 14-16.

A study of West Indian and Asian minorities in Britain as social classes within the welfare state, highlighting their attempts to attain social justice.

125. Rex, John. "A Working Paradigm for Race Relations
     Research," ETHNIC AND RACIAL STUDIES, 4 (1981),
     1-25.

     Develops a theory of the structure of colonial
     societies with reference to precolonial social form-
     ations, colonial modes of production, and imposed
     ethnic stratification, viewing race relations in
     terms of differential group rights.

126. Rhodes, Lodis and Johnny S. Butler. "Sport and
     Racism: A Contribution to Theory Building and
     Race Relations?" SOCIAL SCIENCE QUARTERLY,
     55 (1975), 919-925.

     Racism in competitive athletics is analyzed as a
     microcosm of racism in the society at large.

127. Roucek, Joseph S. "The Power and Ideological Aspects
     of the Majority/Minority Relationship,"
     SOCIOLOGY INTERNATIONAL, 11 (1965), 97-120.

     The dominant-minority situation is explored in terms
     of group consciousness and power politics, viewing
     both cultural pluralism and assimilation as potential
     solutions to the minority problem.

128. Schermerhorn, Richard A. COMPARATIVE ETHNIC RELATIONS:
     A FRAMEWORK FOR THEORY AND RESEARCH. New York:
     Random House, 1970.

     A comparative, multiple-factor approach to inter-
     group relations, highlighting dual perspectives on
     such relations, different types of integration,
     intergroup sequences, types of societies, socio-
     historical approaches, and cross-sectional views.

129. Schoen, Robert. "Towards a Theory of the Demographic
     Implications of Ethnic Stratification,"
     SOCIAL SCIENCE QUARTERLY, 59 (1978), 468-481.

Focuses on demographic opportunity structures with
respect to economic gain and reduced fertility rates.

130. Shibutani, Tamotsu and Kain M. Kwan. ETHNIC
     STRATIFICATION: A COMPARATIVE APPROACH. New
     York: Macmillan, 1965.

     A study of intergroup competition and conflict
     and associated factors behind changes in ethnic
     stratification.

131. Schermerhorn, Richard. "Polarity in the Approach
     to Comparative Research in Ethnic Relations,"
     SOCIOLOGY AND SOCIAL RESEARCH, 51 (1967), 235-
     240.

     A brief attempt to delineate dominant-subordinate
     ethnic group relations using Simmel's dialectical
     approach and the polar relations of integration/
     conflict.

132. Tabb, William K. "Race Relations Models and Social
     Change," SOCIAL PROBLEMS, 18 (1971), 431-444.

     Discusses two theoretical frameworks central to
     radical perspectives: the black ghetto as an intern-
     al colony; and, blacks as a marginal working class.

133. Turner, Jonathan H. "A Theory of Ethnic Oppression:
     Toward a Reintegration of Cultural and Struct-
     ural Concepts in Ethnic Relations Theory,"
     SOCIAL FORCES, 56 (1978), 1001-1018.

     An attempt to incorporate both cultural and
     structural variables into a theory of ethnic
     oppression, highlighting the central role of
     legitimating beliefs.

134. van den Berghe, Pierre L. "The Dynamics of Racial Prejudice: An Ideal Type Dichotomy," SOCIAL FORCES, 37 (1958), 138-141.

Delineation of paternalistic and competitive types of racial prejudice in terms of economic, status, psychological, and historical factors.

135. van den Berghe, Pierre L. RACE AND RACISM: A COMPARATIVE PERSPECTIVE. New York: Wiley, 1967.

A cross-cultural analysis of race relations focusing on paternalistic and competitive types using Mexico, Brazil, South Africa, and the United States as case studies.

136. Williams, John T. "Conflict Theory and Race Conflict," SOCIAL SCIENCE, 51 (1975), 32-36.

The conflict perspective is seen as possibly providing positive values and goals which might contribute to mutual understanding and respect in race relations.

CONTACT THEORY

137. Bernard, S. "Thoughts on the Theory of Colonial Conflicts," R. INST. SOCIOL. 1 (1958), 71-101.

Applies political, psychological, and functional approaches to the study of colonialism, in particular the mechanisms of colonial conflict.

138. Bogardus, Emory S. "Stages in White/Negro Relations in the United States," SOCIOLOGY AND SOCIAL RESEARCH, 45 (1960), 74-79.

Outlines ten major stages in American race relations from enslavement through segregation to gradual integration in the wake of desegregation.

139. Bullock, Charles S. "Contact Theory and Racial Tolerance among High School Students," SCHOOL REVIEW, 86 (1978), 187-216.

A study of racial tolerance among 6,000 high school students in Georgia, revealing that school contact is most highly correlated with tolerance in schools with the least number of blacks.

140. Lyman, Stanford M. "The Race Relations Cycle of Robert E. Park," PACIFIC SOCIOLOGICAL REVIEW, 11 (1968), 16-22.

Delineates some of the major dilemmas contained in Park's "race relations cycle" notion with respect to methodology and theory construction in particular.

141. Mason, Phillip. "An Approach to Race Relations," RACE, 1 (1959), 41-52.

Advocates studying particular race relations situations with respect to historical, psychological, and cultural factors.

142. Moore, Joan W. "American Minorities and New Nation Perspectives," PACIFIC SOCIOLOGICAL REVIEW, 19 (1976), 447-468.

Applies the "internal colonialism" model to American Indian reservations and the "dual economy" approach to urban ghettos. A diversity of models is advocated.

143. Rothstein, David. "Culture Creation and Social Reconstruction: The Socio-Cultural Dynamics of Intergroup Contact," AMERICAN SOCIOLOGICAL REVIEW, 37 (1972), 671-678.

Analyzes intergroup contact in terms of cultural and structural compatibility and oppression with respect to particular configurations.

144. Schermerhorn, Richard A. "Toward a General Theory of
        Minority Groups," PHYLON, 25 (1964), 238-246.

    Minority situations are analyzed in relation to
    modes of domination, "cumulative directionality,"
    and particular types of stratification in societal
    context.

DEPRIVATION THEORY

145. Cohen, Steven M. and Robert E. Kapsis. "Partici-
        pation of Blacks, Puerto Ricans, and Whites in
        Voluntary Associations: A Test of Current
        Theories," SOCIAL FORCES, 56 (1978), 153-171.

    A study of 1,200 New York city residents indicating
    that participation in voluntary associations among
    minorities could not be explained by either
    deprivation or normative theories.

146. Ehrlich, Howard J. THE SOCIAL PSYCHOLOGY OF
        PREJUDICE. New York: Wiley, 1973.

    A systematic attempt to deal with the components of
    prejudice, including its cognitive, conative,
    affectual, and supporting factors.

147. Franklin, Clyde W. and Laurel R. Walum. "Toward a
        Paradigm of Substructural Relations: An
        Application to Sex and Race in the United
        States," PHYLON, 33 (1972), 242-253.

    A paradigm of substructural relations with respect
    to sex and race, focusing on socialization, cognitive
    organization, structural dependence, and perceived
    legitimacy.

148. Klovus, Patricia A. and John N. Edwards. "The Social Participation of Minorities: A Critical Examination of Current Theories," PHYLON, 37 (1976), 150-158.

A critique of studies comparing racial differences in social and political participation, encouraging instead a concern with the effects of subcultural norms, factors related to affiliation, types of participation, and minority population characteristics.

149. McPherson, J. Miller. "Correlates of Social Participation: A Comparison of the Ethnic Community and Compensatory Theories," THE SOCIOLOGICAL QUARTERLY, 18 (1977), 197-208.

A study of 350 black and 362 white residents of Nashville, revealing that voluntary organization participation is correlated with political efficacy and self-esteem among blacks but less so among whites.

LABELING THEORY

150. Klobus-Edwards, Patricia and John N. Edwards, et al. "Differences in Social Participation: Blacks and Whites," SOCIAL FORCES, 56 (1978), 1035-1052.

A study of 100 blacks and 100 whites in Virginia, focusing on organizational involvement, efficacy, system blaming as well as age and occupational prestige as controls. Greater differences within than between races were discovered.

151. Mirande, Alfredo M. "Deviance and Oppression: The Application of Labeling to Racial and Ethnic Minorities," INTERNATIONAL JOURNAL OF CONTEMPORARY SOCIOLOGY, 15 (1978), 375-296.

35

An application of the labeling perspective to deviants
as well as the categorization and stereotyping of
racial and ethnic minorities, using Chicanos as a
case study.

152. Richmond, Anthony H. "Sociological and Psychological Explanations of Racial Prejudice: Some
Light on the Controversy from Recent Research
in Great Britain," PACIFIC SOCIOLOGICAL REVIEW,
4 (1961), 63-68.

An exploration of racial prejudice in terms of the
parts played by introjection and projection in the
perception of racial norms.

153. Rinder, Irwin D. "Minority Orientations: An
Approach to Intergroup Relations Theory through
Social Psychology," PHYLON, 26 (1965), 5-17.

Types of minority group orientation are delineated
according to subordinate group morale and super-
ordinate group acceptance.

154. Rothman, Jack. "Minority Group Status, Mental
Health and Intergroup Relations: An Appraisal
of Kurt Lewin's Thesis," JOURNAL OF INTERGROUP
RELATIONS, 3 (1962), 299-310.

Explains minority group maladjustment as frustration
caused by blocked assimilation into the majority.

155. Roucek, Joseph S. "The Sociological Framework of the
Negro Problem," INDIAN JOURNAL OF SOCIAL RESEARCH,
2 (1961), 7-21.

A sociological analysis of the Negro problem since
the Civil War and Reconstruction, highlighting their
gradual integration.

156. Tajfel, Henri. "The Exit of Social Mobility and the Voice of Social Change: Notes on the Social Psychology of Intergroup Relations," SOCIAL SCIENCE QUARTERLY, 14 (1975), 101-118.

An application of the concepts of "group exit" and "group chorus" to intergroup relations and social conflict.

DEMOGRAPHIC THEORY

157. Coleman, A. Lee. "The Rural-Urban Variable in Race Relations," RURAL SOCIOLOGY, 30 (1965), 393-406.

Highlights the importance of the rural-urban variable in race relations, particularly in the South.

158. Gottlieb, David. "Regional Differences as a Variable in Sociological Research," SOCIAL PROBLEMS, 10 (1963), 251-255.

A study of adolescents at a midwest summer camp, finding that males prefer non-Southern friends while females choose Southern campers more often.

159. Klaff, Vivian Z. "Pluralism as an Alternative Model for the Human Ecologist," ETHNICITY, 7 (1980), 102-118.

Argues that ethnic pluralism, representing a group's sense of community or identity may be positive rather than destructive element.

160. Richmond, Anthany H. "Migration, Ethnicity and Race Relations," ETHNIC AND RACIAL STUDIES, 1 (1978), 1-18.

A discussion of pluralism, racism, and neoclonialism in terms of industrial and postindustrial migration within societies as complex, adaptive systems.

161. Steinnes, Donald N. "Alternative Models of Neighborhood Change," SOCIAL FORCES, 55 (1977), 1043-1057.

A study of the tipping point model as applied to neighborhood change in Chicago during 1950 and 1960.

STRUCTURAL-FUNCTIONAL AND SYSTEM THEORIES

162. Armstrong, Edward G. "The System Paradigm and the Sociological Study of Racial Conflict," PHYLON, 36 (1975), 8-13.

A critique of the "system paradigm" as applied to the study of racial conflict by traditional sociologists - an approach which fails to understand such an issue.

163. Harris, Roland A. "The Applicability of Parsons' Theory of the Social System to Blacks and Urban Places," THE JOURNAL OF NEGRO EDUCATION, 48 (1979), 139-148.

A critique of Parsons' theory of the social system as applied to blacks who live in urban centers for failing to take the effects of discrimination adequately into account.

164. Works, Ernest. "The Pattern Variables as a Framework for the Study of Negro-White Relations," PACIFIC SOCIOLOGICAL REVIEW, 10 (1967), 25-32.

An application of the pattern variables to Negro-white relations, hypothesizing least racial exclusion where performance and universalism are predominant.

38

TYPOLOGIES OF RACE AND ETHNIC RELATIONS

165. Banks, James A. and Geneva Gay. "Ethnicity in Contemporary American Society: Toward the Development of a Typology," ETHNICITY, 5 (1978), 238-251.

A classification of ethnic groups in terms of preferred associations, personality development and identity, and emotional support, producing cultural, economic, political, eco-political, and holistic types.

166. Franklin, Clyde W. and Laurel R. Walum. "Toward a Paradigm of Substructural Relations: An Application to Sex and Race in the United States," PHYLON, 33 (1972), 242-253.

Racial and sexual relations are explored in terms of macrostructures, patterned social relationships, and societal variables.

167. Rex, John. "Race Relations and Minority Groups: Some Convergences," INTERNATIONAL SOCIAL SCIENCE JOURNAL, 33 (1981), 351-373.

Presents a research approach which types colonial situations and relates them to contemporary metropolitan race relations.

168. Schermerhorn, Richard A. "Interethnic Relations: An Attempt at a Typology," CAHIERS INTERNAT. DE SOCIOLOGIE, 44 (1968), 145-156.

A framework designed for comparative research in ethnic relations relating ethnic enclosure and control of scarce values to intergroup relations and conflict as mediated by group goals, patterns of interaction, and the societal context.

169. Young, Warren L. "Multidimenstionality and
      Minoricity: Toward a Taxonomy of Minority-
      Societal Relationships," REVISTA DE SOCIOLOGIA,
      12 (1975), 5-42.

      Minority groups are typified in terms of segmentation,
      power position, and historico-demographic dimensions.

TYPES OF INTERGROUP SITUATIONS

170. Cox, Oliver C. "The Question of Pluralism," RACE,
      12 (1971), 385-400.

      Analyzes the term pluralism with respect to its
      political, legalistic, and societal usages, concluding
      that the concept's utility in understanding race
      relations is limited.

171. Manheim, Henry L. "Experimental Demonstration of
      the Relationship between Group Characteristics
      and Patterns of Intergroup Interaction,"
      PACIFIC SOCIOLOGICAL REVIEW, 6 (1963), 25-29.

      A laboratory study of ten types of intergroup
      interaction, consisting of various combinations
      of status and leadership elements, highlighting
      group rather than individual characteristics.

172. Reitzes, Deitrich C. "Institutional Structure and
      Race Relations," PHYLON, 20 (1959), 48-66.

      Highlights situational and organizational definitions
      of racial situations as more significant than
      individual behavior in specific racial encounters.

173. Turk, Herman and Myron J. Lefcowitz. "Towards a
      Theory of Representation between Groups," SOCIAL
      FORCES, 40 (1962), 337-341.

      Conceptualizes group relations with regard to power
      and legitimation, producing four types of intergroup
      situations and evaluating their implications.

CHAPTER III

RACE AND ETHNIC RELATIONS IN THE UNITED STATES

GENERAL AND COMPARATIVE RACE AND ETHNIC RELATIONS

174. Abramson, Harold J. "Migrants and Cultural Diversity:
      On Ethnicity and Religion and Society," SOCIAL
      COMPASS, 36 (1979), 5-29.

      A study of multicultural societies which focuses on
      migrant-indigenous cultural differences and
      consequences of migration.

175. Bahr, Howard M, Bruce A. Chadwick, et al. AMERICAN
      ETHNICITY. Lexington: Heath, 1979.

      A text which deals with the history of American
      ethnic groups, the impact of ethnic variation,
      social psychological perspectives on ethnicity,
      ethnic communities, and interethnic discrimination
      and conflict.

176. Berry, Brewton and Henry L. Tischler. RACE AND
      ETHNIC RELATIONS. Boston: Houghton Mifflin,
      1978.

      A text organized in terms of basic perspectives and
      definitions, intergroup contact, patterns and
      resolutions of inequality.

177.   Blalock, Hubert M.   RACE AND ETHNIC RELATIONS.
       Englewood Cliffs: Prentice-Hall, 1982.

       A brief text dealing with prejudice, minority
       exchanges, competition and discrimination, status
       attainment, segregation, power and conflict, and
       policy implications.

178.   Bonney, Norman.   "Race and Politics in Chicago in the
       Daley Era," RACE, 15 (1974), 329-350.

       Focuses on the black submachine in Chicago politics
       as well as church-led movements increasingly involved
       in racial conflict.

179.   Breen, T.H.   "A Changing Labor Force and Race Relat-
       ions in Virginia, 1660-1710," JOURNAL OF SOCIAL
       HISTORY, 7 (1973), 3-25.

       A study of indentured servants, black slaves, and
       poor freemen blamed by Virginia's ruling planters
       for civil violence.

180.   Broom, Leonard, Cora Martin, et al.   "Status Profiles
       of Racial and Ethnic Populations," SOCIAL SCIENCE
       QUARTERLY, 52 (1971), 379-388.

       An educational, occupational, and income profile
       of major racial and ethnic groups in American society
       based on the 1960 census.

181.   Brunswick, Ann F.   "What Generation Gap? A Compari-
       son of Some Generational Differences among Blacks
       and Whites," SOCIAL PROBLEMS, 17 (1970), 358-371.

       Based on seven national surveys of racial attitudes,
       this analysis finds that education among both racial
       groups appears positively related to moderate views.

42

182. Castile, George P. and Gilbert Kushner, eds. PERSISTENT PEOPLES. Tucson: University of Arizona Press, 1981.

A set of articles analyzing "enduring cultural systems" with respect to plural interrelationships, opposition and persistency, ritual and persistence, and adaptive perspectives.

183. Davis, F. James, ed. UNDERSTANDING MINORITY-DOMINANT RELATIONS. Arlington Heights: AHM Publishing, 1979.

A reader which focuses on minority-dominant relations in terms of theoretical approaches, prejudice, discrimination, assimilation, and minority protest and change.

184. Davis, F. James. MINORITY-DOMINANT RELATIONS. Arlington Heights: AHM Publishing, 1978.

A text which deals with basic minority concepts and processes, patterns of accommodation, group assimilation, and action toward equality.

185. Dworkin, Anthony G. and Rosalind J. Dworkin, eds. THE MINORITY REPORT. New York: Holt, Rinehart and Winston, 1982.

A reader of articles written by minority group members, focuing on racial, ethnic, and gender relations.

186. Epps, Edgar G., ed. RACE RELATIONS. Cambridge: Winthrop, 1973.

A reader which focuses on theoretical perspectives on race relations, perspectives on minority experiences in America, the black family, and black politics.

187. Farley, John E. MAJORITY-MINORITY RELATIONS.
     Englewood Cliffs: Prentice-Hall, 1982.

     A text which focuses on the study of prejudice,
     perspectives on majority-minority relations, the
     role of institutional discrimination, and major
     issues in intergroup relations.

188. Feagin, Joe R. RACIAL AND ETHNIC RELATIONS.
     Englewood Cliffs: Prentice-Hall, 1978.

     A text which analyzes the background, reactions, and
     institutions of English, Irish, Italian, Jewish,
     Native, Black, Mexican, and Japanese Americans.

189. Fellows, Donald K. A MOSAIC OF AMERICA'S ETHNIC
     MINORITIES. New York: Wiley, 1972.

     An analysis of the historical background, population
     patterns, and socioeconomic characteristics of Ameri-
     can blacks, Mexicans, Indians, Chinese, Japanese,
     and Puerto Rican minorities.

190. Gilman, Stuart C. "Alternative Life Worlds for
     Blacks and Whites: A Research Note," ETHNICITY,
     5 (1978), 14-19.

     Advocates the development of new methodologies to
     analyze minority cultures within the larger society.

191. Gomez, Rudolph, Clement Cottingham, Jr., et al., eds.
     THE SOCIAL REALITY OF ETHNIC AMERICA. Lexington:
     Heath, 1974.

     A reader which deals with Afro-Americans, American
     Indians, Japanese and Mexican Americans.

192. Griessman, B. Eugene. MINORITIES. Hinsdale:
     Dryden, 1975.

44

A text with readings, focusing on Western thought,
social differentiation, assimilation, organizations,
the individual, social control, and conflict.

193. Gurak, Douglas T. "Sources of Ethnic Fertility
     Differences: An Examination of Five Minority
     Groups," SOCIAL SCIENCE QUARTERLY, 59 (1978), 295-
     310.

     A study of fertility rates among five minority
     groups, finding that minority status does not explain
     these rates; instead, cultural background may be
     more relevant.

194. Handlin, Oscar. RACE AND NATIONALITY IN AMERICAN
     LIFE. Garden City: Doubleday, 1957.

     Deals with issue of race and exploitation, the
     nature of prejudice, and future trends in intergroup
     relations.

195. Halpern, Ben. "Ethnic and Religious Minorities:
     Subcultures and Subcommunities," JEWISH SOCIO-
     LOGICAL STUDIES, 27 (1965), 37-44.

     Compares Jewish and Negro subcommunities, arguing
     that they have developed similarly alienated pers-
     pectives but with differing solutions.

196. Harris, Edward E. SOME SOCIAL EFFECTS OF RACE
     RELATIONS. New York: American Press, 1967.

     A book of essays focusing on racial discrimination
     with respect to academic hiring, the clergy role,
     and the American Dream.

197. Hernton, Calvin C. SEX AND RACISM IN AMERICA: AN
ANALYSIS OF THE INFLUENCE OF SEX ON THE RACE
PROBLEM. Garden City: Doubleday, 1965.

Deals with the sexual aspect of racism, including the
taboo against interracial relationships, racist
stereotypes, and sexual paranoia.

198. Hicks, George L. and Philip E. Leis, eds. ETHNIC
ENCOUNTERS: IDENTITIES AND CONTEXTS. North
Scituate: Duxbury, 1977.

A reader on ethnicity dealing with its relationship
to identity, social life, and inequality on a worldwide basis.

199. Howard, John R., ed. AWAKENING MINORITIES. New
Brunswick: Transaction, 1970.

A set of articles analyzing ethnic stratification as
it applies to American Indians, Mexicans, and Puerto
Ricans.

200. Hughes, Everett C. THE SOCIOLOGICAL EYE. Chicago:
Aldine-Atherton, 1971.

A set of wide-ranging essays, including a focus on
the relationship between institutions and race, and
the meeting of races and cultures.

201. Hughes, Helen M., ed. RACIAL AND ETHNIC RELATIONS.
Boston: Holbrook, 1970.

A set of articles dealing with caste in India,
Japanese outcasts, white-black relations in the
United States, the changing South, high school
integration, prejudice and discrimination, desegregation, integration in the military, and changing
minority status.

202. Jiobu, Robert M. "Earnings Differentials between Whites and Ethnic Minorities: The Cases of Asian Americans, Blacks and Chicanos," SOCIOLOGY AND SOCIAL RESEARCH, 61 (1976), 24-39.

A comparative study of whites and racial minorities in California with respect to differential earnings, finding that Japanese and Chinese Americans have largely achieved parity with whites while blacks and Chicanos remain deprived.

203. Jones, Rhett S. "Race Relations in the Colonial Americas: An Overview," HUMBOLDT JOURNAL OF SOCIAL RELATIONS, 1 (1974), 73-82.

A study of literature on comparative colonial race relations in the New World, highlighting religion, nationality, economics, minorities, demographic factors, and kinship.

204. Killian, Lewis M. and Charles M. Grigg. "Race Relations in an Urbanized South," JOURNAL OF SOCIAL ISSUES, 22 (1966), 20-29.

A discussion of the effects of urbanization on southern race relations, predicting that Negroes will experience impersonality, exclusion, and hostility in this new context.

205. Kitano, Harry H.L. RACE RELATIONS. Englewood Cliffs: Prentice-Hall, 1974.

A text which deals with major aspects of prejudice and discrimination, as well as ethnic groups, including American Indians, Afro-Americans, Chinese, Japanese, and Mexican Americans, as well as Filipinos and Puerto Ricans.

206. Kurokawa, Minako, ed. MINORITY RESPONSES. New York: Random House, 1970.

A reader organized around major theoretical frameworks and types of minority response to subordination, including attempted assimilation, accommodation, submission, contention, and revitalization.

207. Lee, Frank F. "A Cross-Institutional Comparison of Northern and Southern Race Relations," SOCIO-LOGY AND SOCIAL RESEARCH, 42 (1958), 185-191.

Contends that the major Northern-Southern difference is the acceptance of school integration in the case of the North and its rejection among Southerners as threatening other forms of segregation.

208. Lambert, Richard D. "Ethnic/Racial Relations in the United States in Comparitive Perspective," ANNALS OF THE AMERICAN ACADEMY OF POLITICAL AND SOCIAL SCIENCE, 454 (1981), 189-205.

Views the U.S. situation as distinctive in terms of the increasing salience of intergroup relations, bipolar perceptions despite the melting pot theory, ideology, and emphasis on hierarchy, a view of government as a protagonist for the underclass, and ethnic violence.

209. Lieberson, Stanley and Donna K. Carter. "Making it in America: Differences between Eminent Blacks and White Ethnic Groups," AMERICAN SOCIOLOGICAL REVIEW, 44 (1979), 347-366.

A study of inclusion by race and ethnicity in WHO'S WHO for the years 1924/25, 1944/45, and 1974/75, finding that the English exceed the national average while the black rate is the lowest.

210. Luhman, Reid and Stuart Gilman. RACE AND ETHNIC RELATIONS. Belmont: Wadsworth, 1980.

A text which concentrates on the historical, political, economic, cultural, and ideological dimensions of racial and ethnic relations.

211. Makielski, Jr., S.J. BELEAGURED MINORITIES. San Francisco: Freeman, 1973.

A discussion of the historical evolution of America's minorities and their political activities.

212. Marden, Charles F. and Gladys Meyer. MINORITIES IN AMERICAN SOCIETY. New York: Van Nostrant, 1978.

A text which discusses basic approaches to analyzing American minorities and proceeds to discuss the society's major racial groups.

213. Martin, James G. and Clyde W. Franklin. MINORITY GROUP RELATIONS. Columbus: Merrill, 1973.

A text which highlights prejudice and discrimination as major dimensions of intergroup relations.

214. McLemore, S. Dale. RACIAL AND ETHNIC RELATIONS IN AMERICA. Boston: Allyn and Bacon, 1980.

A text which focuses on the inclusion process, Anglo conformity, prejudice and discrimination, Japanese, Chicano, and black Americans, and increased ethnicity.

215. Mirowski, John and Catherine E. Ross. "Minority Status, Ethnic Culture, and Distress: A Comparison of Blacks, Whites, Mexicans, and Mexican-Americans," AMERICAN JOURNAL OF SOCIOLOGY, 86 (1980), 479-495.

A study of 429 El Paso and Juarez residents which concludes that distress is explained by ethnic-culture rather than minority status.

49

216. Patterson, Orlando. "On Guilt, Relativism, and
     Black/White Relations," THE AMERICAN SCHOLAR,
     43 (1973-74), 122-132.

     Critiques white relativists for assuming their
     values are superior to those of people they study,
     emphasizing instead that each individual is autono-
     mous and unique.

217. Raab, Earl, ed. AMERICAN RACE RELATIONS TODAY.
     Garden City: Doubleday, 1962.

     A set of articles on desegregation, the prejudiced
     society, Negro student reaction, metropolitan
     situations, schools and the slums, and the reactions
     of Mexicans, Puerto Ricans, and Black Muslims.

218. Rose, Peter I. THEY AND WE: RACIAL AND ETHNIC
     RELATIONS IN THE UNITED STATES. New York:
     Random House, 1964.

     An introduction to the field, dealing with key
     concepts, the history of U.S. minorities, the
     characteristics of discrimination, the nature of
     prejudice, and reaction of minorities.

219. Rose, Peter I. NATION OF NATIONS. New York:
     Random House, 1972.

     A reader which focuses on the history, character-
     istics of, and competition between America's racial
     and ethnic minorities.

220. Roucek, Joseph S. "Education and Americanization in
     Its Sociological Aspects," INDIAN JOURNAL OF
     SOCIAL RESEARCH, 1 (1960), 38-46.

     A discussion of the public school as an important
     media of acculturation and assimilation with regard
     to immigrants, particularly during post W.W.II.

221. Roucek, Joseph S. "Special Characteristics of the Problem of Racial Minorities in the U.S.A.," REVISTA INTERNACIONAL DE SOCIOLOGIA, 23 (1965), 37-54.

While there are no legally defined minorities in the U.S., Jeffersonian racism, discriminatory immigration laws, and the economic position of various racial groups have all contributed to the minority situation.

222. Roucek, Joseph S. "Unique Features of Racial Minorities in the United States," INDIAN SOCIOLOGICAL BULLETIN, 7 (1969), 25-38.

Outlines the extent and effects of racism in the historical development of America, particularly in regard to the treatment of Negroes.

223. Schaefer, Richard T. RACIAL AND ETHNIC GROUPS. Boston: Little, Brown, 1979.

A text which outlines basic perspectives on racial and ethnic groups, racial and ethnic minorities in the United States, and other forms of dominance such as sexism.

224. Simpson, George E. and J.M. Yinger. RACIAL AND CULTURAL MINORITIES. New York: Harper and Row, 1972.

A text which deals with the causes and consequences of prejudice and discrimination, institutional patterns of intergroup relations, as well as prejudice, discrimination, and democratic values.

225. Singh, Krishna, R. Lewis Donohew, et al., "Foreign Students as Minority Group Members in American Society: An Exploration," INTERNATIONAL JOURNAL OF CONTEMPORARY SOCIOLOGY, 11 (1974), 207-217.

A questionnaire study of 193 foreign students delineating their attitudes as a minority as well as pluralistic, isolated, and assimilative orientations.

226. Turner, Jonathan H. "Structural Conditions of Achievement among Whites and Blacks in the Rural South," SOCIAL PROBLEMS, 19 (1972), 496-508.

Structural conditions such as community oppression, minority socialization, and mobility perceptions are used to account for differential racial achievement.

227. Yetman, Norman and C. Hoy Steele, eds. MAJORITY AND MINORITY. Boston: Allyn and Bacon, 1975.

A reader dealing with perspectives on race and ethnic relations (including comparative analyses), the historical background to American minorities, intergroup contact, attitudinal and institutional discrimination, and the resurgence of ethnicity.

228. Young, Richard P. SOCIETAL CHANGE AND THE EVOLUTION OF AMERICAN RACE RELATIONS. Diss. Stanford Univ., 1979.

An historical analysis of political and cultural changes in American race relations since 1915, focusing on political incorporation and the decline of white racist attitudes.

229. Weiss, Karel, ed. UNDER THE MASK. New York: Dell, 1972.

A set of documents delineating the history, experience, control, segregation, and resistance of America's racial minorities.

230. Zeigler, Harmon and Michael Ross. "Racial Problems and Policy in American Public Schools," SOCIOLOGY OF EDUCATION, 47 (1974), 319-336.

A study of 81 school districts, revealing school
board insensitivity and ambiguity towards racial
problems.

WHITE AMERICANS: SOUTHERNERS AND ETHNIC IMMIGRANTS

231. Anderson, Charles H. WHITE PROTESTANT AMERICANS.
Englewood Cliffs: Prentice-Hall, 1970.

An analysis of the assimilation of protestant national
origin groups in America, as well as the past and
present status of white protestantism in American
life.

232. Barksdale, Richard K. "White Tragedy-Black Comedy:
A Literary Approach to Southern Race Relations,"
PHYLON, 22 (1961), 226-233.

Applies the literary notions of tragedy and comedy
to changes in white-black race relations in the
South.

233. Berg, Phillip L. "Racism and the Puritan Mind,"
PHYLON, 36 (1975), 1-7.

A study of the American Puritans of Massachusetts
Bay and their view of Indians as heathens requiring
saving grace.

234. Binzen, Peter. WHITETOWN USA. New York: Vintage,
1970.

A portrait of how the "silent majority" lives,
learns, works and thinks.

235. Black, Merle. "Racial Composition of Congressional
Districts and Support for Federal Voting Rights
in the American South," SOCIAL SCIENCE QUARTERLY,
59 (1978), 435-450.

Outlines the shift of white southerners from rejectors
to supporters of minority voters rights during the
period 1957 through 1975.

236. Bromley, David G. and Charles F. Longino, eds.
     WHITE RACISM AND BLACK AMERICANS. Cambridge:
     Schenkman, 1972.

A collection of articles which deals with major
processes (ecological, victimization and socialization) and institutions (the family, education,
economics, politics, religion, and health) involved
in white racism as well as the major dimensions of
black culture.

237. Cramer, M. Richard. "Race and Southern White Workers'
     Support for Unions," PHYLON, 39 (1978), 311-321.

A survey of 887 residents of a North Carolina town
which finds that blacks tend to be more favorable to
unions and racial integration.

238. Cummings, Scott and Charles W. Pinnel. "Racial
     Double Standards of Morality in a Small Southern
     Community: Another Look at Myrdal's American
     Dilemma," JOURNAL OF BLACK STUDIES, 9 (1978),
     67-86.

A study which documents the manner in which whites
apply differential moral and ethical standards to
blacks in comparison to themselves.

239. Fallows, Marjorie R. IRISH AMERICANS. Englewood
     Cliffs: Prentice-Hall, 1979.

Deals with Irish Americans in terms of their historical background, early years in America, community
structures, social mobility, politics, religious
activities, family characteristics, ethnic identity,
and patterns of assimilation.

240. Greeley, Andrew M. and William C. McCready. "Does
     Ethnicity Matter?" ETHNICITY, 1 (1974), 91-108.

     A study of second and third generation Irish Catholics
     and Italians compared with Anglo-Saxons, finding most
     attitudinal similarities between the Irish and Anglo-
     Saxon.

241. Howe, Louise K., ed. THE WHITE MAJORITY. New York:
     Vintage, 1970.

     A reader on the social, economic, and political
     life of America's white majority.

242. Katzman, Marton T. "Opportunity, Subculture, and
     the Economic Performance of Ethnic Groups,"
     AMERICAN JOURNAL OF ECONOMICS AND SOCIOLOGY,
     28 (1969), 351-366.

     A study of economic achievement among 14 ethnic
     groups in metropolitan areas based on 1950 census
     data and accounted for in terms of urban opportunities,
     group size, education, and ethnic factors.

243. Lewis, Herbert S. "European Ethnicity in Wisconsin:
     An Exploratory Formulation," ETHNICITY, 5 (1978),
     174-188.

     Documents the continuation of cultural values and
     traditions among European ethnic communities in rural
     Wisconsin.

244. Martin, Walter T. "On the Social Mechanisms of White
     Supremacy," PACIFIC SOCIOLOGICAL REVIEW, 15
     (1972), 203-224.

     A study of variation among states with respect to
     white-black occupational dissimilarity based on the
     historical, attitudinal, and political traits of
     each area.

245. Moynihan, Daniel P. "The Irish of New York," COMMENTARY, 36 (1963), 93-107.

A discussion of Irish assimilation and the continuing effects of religion on their socioeconomic position in New York.

246. Rabitsa, Bogdan. "Clash of Two Immigrant Generations" COMMENTARY, 25 (1958), 8-15.

Differences between pre and post-1945 Croatian immigrants are outlined, highlighting the resentment of the latter over the success of the former.

247. Rohrer, Wayne C. BLACK PROFILES OF WHITE AMERICANS. New York: Davis, 1970.

A study of white Americans in respect to their typical responses to racial change, including democrats, civil rights activists, laissez-faire immigrants, and undemocratic whites.

248. Saloutow , Theodore. GREEKS IN THE UNITED STATES. Cambridge: Harvard University Press, 1964.

A study of Greek Americans which deals with migration conditions, community structure, old and new world politics, economic and cultural assimilation.

249. Schwartz, Barry N. and Robert Disch. WHITE RACISM. New York: Dell, 1970.

A set of articles on the white psyche, pathological nature of white society, anonymous racism, stereotypes, myths and images, contemporary responses to racism, and the future.

250. Vrga, Djuro J. and Frank J. Fahey. "Structural Sources of Ethnic Factionalism," SOCIAL SCIENCE, 44 (1969), 12-19.

Ethnic factionalism among Serbs is accounted for by
conditions of and reasons for migration.

251. Vrga, Djuro J. "Differential Associational Involve-
     ment of Successive Ethnic Immigrants: An
     Indicator of Ethno-religious Factionalism and
     Alienation of Immigrants," SOCIAL FORCES, 50
     (1971), 239-248.

     A study of Serbian immigrants which explains status-
     oriented voluntary association activity as a response
     to prestige loss and limited mobility opportunities.

JEWISH AMERICANS

252. Gould, Julius. "American Jewry - Some Social Trends,"
     JEWISH JOURNAL OF SOCIOLOGY, 3 (1961), 55-73.

     A discussion of studies of Jewish life which finds
     no religious awakening, on the one hand, with main-
     tenance of self-segregation and endogamy, on the
     other.

253. Kramer, Judith R. and Seymour Leventman. CHILDREN
     OF THE GILDED GHETTO: CONFLICT RESOLUTIONS OF
     THREE GENERATIONS OF AMERICAN JEWS. New Haven:
     Yale University Press, 1961.

     A study of generational differences among American
     Jews, highlighting class and ethnic tensions and the
     shift from ethnic to status community over the
     generations.

254. Newman, William M. and Peter L. Halvorson. "American
     Jews: Patterns of Geographic Distribution and
     Change, 1952-1971," JOURNAL FOR THE SCIENTIFIC
     STUDY OF RELIGION, 18 (1979), 183-193.

     A study of geographical changes in distribution which
     finds high metropolitan concentrations and areas
     of religious pluralism.

255. Reid, John S. "Ethnicity in the South: Some
     Observations on the Acculturation of Southern
     Jews," ETHNICITY, 6 (1979), 79-106.

     56 Gallup polls conducted between 1968 and 1972
     reveal that Southern Jews tend to be urban, well-
     educated, professional, and politically conservative.

256. Rose, Arnold. "America is Changing the Mutual Images
     of Jews and Catholics," SOCIAL ORDER, 13 (1963),
     19-28.

     Mutual Jewish-Catholic images are examined for
     changes over time with respect to cultural traits,
     views of Christ, birth control and censorship, and
     orientations towards life.

257. Rosenthal, Erich. "Culturalization without Assimi-
     lation? The Jewish Community of Chicago,
     Illinois," AMERICAN JOURNAL OF SOCIOLOGY, 66
     (1960), 275-283.

     A study of the manner in which high status voluntary
     segregation and Jewish education appear to be inhib-
     iting large-scale assimilation.

258. Senn, Milton. "Race, Religion, and Suburbia,"
     JOURNAL OF INTERGROUP RELATIONS, 2 (1962), 159-
     170.

     The desire for security, avoidance of rejection, and
     ethnic identification are used to explain the
     process of "selfghettoization" among Jews who move
     to the suburbs.

259. Sherman, C. Bezalel. THE JEW WITHIN AMERICAN SOCIETY:
     A STUDY IN ETHNIC INDIVIDUALITY. Michigan:
     Wayne State University Press, 1961.

     A study of Jewish immigrants and their accommodation
     to American society, including conflicting tendencies,

ethnic isolation, upward mobility, and self-images.

260. Sherman, C. Bezalel. "Emerging Patterns and Attitudes in an American Jewish Life," JEWISH JOURNAL OF SOCIOLOGY, 5 (1963), 47-54.

Deals with the ambivalent character of Jewish acculturation involving both assimilation and maintenance of tradition.

ITALIAN AMERICANS

261. Vecoli, Rudolph J. "The Coming of Age of the Italian Americans: 1945-1974," ETHNICITY, 5 (1978), 119-146.

A discussion of the history of Italian immigrants, the negative conditions of their arrival, limited upward mobility, and maintenance of values such as family loyalty, male dominance, hospitality, and respect for authority.

LATIN AMERICANS

262. Knowlton, Clark S. "The Spanish Americans in New Mexico," SOCIOLOGY AND SOCIAL RESEARCH, 45 (1961), 448-454.

A discussion of the relative uniqueness and changing character of Spanish Americans in southern Colorado and northern New Mexico.

263. Portes, Alejandro, Robert N. Parker, et al. "Assimilation or Consciousness: Conceptions of United States Society among the Recent Latin American Immigrants to the United States," SOCIAL FORCES, 59 (1980), 200-224.

A longitudinal study of 439 Mexican and 427 Cuban
immigrants which supports the conflict rather than
assimilationist view of immigrants' perceptions of
American society.

264. Ramsey, Glenn V. "Anglo-Latin Problems as Perceived
        by Public Service Personnel," SOCIAL FORCES, 37
        (1959), 339-348.

150 public service personnel outline problems in
cultural relations, highlighting Latin-Anglo attitudes
as well as institutional issues.

BLACK AMERICANS

ATTITUDES AND IDENTITY

265. Baughman, E. Earl. BLACK AMERICANS. New York:
        Academic Press, 1971.

A psychological analysis of the concept of race,
and its relationship to intelligence, scholastic
performance, self-esteem, aggression, psychopathology,
the family, and leadership among blacks.

266. Bellwig, David J. "Afro-American Reactions to the
        Japanese and the Anti-Japanese Movement, 1906-
        1924," PHYLON, 38 (1977), 93-104.

A study which indicates that black opposition to
Japanese immigration was rare; on the contrary,
many admired Japanese ability to overcome adversity.

267. Benjamin, Rommel. CONCEPTIONS OF THE MALE FAMILIAL
        ROLE BY BLACK MALE YOUTH. Diss. Mississippi State
        Univ., 1971.

Male conceptions of the male familial role among 344
black college and high school blacks were found

60

to be most closely related to the respondent's
father's familial role.

268. Bond, Horace M. "Negro Attitudes towards Jews,"
     JEWISH SOCIAL STUDIES, 27 (1965), 3-9.

     Argues that Negroes have absorbed anti-semitism from
     the larger American culture and is part of their
     anti-white sentiment.

269. Cleaver, Eldridge. SOUL ON ICE. New York:
     Delta, 1968.

     A set of essays which attempt to identify the nature
     of black soul in the context of America's colonial-
     type society.

270. Cruse, Harold. THE CRISIS OF THE NEGRO INTELLECTUAL.
     New York: Morrow, 1967.

     A study of the complex problem Negro intellectuals
     face in being spokesmen for the Negro masses as a
     whole.

271. David, Jay and Elaine Crane, eds. LIVING BLACK IN
     WHITE AMERICA. New York: Morrow, 1971.

     A reader which deals with the black experience in
     America, the "seeds of bitterness," as well as
     black protest.

272. Elifson, Kirk W. and Joseph Irwin. "Black Ministers'
     Attitudes toward Population Size and Birth
     Control,' SOCIOLOGICAL ANALYSIS, 38 (1977),
     245-252.

     A study of population policy attitudes among 154
     black clergy in Nashville, indicating the relevance
     of a number of demographic and experiential factors.

273. Foster, Lorn S. "Black Perceptions of the Mayor: An Empirical Test," URBAN AFFAIRS QUARTERLY, 14 (1978), 245-252.

The attitudes of white and black students to a white and black mayor are studied in East St. Louis and Peoria, finding that mayors of one's own race are better known and more positively evaluated.

274. Garza, Joseph M. RACE, THE ACHIEVEMENT SYNDROME, AND PERCEPTION OF OPPORTUNITY. Diss. Univ. Kentucky, 1966.

A study of low-income Negro and white mothers and their 11 year old sons which suggests a clear distinction between group values and expectations regarding their implementation.

275. Giles, Michael W. "Percent Black and Racial Hostility: An Old Assumption Re-examined," SOCIAL SCIENCE QUARTERLY, 58 (1977), 412-417.

A study of white racial attitudes which indicates that negative views are associated with higher concentrations of blacks only in the case of southerners.

276. Gordon, Daniel N. "A Note on Negro Alienation," AMERICAN JOURNAL OF SOCIOLOGY, 70 (1965), 477-478.

Critiques Coleman's analysis of Negro alienation and argues that such disaffection is a product of the urban rather than southern environment.

277. Grier, William H. and Price M. Cobbs. BLACK RAGE. New York: Bantam, 1968.

An analysis of types of black reaction to white domination, in particular anger and desperation, and how these affect adulthood, family life, and black personality among black males in America.

278. Grossack, Martin M. "Group Belongingness and Authoritarianism in Southern Negroes - A Research Note," PHYLON, 18 (1957), 261-266.

A questionnaire study of 148 Negro college students which discovers favorable mobility expectations, opposition to segregation, assertion of self-pride, rejection of "passing," and support for the NAACP.

279. Hatton, John M. "Reactions of Negroes in a Biracial Bargaining Situation," JOURNAL OF PERSONALITY AND SOCIAL PSYCHOLOGY, 7 (1967), 301-306.

An experimental study of Negro-white bargaining behavior which revealed the effects of perceived white power and prejudice.

280. Heller, Celia S. and Alphonso Pinkney. "The Attitudes of Negroes toward Jews," SOCIAL FORCES, 43 (1965), 364-369.

Data from a *Newsweek* poll indicate that a majority of Negroes view Jews as helpful to their cause, particularly respondents who are leaders and have higher incomes.

281. Hesslink, George K. NEGROES IN A NORTHERN RURAL COMMUNITY. Indianapolis: Bobbs-Merrill, 1968.

An analysis of a rural northern community that has remained bi-racial in nature for more than a century, maintaining stable and egalitarian race relations.

282. Killian, Lewis M. and Charles M. Grigg. "Negro Perceptions of Organizational Effectiveness," SOCIAL PROBLEMS, 11 (1964), 380-388.

549 Negroes in a southern city were asked to rank the effectiveness of 16 organizations and were found to rank the NAACP, Democratic Party, Federal Government, and Urban League the highest.

283. Lacy, Leslie A. THE RISE AND FALL OF A PROPER
     NEGRO. New York: Macmillan, 1970.

     An autobiography written by a southern Negro
     and concerned with his provocative racial experiences
     in America and Africa.

284. Lash, John. "The Conditioning of Servitude: A
     Critical Summary of Literature by and about
     Negroes in 1957," PHYLON, 19 (1958), 143-153.

     A critique of the literature on race and culture as
     distinguished by quantity rather than quality,
     stifling rather than encouraging the creative impulse.

285. McDaniel, Paul A. and Nicholas Babchuk. "Negro
     Conceptions of White People in a Northeastern
     City," PHYLON, 21 (1960), 7-19.

     26 stereotypes of whites were presented to a sample
     of 100 Negroes of varying social classes, indicating
     considerable consensus between the sample and the
     responses of southern Negroes. Lower class groups
     in both samples were most intensely unfavorable.

286. McDowell, Sophia. "Patterns of Preference by Negro
     Youth for White and Negro Associates," PHYLON,
     32 (1971), 290-301.

     Interracial preferences among 582 Negro youth in
     Washington, D.C. highlighted the importance of white
     racial attitudes rather than personal traits or
     socioeconomic characteristics.

287. Melish, Ilene H. "Attitudes toward the White
     Minority on a Black Campus: 1966-1968,"
     SOCIOLOGICAL QUARTERLY, 11 (1970), 321-330.

     A questionnaire study of 343 students and 34 faculty
     at a predominantly Negro southern college, docu-
     menting hostility toward the white minority as based
     on the perception of their alien nature.

288. Parker, Seymore and Robert Kneiner. "Status Position, Mobility, and Ethnic Identification of the Negro," JOURNAL OF SOCIAL ISSUES, 20 (1964), 85-102.

A study of Negro psychopathology, focusing on conflicting attitudes concerning ethnic identification as influenced by upward and downward mobility.

289. Ransford, H. Edward. "Skin Color, Life Chances, and Anti-White Attitudes," SOCIAL PROBLEMS, 18 (1970), 164-178.

Interviews of 312 Negro males after the Watts riot find that lower socioeconomic status and higher racial hostility tend to be associated with darker skin color.

290. Record, Wilson. "Changing Patterns of Internal Differentiation among Negroes in the United States," SOCIOLOGUS, 9 (1959), 115-131.

Negro group differentiation is defined as based on differential slave status, skin color, socioeconomic position, education, urbanization, and religion.

291. Scanzoni, John H. THE BLACK FAMILY IN MODERN SOCIETY. Boston: Allyn and Bacon, 1971.

A study of the black family which focuses on structural background, parental functionality, achievement and mobility, husband-wife and parent-child relationships, based on a wide variety of available data.

292. Turner, Castellano B. and William J. Wilson. "Dimensions of Racial Ideology: A Study of Urban Black Attitudes," THE JOURNAL OF SOCIAL ISSUES, 32 (1976), 139-152.

The racial views of 1,900 northern and southern blacks are analyzed in interviews, revealing that support for racial violence is most prevalent among the young, poorer northerners.

293. Weisborg, R. "Africa, Africans and the Afro-
Americans: Images and Identities in Transition,"
RACE, 10 (1969), 305-322.

An historical analysis of the continuity of African
identity among American blacks.

294. Works, Ernest. "Prejudice-Interaction Hypothesis
from the Point of View of the Negro Minority
Group," AMERICAN JOURNAL OF SOCIOLOGY, 67 (1961),
47-52.

A study which finds that for Negroes, as for whites,
racial prejudice tends to decline through intimate
and interracial contacts of individuals equal in
status.

ECONOMIC AND OCCUPATIONAL CONDITIONS

295. Bonacich, Edna. "Advanced Capitalism and Black/White
Relations in the United States: A Split Labor
Market Interpretation," AMERICAN SOCIOLOGICAL
REVIEW, 41 (1976), 34-51.

A discussion of the black/white split labor market
(i.e., differential labor prices) between W.W.I and
the New Deal, revealing how blacks were used to undermine white workers and unions until labor legislation,
use of overseas labor, and automation created the
hard-core unemployed.

296. Brimmer, Andrew F. "Economic Developments in the
Black Community," THE PUBLIC INTEREST, 34 (1974),
146-163.

While blacks have made income, educational, employment, and professional gains, their white collar
employment and advancement of black capitalism appear
limited.

297. Bush, Louis F. INTERRELATIONSHIPS AMONG RACIAL-ETHNIC
     BACKGROUND, FAMILY SIZE, AND INDIVIDUAL SOCIO-
     ECONOMIC DEVELOPMENT. Diss. U.S. International
     University, 1969.

     A study of 150 Mexican American, 1,400 Negro, and
     1,400 Caucasian eleventh-grade students, highlighting
     racial differences with regard to I.Q., values, and
     age of marriage but similar within-class career
     aspirations regardless of race.

298. Cook, Thomas J. "Benign Neglect: Minimal Feasible
     Understanding," SOCIAL PROBLEMS, 18 (1970), 145-
     151.

     1959-1968 Negro-white income differentials, while
     somewhat narrowed, continue to reveal significant
     regional and racial differences.

299. Davis, King E. "Jobs, Income, Business and Charity
     in the Black Community," THE BLACK SCHOLAR, 9
     (1977), 2-11.

     A study of changes in black income between 1947 and
     1977 which, while indicating increases, reveals no
     change in income sources or black wealth.

300. Duncan, Otis D. "Discrimination against Negroes,"
     THE ANNALS OF THE AMERICAN ACADEMY OF POLITICAL
     AND SOCIAL SCIENCE, 371 (1967), 85-103.

     Highlights statistical problems involved in developing
     reliable inferences and realistic recommendations
     regarding Negro discrimination. The relevance of
     research funding, the cooperation of official state
     agencies, freedom to study sensitive problems, and
     improved analytical and interpretive models to a
     fuller understanding of this issue is emphasized.

301. Geisel, Paul N. IQ PERFORMANCE, EDUCATIONAL AND OCCU-
      PATIONAL ASPIRATIONS OF YOUTH IN A SOUTHERN CITY:
      A RACIAL COMPARISON. Diss. Vanderbilt Univ.,1962.

      A study of 1,700 Negro and white school children which
      finds that while Negro IQ and aptitude scores are
      consistently lower than those of whites, their edu-
      cational and occupational aspirations are consistently
      higher.

302. Foner, Phillip S. "Organized Labor and the Black
      Worker in the 1970's," THE INSURGENT SOCIOLOGIST,
      8 (1978), 87-95.

      While changes occurred in the 1960's, minority
      workers remain concentrated among low-paying, un-
      skilled-semi-skilled, and low seniority positions
      in the 1970's.

303. Henderson, William L. and L.C. Ledebur. ECONOMIC
      DISPARITY: PROBLEMS AND STRATEGIES FOR BLACK
      AMERICANS. New York: Free Press, 1970.

      A discussion of various black and economic ideologies
      as they relate to the problem of racial economic
      disparity.

304. Hill, Robert. "The Illusion of Black Progress,"
      THE BLACK SCHOLAR, 10 (1978), 18-24.

      A study indicating that the proportion of upper
      class or upper middle class black families has not
      increased and may have declined.

305. Kelly, William R. and David Snyder. "Racial Violence
      and Socioeconomic Changes among Blacks in the
      United States," SOCIAL FORCES, 58 (1980), 739-
      760.

      An examination of the socioeconomic effects of racial
      violence, finding no relationship between such
      disruption and black gains.

306. Karnig, Albert K. "Black Economic, Political, and Cultural Development: Does City Size Make a Difference?" SOCIAL FORCES, 57 (1979), 1194-1211.

The effects of city size on black development are examined, finding a generally positive correlation - interpreted in terms of demographic, political, institutional, and economic factors.

307. Norman, Alex J. "Mutual Aid: A Key to Survival for Black Americans," THE BLACK SCHOLAR, 9 (1977), 44-49.

53 members of the L.A. Brotherhood Crusade are interviewed, highlighting their similar non-nationalistic, mutual aid and self-help orientations.

308. Pettigrew, Thomas F. A PROFILE OF THE NEGRO AMERICAN. Princeton: Van Nostrand, 1964.

A study of the Negro American with respect to personality traits, health, intelligence, crime, and protest.

309. Siegel, Paul M. "On the Cost of Being a Negro," SOCIOLOGICAL INQUIRY, 35 (1965), 41-57.

Using Census data, the financial cost of being a Negro is $1,000 - a racial differential which increases in relation to education, thereby belying the notion of a closing income gap.

310. Mhatia, O.L.E. "The Economic Effects of Fair Employment Laws on Occupations: The Application of Information Theory to Evaluate the Progress of Black Americans, 1954-1972," JOURNAL OF BLACK STUDIES, 8 (1978), 259-278.

While Fair Employment laws have reduced discrimination in skilled occupations, discrimination in the categories of managers, officials, and proprietors appears to continue.

311. Parham, T.D. "Black Job Expectations: A Comparative
     Analysis," JOURNAL OF BLACK STUDIES, 8 (1978),
     299-307.

     A study of 700 high school students in three southern
     communities which reveals the relationship between
     race, attitudes, and occupational expectations, with
     blacks higher in humanitarianism than whites.

312. Wilburn, Adolph Y. "Careers in Science and Engin-
     eering for Black Americans," SCIENCE, 184 (1974),
     1148-1154.

     A study of 12,000 blacks in science and engineering
     who graduated between 1940 and 1979, with recommen-
     dations regarding increased minority recruitment.

313. Yinger, J. Milton. A MINORITY GROUP IN AMERICAN
     SOCIETY. New York: McGraw-Hill, 1965.

     A discussion of the basis of minority-majority
     relations generally and Negro segregation, discrim-
     ination, and their reduction specifically.

EDUCATION

314. Anderson, William and Henry Frierson. "Black Sur-
     vival in White Academe," JOURNAL OF NEGRO
     EDUCATION, 48 (1979), 92-102.

     A case study of 42 black faculty at the University
     of North Carolina, highlighting perceived barriers
     and white prejudice.

315. Johnson, Nan E. "Minority Group Status and the
     Fertility of Black Americans,1970: Another
     Look," AMERICAN JOURNAL OF SOCIOLOGY, 84 (1979)
     1386-1400.

An examination of the effects of race and education on fertility among a group of 6,597 whites and blacks, highlighting the influence of education rather than minority group status.

316. Lincoln, C. Eric. "Black Studies and Cultural Continuity," THE BLACK SCHOLAR, 10 (1978), 12-17.

Emphasizes the importance of black studies programs to black cultural continuity and increased white understanding.

317. McCord, William M. and Nicholas J. Demerath, III. "Negro versus White Intelligence: A Continuing Controversy," HARVARD EDUCATIONAL REVIEW, 28 (1958), 120-135.

A rejection of assumed Negro intellectual inferiority as revealed by a number of studies indicating no significant differences in intelligence.

318. Morris, Frank. "The Jensen Hypothesis: Was it the White Perspective or White Racism?" JOURNAL OF BLACK STUDIES, 2 (1972), 371-386.

Critiques Jensen for being unscientific, unfair, value laden and biased towards a racist perspective of blacks and negative environments.

319. Morsell, John A. "Schools, Courts and the Negro's Future," HARVARD EDUCATIONAL REVIEW, 30 (1960), 179-194.

Discusses the persistence of Negro-white educational gaps nationwide as reflected in inferior instruction, curricula, and buildings, particularly in the South.

320. Walters, Ronald and Robert Smith. "The Black Education Strategy in the 1970's," THE JOURNAL OF

NEGRO EDUCATION, 48 (1979), 156-170.

An assessment of the impact of 1960's changes on
black students in the 1970's, revealing that such
students appear to be generally satisfied with their
education and optimistic career-wise although
alienation persists also.

THE BLACK GHETTO

321. Aldrich, Howard. "Employment Opportunities for
      Blacks in the Black Ghetto: The Role of White
      Owned Businesses," AMERICAN JOURNAL OF SOCIOLOGY,
      78 (1973), 1403-1425.

      A study of small businesses in Boston, Chicago, and
      Washington, D.C., documenting white business dominat-
      ion of the labor market and economics of black ghettos.

322. Clark, Kenneth B. DARK GHETTO. New York: Harper
      and Row, 1965.

      A study of the Negro ghetto which attempts to "...
      understand the combined problems of the confined
      Negro and the problem of the slum." It deals with
      the ghetto's dynamics, psychology, pathology, power
      structure, school system, and need for change.

323. Etzioni, Amitai. "Ghetto - A Re-evaluation," SOCIAL
      FORCES, 37 (1959), 255-262.

      A critique of Wirth's model of "the ghetto" as un-
      specific, equilibrium-oriented, and assimilationist-
      oriented.

324. Feagin, Joe R. "Social Organization in the Black
      Ghetto," INTERNATIONAL JOURNAL OF CONTEMPORARY
      SOCIOLOGY, 9 (1972), 108-116.

72

Interviewing 20 Negro leaders in Boston, the author argues for reconceptualizing the slum as an urban village containing positive social forces.

325. LaGuerre, Michele S. "Internal Dependency: The Structural Position of the Black Ghetto in American Society," THE JOURNAL OF ETHNIC STUDIES, 6 (1979), 29-44.

The black ghetto is discussed within the context of dependency theory and the internal colonialism model, emphasizing the need to investigate critical zones in order to understand such a ghetto.

326. Lake, Robert W. "Racial Transition and Black Home Ownership in American Suburbs," THE ANNALS OF THE AMERICAN ACADEMY OF POLITICAL AND SOCIAL SCIENCE, 441 (1979), 142-156.

A study of black suburbanization in 1974 and 1975, revealing that this process is not synonymous with homeownership nor the development of black wealth.

327. Moore, Jr., William. THE VERTICAL GHETTO. New York: Random House, 1969.

A study of the pathology of a low-income, high-rise public housing project and its negative impact on its residents, particularly the children.

328. Osofsky, Gilbert. "The Enduring Ghetto," JOURNAL OF AMERICAN HISTORY, 55 (1968), 243-255.

Historically, while Negro status has changed, the structure of the Negro ghetto has remained largely the same with respect to occupational discrimination and the maintenance of second-class citizenship.

329. Rosenthal, Robert, Bernard Bruce, et al. DIFFERENT STROKES. Boulder: Westview, 1976.

A study of the institutions, types of people, and implications involved in a Boston ghetto.

330. Staples, Robert. "Land of Promise, Cities of Despair: Blacks in Urban America," THE BLACK SCHOLAR, 10 (1978), 2-11.

Argues that while southern black peasant culture was largely positive, northern urban life has been largely negative in respect to taxes, school closings, and limited social services.

BLACK HISTORY

331. Bell, Howard. "Negroes in California, 1849-1859," PHYLON, 28 (1957), 151-160.

A study of race relations during the gold rush, revealing media emphases on the need for minority educational and political participation but little implementation of such goals.

332. Blassingame, John W. THE SLAVE COMMUNITY. New York: Oxford University Press, 1972.

An original study which analyzes the institution of slavery from the perspective of the slaves themselves in contrast to their white owners, highlighting the strength of slave community structure.

333. Bonacich, Edna. "Abolition, the Extension of Slavery, and the Position of Free Blacks: A Study of Split Labor Markets in the United States, 1830-1863," AMERICAN JOURNAL OF SOCIOLOGY, 81 (1975), 601-628.

Race relations in pre-Civil War America are analyzed with respect to white labor interests in the North, South, and West reflected in varying attitudes towards abolition, slavery, and free blacks.

334. Berwanger, Eugene H. "Negro Phobia in Northern
      Pro-Slavery and Anti-Slavery Thought," PHYLON,
      33 (1972), 266-275.

      Anti-Negro prejudice is discovered in both pro and
      anti-slavery writing prior to the Civil War,
      reflecting the extent of racism throughout the
      society.

335. Chace, William M. and Peter Collier, eds. JUSTICE
      DENIED. New York: Harcourt, Brace and World,
      1970.

      A reader which deals with the historical periods of
      slavery and resistance, abolition to Jim Crow, through
      World War II, the awakening of civil rights, the
      urban crisis, and black power.

336. Fogel, Robert W. and Stanley L. Engerman, TIME ON THE
      CROSS, Vols. I,II. Boston: Little, Brown, 1974.

      An empirical examination of the economic foundations
      of American Negro slavery, challenging previous
      assumptions concerning the material conditions of
      slavery.

337. Hills, Stuart L. "Negroes and Immigrants in America,"
      SOCIOLOGICAL FOCUS, 3 (1970), 85-96.

      European immigrants and Negroes are compared in terms
      of visibility, effects of slavery, economic position,
      group action, government intervention, and ethnicity.

338. Romero, Patricia W., ed. IN BLACK AMERICA. New
      York: United, 1969.

      A pictorial tour of black America dealing with black
      history, the characteristics of institutionalized
      racism, major personalities, bibliographies of
      relevant articles, statistical data, and civil rights
      legislation.

339. Shepperson, G. "The Negro on the New Frontier,"
POLITICAL QUARTERLY, 33 (1962), 172-182.

A positive evaluation of J.F. Kennedy's impact on
civil rights compared with previous administrations.

340. Wilson, William J. "Class Conflict and Jim Crow
Segregation in the Postbellum South," PACIFIC
SOCIOLOGICAL REVIEW, 19 (1976), 431-446.

Analyzes southern race relations between 1865 and
1900 in relation to changing types of production,
ending with Populists competing with the upper
classes.

341. Wye, Christopher G. "The New Deal and the Negro
Community: Toward a Broader Conceptualization,"
JOURNAL OF AMERICAN HISTORY, 59 (1972), 621-639.

A study of public housing projects effected in
Cleveland during the New Deal, finding that, while
areas were improved, residential segregation increased
also.

BLACKS AND THE LAW

342. Bacon, Emory F. "Race Relations in an Industrial
Society," RACE, 4 (1963), 32-38.

While union grievance procedures have attempted to
improve Negro occupational and wage conditions,
relatively few charges are filed.

343. Cross, Granville J. "The Negro, Prejudice, and
the Police," JOURNAL OF CRIMINAL LAW, CRIMINOL-
OGY AND POLICE SCIENCE, 55 (1964), 405-411.

A discussion of procedures designed to prevent riots
through increased police professionalism and
preventive work.

76

344. Murray, Paul T. "Blacks and the Draft: A History of Institutional Racism," JOURNAL OF BLACK STUDIES 2 (1971), 57-76.

A study of disproportionate numbers of blacks drafted in W.W.I, Korea and Vietnam, reflecting predominant military opinions and domestic politics.

345. Newton, I.G. "The Negro and the National Guard," PHYLON, 23 (1962), 18-28.

The low number of Negroes in the National Guard is attributed to informal racially restrictive policies regarding recruitment and the dual control of federal and state agencies.

346. Rose, Arnold M. "New and Emerging Negro Problems," JOURNAL OF INTERGROUP RELATIONS, 1 (1960), 71-74.

During what is viewed as a transitional phase, continuing occupational, political, personal, and residential discrimination is associated with limited Negro labor market skills and familiarity with the urban context.

BLACK POLITICS

347. Baldwin, Charles H. A TREND ANALYSIS OF BLACK AMERICANS' POLITICAL AND RACIAL ATTITUDES. Diss. Univ. of North Carolina at Chapel Hill, 1977.

An examination of trends in black political and racial attitudes between 1952 and 1972 with respect to age, education, region, and political involvement, finding no consistent effects over time.

348. Brotz, Howard. "The Negro-Jewish Community and the Contemporary Race Crisis," JEWISH SOCIAL STUDIES, 27 (1975), 10-17.

A case study of the Black Jews or Ethiopian Hebrew
sect in New York, highlighting their self-sufficiency,
pride, emphasis on self-help and morals in their
family lives. The importance of ethnic community
development to improving race relations is emphasized.

349. Bullock, Charles, III. "The Election of Blacks in
     the South: Preconditions and Consequences,"
     AMERICAN JOURNAL OF POLITICAL SCIENCE, 19 (1975),
     727-739.

A study of electoral, demographic, and political
factors behind the successful election of black
candidates to political office in the South.

350. Burgess, M. Elaine. NEGRO LEADERSHIP IN A SOUTHERN
     CITY. Chapel Hill: University of North
     Carolina Press, 1962.

A case study of power and decision-making within an
urban Negro community with respect to the issue of
desegregation and white response.

351. Burns, W. Haywood. "Black Muslims in America:
     A Reinterpretation," RACE, 5 (1963), 26-37.

An interpretation of the Black Muslim movement as
a desire for access to scarce values, providing its
members with a sense of identity, respectability,
and acceptance.

352. Cannon, J. Alfred. "Re-Africanization: The Last
     Alternative for Black America," PHYLON, 38
     (1977), 203-210.

Advocates Africanization (identification with the
black cultures of Africa and the Caribbean) as vital
to the survival of the black community.

78

353. Carmichael, Stokely and Charles V. Hamilton. BLACK
     POWER. New York: Vintage, 1967.

     A discussion of white power as colonialism and the
     politics of black liberation necessary to deal with
     and overcome it.

354. Clute, William T. COMMUNITY INVOLVEMENT AND ASSOC-
     IATIONAL PARTICIPATION IN A RACIALLY MIXED URBAN
     AREA. Diss. Univ. of Minnesota, 1969.

     A study of the relationship between race, neighborhood
     evaluation, and community involvement, finding that
     Negroes had a greater attachment to and interaction
     within the neighborhood than whites.

355. Cruse, Harold. REBELLION OR REVOLUTION? New York:
     Morrow, 1968.

     A set of essays analyzing different facets of
     black nationalism and its alternatives.

356. Danigelis, Nicholas L. RACE AND POLITICAL ACTIVITY
     IN THE UNITED STATES, 1948-1968: A TREND
     ANALYSIS. Diss. Indiana Univ., 1973.

     Six presidential year surveys highlight the
     continuing importance of political climate to
     the extent of black political activity.

357. Feagin, Joe R. "The Second Reconstruction: Black
     Political Strength in the South," SOCIAL SCIENCE
     QUARTERLY, 51 (1970), 42-56.

     Outlines the conditions required for minority
     political achievement, including experience, leader-
     ship, legal safeguards, and gradualistic attitudes.
     Concludes that blacks possess many of these
     qualities.

358. Flaming, Carl H., John Patten, et al. "Black Power-
      lessness in Policy-Making Decisions," SOCIOLOGICAL
      QUARTERLY, 13 (1972), 126-133.

      A study of Milwaukee blacks in business, public,
      academic, and voluntary policy-making positions,
      revealing their low numbers and underrepresentation.

359. Ginzberg, Eli and Alfred S. Eichner. THE TROUBLE-
      SOME PRESENCE: AMERICAN DEMOCRACY AND THE
      NEGRO. New York: Free Press, 1964.

      A history of Negro-white confrontation in reference
      to significant stages and increasing minority
      political power.

360. Glazer, Nathan. "Blacks and Ethnic Groups: The
      Difference and the Political Difference It
      Makes," SOCIAL PROBLEMS, 18 (1971), 444-461.

      Views the internal colonialism model as more relevant
      to southern race relations with pluralism operative
      in the north. Black political decisions are seen as
      having important repercussions on other racial
      minorities.

361. Killian, Lewis M. and Charles M. Grigg. "Race
      Relations in an Urbanized South," JOURNAL OF
      SOCIAL ISSUES, 22 (1966), 20-29.

      A discussion of the impact of urban Negroes on race
      relations in the South.

362. Lincoln, C. Eric. THE BLACK MUSLIM IN AMERICA.
      Boston: Beacon Press, 1961.

      A study of the background and motives of Black Muslim
      members as well as the functions and impact of the
      movement for the larger society.

363. Long, Herman H. "The Challenge to Negro Leadership," JOURNAL OF INTERGROUP RELATIONS, 1 (1960), 75-78.

Outlines the dilemma posed by maintaining group solidarity while attempting societal integration.

364. McCarthy, John D. RACE AND POLITICAL ACTIVITY IN AN URBAN CONTEXT. Diss. Univ. of Oregon, 1968.

Survey data from Portland, Oregon, indicate that whites are more likely to engage in local informal political activities than Negroes.

365. Olsen, Marvin E. "Social and Political Participation of Blacks," AMERICAN SOCIOLOGICAL REVIEW, 35 (1970), 682-689.

When socioeconomic status and other background variables are controlled, blacks are found to participate highly in a wide range of social and political activities.

366. Williams, Joyce E. BLACK COMMUNITY CONTROL. New York: Praeger, 1973.

A detailed account of the emergence of a black community in Texas and its struggle for community control, as a case study in black protest.

367. Wilson, James Q. "The Negro in Politics," DAEDALUS, 94 (1965), 949-973.

Discusses characteristics of the Negro voter in the South and North as well as future possible developments.

ASIAN AMERICANS

368. Boyd, Monica. "Oriental Immigration: The Experience
of the Chinese, Japanese, and Filipino Population
in the United States," INTERNATIONAL MIGRATION
REVIEW, 5 (1971), 48-61.

Analyzes the pre-1960 historical and demographic
character of minority migration to the United States,
highlighting regional concentration, past immigrations,
and male labor force characteristics.

369. Fong, Stanley L.M. "Assimilation of Chinese in
America: Changes in Orientation and Social
Perception," AMERICAN JOURNAL OF SOCIOLOGY, 71
(1965), 265-273.

A study of the attitudes of 336 Chinese college
students, revealing their progressive acculturation,
declining tradition, and internalization of American
norms.

370. Gupta, Santosh P. "Changes in the Food Habits of
Asian Indians in the United States: A Case
Study," SOCIOLOGY AND SOCIAL RESEARCH, 60 (1975),
87-99.

Changing food habits among 50 Asian Indians are found
to be related to marital status, age, sex, length
of U.S. residence, caste and rural versus urban
background.

371. Jones, Dorothy M. "Race Relations in an Alaska
Native Village," ANTHROPOLOGICA, 15 (1973),
167-190.

White-Aleut relations highlight the manner in which
the former undermine the latter's self-esteem by
socializing them in denigrating and humiliating ways,
assigning them a subservient status in the community.

372. Kung, S.W. CHINESE IN AMERICAN LIFE. Seattle:
     University of Washington Press, 1962.

     A study of the historical, demographic, and political
     conditions affecting Chinese Americans, concluding
     with a discussion of the mutual benefits produced
     by freer Chinese-American interaction.

373. Kitano, Harry H.L. JAPANESE AMERICANS. Englewood
     Cliffs: Prentice-Hall, 1969.

     Deals with the history of Japanese Americans, their
     family, community, and cultural characteristics
     and aberrant behavior.

374. Kitano, Harry H.L. and Sue Stanley. "The Model
     Minorities," JOURNAL OF SOCIAL ISSUES, 29 (1972),
     1-9.

     A study of the significant gains made by Asian
     American minorities (Chinese, Filipino, Japanese,
     Korean) which questions the degree to which such
     success has produced satisfaction also.

375. Kuo, Wen H. "On the Study of Asian Americans: Its
     Current State and Agenda," THE SOCIOLOGICAL
     QUARTERLY, 29 (1979), 279-290.

     A critique of Asian American assimilation studies
     for being ahistorical, ignoring activism, and low
     cross-cultural orientation.

376. Lee, Rose H. "The Stranded Chinese in the United
     States," PHYLON, 19 (1958), 180-194.

     A study of a group of stranded Nationalist Chinese
     students in the U.S., highlighting their marginality,
     deferred gratification, and reduced status.

377. Montero, Darrel and Ronald Tsukashima, "Assimilation and Educational Achievement: The Case of the Second Generation Japanese American," THE SOCIO-LOGICAL QUARTERLY, 18 (1977), 490-503.

378. Petersen, William. JAPANESE AMERICANS. New York: Random House, 1971.

An analysis of Japanese Americans in terms of their migration, internment experience, social mobility, social problems, religious and family characteristics.

HAWAII

379. Kinloch, Graham C. "Race, Socioeconomic Status, and Social Distance in Hawaii," SOCIOLOGY AND SOCIAL RESEARCH, 57 (1973), 156-167.

1,346 students at the University of Hawaii were administered the Bogardus Social Distance Scale, revealing that Chinese, Japanese, and Korean students tended to be more prejudiced than Filipinos, Negroes and Caucasians.

380. Lind, Andrew W. HAWAII'S PEOPLE. Honolulu: University of Hawaii Press, 1967.

A demographic analysis of Hawaii's population, with particular reference to racial background, age, sex, geographic distribution, socioeconomic traits, education, political status, and mortality.

381. Lind, Andrew W. HAWAII, THE LAST OF THE MAGIC ISLES. London: Oxford University Press, 1969.

A case study of the historical factors behind and demographic characteristics associated with race relations in Hawaii.

382. Samuels, Frederick. "The Oriental In-Group in Hawa-
     ii," PHYLON, 31 (1970), 148-156.

     210 interviews of Japanese and Caucasian respondents
     in Honolulu were carried out. Class background was
     found to be positively associated with acceptance of
     racial out-groups.

383. Samuels, Frederick. THE JAPANESE AND HAOLES OF
     HONOLULU: DURABLE GROUP INTERACTION, New Haven:
     College and University Press, 1971.

     A detailed analysis of Japanese-Caucasian relations
     in Honolulu based on interviews, participant observ-
     ation, and demographic data.

384. Yinger, J. Milton. "Integration and Pluralism
     Viewed from Hawaii," ANTIOCH REVIEW, 22 (1962),
     397-410.

     A discussion of undesirable segregation versus
     legitimate pluralism comparing Hawaii with the
     larger U.S. The latter is considered a case of
     undesirable segregation.

INDIAN AMERICANS

385. Beuf, Ann H. THE INNER ALCATRAZ: A STUDY OF RACIAL
     ATTITUDES IN AMERICAN PRE-SCHOOL CHILDREN.
     Diss. Bryn Mawr Coll., 1972.

     Racial awareness, preferences, and self-identifi-
     cation were studied among 200 young American Indian
     and Anglo children, revealing significant racial
     differences.

386. Brown, Dee. BURY MY HEART AT WOUNDED KNEE. New
     York: Holt, Rinehart and Winston, 1970.

A narrative of the conquest of the American West constructed from the Indians' own words and reactions where possible.

387. Chadwick, Bruce A. and Joseph Stous, et al. "Confrontation with the Law: The American Indians in Seattle," PHYLON, 37 (1976), 163-171.

300 American Indians in Seattle were interviewed and found not to perceive white exploitation nor be aware of social service agencies.

388. David, Jay, ed. THE AMERICAN INDIAN, THE FIRST VICTIM. New York: Morrow, 1972.

A set of documents dealing with growing up as an Indian, the Indian "way of life," encounters with whites, and the Indian in the twentieth century.

389. Hoebel, E. Adamson. THE CHEYENNES. New York: Holt, Rinehart and Winston, 1960.

Discusses the Cheyennes in terms of their ritual and tribal integration, social structures, warfare, culture, and personality traits.

390. Josephy, Alvin M. THE INDIAN HERITAGE OF AMERICA. New York: Knopf, 1970.

A discussion of the history, archeology, and ethnology of all major Indian cultures in the United States.

391. Margon, Arthur. "Indians and Immigrants: A Comparison of Groups New to the City," THE JOURNAL OF ETHNIC STUDIES, 4 (1977), 17-28.

While Indians appear to have similar urban experiences to other minorities, tribalism appears to put different pressures on the individual.

392. Marriott, Alice and Carol K. Rachlin. AMERICAN
     EPIC: THE STORY OF THE AMERICAN INDIAN. New
     York: Mentor, 1969.

     A discussion of the American Indian which focuses
     specifically on the effects of European and Euro-
     American contacts on cultural relations in the New
     World.

393. Schusky, Ernest L. "An Indian Dilemma," INTERNATIONAL
     JOURNAL OF COMPARATIVE SOCIOLOGY, 11 (1970), 58-
     66.

     A discussion of the dilemma between tribal rights
     and civil rights as it affects the treatment of
     crime, property rights, and land ownership.

394. Sorkin, Alan. "Some Aspects of American Indian
     Migration," SOCIAL FORCES, 48 (1969), 243-250.

     A study of American Indian urban relocation which
     finds that while standards of living are improved,
     surplus labor on the reservations is not sufficiently
     reduced.

395. Sorkin, Alan. "The Economic and Social Status of the
     American Indian, 1940-1970," THE JOURNAL OF
     NEGRO EDUCATION, 45 (1976), 432-447.

     A comparison of reservation and urban Indians,
     indicating the increasing socioeconomic disparity
     between the two.

396. Steiner, Stan. THE NEW INDIANS. New York: Delta,
     1968.

     Discusses the survival of the "old Indian" and
     emergence of the "new Indian" as told in their own
     words.

397. Terrell, John U. APACHE CHRONICLE. New York:
     World, 1972.

     A detailed chronicle of the destruction of the Apache
     nation as well as their customs, diverse tribes,
     and flamboyant leaders.

398. Thornton, Russell and Mary K. Grasmick. "Sociolog-
     logical Study of American Indians: A Research
     Note on Journal Literature," ETHNICITY, 6 (1979),
     299-305.

     273 sociological articles indicate increased concern
     with pan-Indianism and social science concerns.

399. Wax, Rosalie and Robert A. Thomas. "American Indians
     and White People," PHYLON, 22 (1961), 305-317.

     Racial differences in levels of activity and aggress-
     ion are seen as making interracial interaction
     troubled and difficult.

400. Wax, Murrey L. et al. "Formal Education in an
     American Indian Community," SOCIAL PROBLEMS,
     11 (1964), Supplement.

     A monograph study of the education system on Pine
     Ridge Reservation, highlighting its general isolation
     from the mainstream of American life.

401. Wicker, Leslie C. RACIAL AWARENESS AND RACIAL
     IDENTIFICATION AMONG AMERICAN INDIAN CHILDREN AS
     INFLUENCED BY NATIVE-AMERICAN POWER IDEOLOGY
     AND SELF-CONCEPT. Diss. Univ. of North Carolina
     at Greensboro, 1977.

     The effects of exposure to a native-American move-
     ment on racial awareness and identification among
     American Indian children was examined with little
     apparent relationship.

402. Aguirre, Alberto. "Intelligence Testing in Chicano: A Quality of Life Issue," SOCIAL PROBLEMS, 26 (1979), 186-195.

Defines intelligence tests as ideological devices used to legitimate Chicano educational inequality.

403. Alford, Harold J. THE PROUD PEOPLES. New York: David McKay, 1972.

An analysis of the heritage and culture of Spanish-speaking peoples in the United States.

404. Antunes, George and Charles M. Gaitz. "Ethnicity and Participation: A Study of Mexican Americans, Blacks, and Whites," AMERICAN JOURNAL OF SOCIO-LOGY, 80 (1975), 1192-1211.

A community survey of Houston finds that Mexican American social and political participation is lower than that of other groups, even when social class is controlled for.

405. Dworkin, Anthony G. "Stereotypes and Self-Images Held by Native Born and Foreign Born Mexican Americans, "SOCIOLOGY AND SOCIAL RESEARCH, 49 (1965), 214-224.

A study of 280 U.S. born and Mexican born Mexican Americans found that the latter more often hold favorable stereotypes and self-images.

406. Edwards, John N. and Patricia A. Clobus. "Ethnicity and Participation: A Commentary," AMERICAN JOURNAL OF SOCIOLOGY, 82 (1976), 423-427.

Low social and political participation among Mexican Americans is explained using the "isolation hypothesis."

407. Forbes, Jack D. "Race and Color in Mexican American
        Problems," JOURNAL OF HUMAN RELATIONS, 16 (1968),
        55-68.

        Attempts to clarify the Mexican American problem by
        discussing evidence indicating that their self-
        esteem has been damaged by anti-Indian prejudice,
        producing high levels of shame.

408. Grebler, Leo, Joan W Moore, et al. THE MEXICAN
        AMERICAN PEOPLE: THE NATION'S SECOND LARGEST
        MINORITY. New York: Free Press, 1970.

        A large-scale study of Mexican American socioeconomic
        status, dealing with historical background, immi-
        gration, occupations, social mobility, housing
        conditions, religion, the family, ethnic relations,
        and politics.

409. Hernandez, Carrol A., Marsha J. Haug, et al., eds.
        CHICANOS, SOCIAL AND PSYCHOLOGICAL PERSPECTIVES.
        St Louis: Mosby, 1976.

        A collection of articles on Mexican Americans,
        focusing on the justice issue, personality studies,
        education, and mental health.

410. Lampe, Phillip E. "Ethnic Identity among Minority
        Groups and Public Parochial Schools," ETHNIC
        GROUPS, 1 (1977), 337-352.

        A study of 750 black and Mexican American school
        students which finds that ethnic identity is un-
        related to type of school (parochial versus public).

411. Lampe, Phillip E. "Ethnic Self-Referent and the
        Assimilation of Mexican Americans," INTERNATIONAL
        JOURNAL OF COMPARATIVE SOCIOLOGY, 19 (1978), 259-
        270.

368 eighth-grade Mexican Americans were administered
a questionnaire on ethnic identity, finding that
the most assimilated were American in self-referent,
followed by Mexican Americans, Spanish or Latin
Americans, and Chicanos.

412. Marrett, Cora B. "The Brown Power Revolt: A True
      Social Movement," JOURNAL OF HUMAN RELATIONS,
      19 (1971), 356-366.

      Examines minority movements in terms of their
      cooptation by the larger society by focusing on
      movement goals rather than activist rhetoric.

413. McLenore, Dale S. "The Origins of Mexican American
      Subordination in Texas," SOCIAL SCIENCE QUARTERLY,
      53 (1973), 656-670.

      Applies the theory of resource-competition to
      explain the historical subordination of Mexican
      Americans in Texas.

414. Moerk, Ernst. "The Acculturation of the Mexican
      American Minority to the Anglo Society in the
      United States," JOURNAL OF HUMAN RELATIONS, 20
      (1972), 317-325.

      A study of acculturation among Mexican Americans
      over time, finding rising expectations and cultural
      assimilation.

415. Moore, Joan W. "Colonialism: The Case of the
      Mexican Americans," SOCIAL PROBLEMS, 17 (1970),
      463-472.

      Delineation of classic conflict and economic colon-
      ialism as they have influenced Mexican Americans in
      different parts of Mexico and the U.S.

416. Moore, Joan W. MEXICAN AMERICANS. Englewood Cliffs:
     Prentice-Hall, 1970.

     A book on Mexican Americans focusing on historical
     background, immigration, and education.

417. Parades, Raymond A. "The Origins of Anti-Mexican
     Sentiment in the United States," THE NEW SCHOLAR,
     6 (1977), 139-165.

     The sources of anti-Mexican sentiment are traced to
     English notions concerning Catholicism, Spanish
     character, and Mexican aborigines.

418. Penalosa, Fernando and E.C. McDonagh. "Social
     Mobility in a Mexican-American Community,"
     SOCIAL FORCES, 44 (1966), 498-505.

     An analysis of Mexican American social mobility in
     Southern California which indicates that such mobility
     is associated with second-generation status, main-
     tenance of ethnic identity, and Catholicism.

419. Penalosa, Fernando. "The Changing Mexican American
     in Southern California," SOCIOLOGY AND SOCIAL
     RESEARCH, 51 (1967), 405-417.

     Given integration, assimilation, upward mobility,
     and increased political power, the predominant
     view of Mexican Americans as largely employed in
     migratory labor is condemned as a sociological
     stereotype.

420. Penalosa, Fernando. "Recent Changes among the
     Chicanos," SOCIOLOGY AND SOCIAL RESEARCH, 55
     (1970), 47-53.

     A discussion of the emergence of political and
     educational militancy among Chicanos.

421. Poston, Dudley L., David Alvirez, et al. "Earnings
     Differences between Anglo and Mexican American
     Male Workers in 1960-1970: Changes in the Cost
     of Being Mexican American," SOCIAL SCIENCE
     QUARTERLY, 57 (1976), 618-631.

     A study which shows that the economic cost of being
     Mexican American has increased during the 1960's,
     belying images of significant improvement.

422. Schoen, Robert and Lawrence E. Cohen. "Ethnic
     Endogamy among Mexican American Groups: A Re-
     analysis of Generational and Occupational Effects,"
     AMERICAN JOURNAL OF SOCIOLOGY, 86 (1980), 359-
     366.

     Generational rather than occupational factors are
     found to explain Mexican American endogamy.

423. Simmons, Ozzie G. "Mutual Images and Expectations
     of Anglo-American and Mexican Americans,"
     DAEDALUS, 90 (1961), 286-299.

     Mutually negative images and expectations between
     Anglo and Mexican Americans are documented with the
     former demanding assimilation of the latter as a
     condition of acceptance.

424. Steinman, Michael. "Low Income and Minority Group
     Participation in Administrative Processes:
     Mexican American Orientations to Healthcare
     Services," URBAN AFFAIRS QUARTERLY, 11 (1976),
     523-544.

     149 Mexican Americans in Omaha indicate interest in
     healthcare operational problems and their partici-
     pation should be encouraged.

425. Bonilla, E. Seda. "Patterns of Social Accommodation
      of the Migrant Puerto Rican in the American
      Social Structure," REV. CIE. SOC., 2 (1958),
      189-200.

      Puerto Ricans in the U.S. are viewed as experiencing
      a loss of status upon entering the society, given
      its rigid racial structure.

426. Fitzpatrick, Joseph P. "Attitudes of Puerto Ricans
      toward Color," AMERICAN CATHOLIC SOCIOLOGICAL
      REVIEW, 20 (1959), 219-233.

      Puerto Rican tolerance towards intermarriage is
      found to decline in the context of American society,
      particularly among the middle class.

427. Fitzpatrick, Joseph P. PUERTO RICAN AMERICANS.
      Englewood Cliffs: Prentice-Hall, 1971.

      Deals with Puerto Rican migration, identity,
      community and family characteristics, religious
      institutions, social problems, and experiences in
      New York City.

428. Glazer, Nathan. "The Puerto Ricans," COMMENTARY,
      36 (1963), 1-9.

      Puerto Rican island background and culture are
      used to explain the weakness of their community
      organization and leadership in New York.

429. Macisco, John J. "Assimilation of Puerto Ricans on
      the Mainland: A Socio-demographic Approach,"
      INTERNATIONAL MIGRATION REVIEW, 2 (1968),
      21-37.

Using 1960 census data, this study shows that
second generation Puerto Ricans are moving towards
average demographic characteristics in the U.S. at
large.

430. Maldonado-Denis, Manuel. "The Puerto Ricans: Protest
or Submission?" ANNALS OF THE AMERICAN ACADEMY
OF POLITICAL AND SOCIAL SCIENCE, 382 (1969),
26-31.

Argues that Puerto Ricans need to achieve de-
colonization politically as well as psychologically
in order to develop as a true protest movement.

RACIAL AND ETHNIC ATTITUDES

RACIAL AND ETHNIC PERCEPTIONS AND STEREOTYPES

431. Bennett, Stephen E. "On the Existence of an Underlying 'Vertical Structure' in Whites' Racial
Attitudes," SOCIAL SCIENCE QUARTERLY, 53 (1972),
583-589.

A critique of the notion of "vertical structure" in
racial attitudes based on 1968 Survey Research Center
survey data which reveal a high rate of "socially
acceptable" replies.

432. Blake, Robert R. and Jane S. Mouton. "Comprehension
of Points of Communality in Competing Solutions,"
SOCIOMETRY, 25 (1962), 56-63.

A study of in-group perception of issues which
protects interests and creates barriers which
prevent the resolution of group conflict.

433. Brink, William and Louis Harris. BLACK AND WHITE.
New York: Clarion, 1966.

95

A study of racial attitudes based on poll data, and dealing with progress, leadership, Negro politics, white attitudes, the Negro family, and race relations in the military.

434. Broom, Leonard and Norval D. Glenn. "Negro-White Differences in Reported Attitudes and Behavior," SOCIOLOGY AND SOCIAL RESEARCH, 50 (1965), 187-200.

A research project which finds significant convergence in Negro and white attitudes and behavior and a persistent Negro subculture.

435. Campbell, Angus. WHITE ATTITUDES TOWARD BLACK PEOPLE. Ann Arbor: University of Michigan Press, 1971.

A 15 city study of racial attitudes collected in a series of surveys carried out by the Survey Research Center between 1964 and 1970, highlighting attitudes towards specific issues over time, analyzed according to background characteristics.

436. Campbell, Angus and Shirley Hackett. "Racial Attitude Trends: 1964-1974," INTEGRATED EDUCATION, 14 (1976), 40-42.

Institute for Social Research surveys in 1964 and 1974 indicate declining support for total integration and feel race relations have improved while blacks similarly view interracial contacts in a positive fashion.

437. Carter, Barbara L. and Dorothy K. Newman. "Perceptions about Black Americans," ANNALS OF THE AMERICAN ACADEMY OF POLITICAL AND SOCIAL SCIENCE, 435 (1978), 179-206.

Delineates the extent of institutionalized racism in America, subjecting blacks to political, social, and economic racism.

438. Daniels, Roger and Harry L. Kitano. AMERICAN
RACISM: EXPLORATION OF THE NATURE OF PREJU-
DICE. Englewood Cliffs: Prentice-Hall, 1970.

A book which deals with racial stratification in
America, historical changes, and the present ethnic
crisis.

439. Edwards, Ozzie L. "Intergenerational Variation and
Racial Attitudes," SOCIOLOGY AND SOCIAL RESEARCH,
57 (1972), 22-31.

Racial attitudes of parent-child pairs reveal greater
similarity than variations within black and white
families.

440. Edwards, Ozzie L. "Skin Color as a Variable in
Racial Attitudes of Black Urbanites," JOURNAL OF
BLACK STUDIES, 3 (1973), 473-483.

Degree of darkness is found to be negatively associated with socioeconomic status and positively
correlated with awareness of discrimination.

441. Ehrlich, Howard J. "Stereotyping and Negro-Jewish
Stereotypes," SOCIAL FORCES, 41 (1962), 171-176.

A study of student stereotypes of Negroes and Jews,
highlighting their consistency and generality.

442. Fauman, S. Joseph. "Status Crystallization and
Interracial Attitudes," SOCIAL FORCES, 47 (1968),
53-59.

Using Detroit Area Study data, it is discovered that
high status crystallization tends to be associated
with acceptance of racial integration.

97

443. Gordon, Leonard and John W. Hudson. "Emergent White
     Protestant Student Perceptions of Jews," JOURNAL
     FOR THE SCIENTIFIC STUDY OF RELIGION, 9 (1970),
     235-238.

     A study of how secularization and pluralism have
     reduced the independent influence of religion on
     attitudes and behavior.

444. Greeley, Andrew M. "Ethnicity and Racial Attitudes:
     The Case of the Jews and the Poles," AMERICAN
     JOURNAL OF SOCIOLOGY, 80 (1975), 909-932.

     A 1968 survey of racial attitudes among ten ethnic
     groups revealed that Poles were the least sympathetic
     to black militancy with Jews the most sympathetic.

445. Guichard, Carles P. and Margaret A. Connolly.
     "Ethnic Group Stereotypes: A New Look at an
     Old Problem," THE JOURNAL OF NEGRO EDUCATION,
     46 (1977), 344-357.

     A study of perceived traits among blacks, Chicanos,
     American Indians, Asians, and whites which finds
     that groups tend to perceive others as having
     positive and negative traits in fairly similar
     proportions attributed to themselves.

446. Hamblin, Robert L. "The Dynamics of Racial
     Discrimination," SOCIAL PROBLEMS, 10 (1962),
     103-121.

     An empirical study which concludes that a major
     factor behind discrimination is the actual and
     feared frustration produced by competition with
     minorities.

447. Hesselbart, Susan and Howard Schuman. "Racial
     Attitudes, Educational Level, and a Personality
     Measure," THE PUBLIC OPINION QUARTERLY, 40
     (1976), 108-114.

A sample of 640 Detroit Area whites reveals that
racial perceptions are associated with education and
punitiveness as a personality variable.

448. Heyne, Clare D. RACIAL CONCEPTIONS OF COLLEGE
      STUDENTS ABOUT MEMBERS OF THE BLACK AND WHITE
      RACES. Diss. St. Louis Univ., 1973.

      A study of racial conceptions among black and white
      college students which finds a higher level of
      racial consciousness among the former, particularly
      for females.

449. Himmelfarb, Milton. "Some Attitudes toward Jews,"
      COMMENTARY, 35 (1963), 424-429.

      Attitudes towards Jews in the U.S.S.R. and U.S. among
      Unitarians and Neo-Orthodox groups are analyzed,
      revealing widespread anti-Semitism in Russia but
      positive views of Judaism among American Unitarians.

450. Hough, Richard L., Jene F. Summers, et al. "Parental
      Influence, Youth Contraculture, and Rural Adol-
      escent Attitudes toward Minority Groups," RURAL
      SOCIOLOGY, 34 (1969), 383-386.

      A sample of 740 rural high school students reveals
      a high degree of parent-child consistency with
      regards to racial social distance.

451. Insko, Chester A. and James E. Robinson. "The Leaf
      Similarity versus Race as a Determinant of
      Reactions to Negroes by Southern White Adolescents
      S further Test of Rokeach's Theory," JOURNAL OF
      PERSONALITY AND SOCIAL PSYCHOLOGY, 7 (1967), 216-
      221.

      80 ninth grade students in a North Carolina community
      reveal the importance of race rather than belief
      on racial stereotypes.

452. Johnson, David W. "Racial Attitudes of Negro Freedom
     School Participants and Negro and White Civil
     Rights Participants," SOCIAL FORCES, 45 (1966),
     266-272.

     Racial attitudes of Negro freedom school and civil
     rights participants reveal positive attitudes towards
     Negroes despite white prejudice.

453. Kosa, John. "The Rank Order of Peoples: A Study in
     National Stereotypes," JOURNAL OF SOCIAL PSYCH-
     OLOGY, 46 (1957), 311-320.

     A sample of Hungarian immigrants in Canada indicates
     highest acceptance of the English and most rejection
     of Negroes.

454. Kurokawa, Minako. "Mutual Perceptions of Racial
     Images: White, Black, and Japanese Americans,"
     JOURNAL OF SOCIAL ISSUES, 27 (1971), 213-235.

     College students and school children in California
     are found to portray whites as materialistic and
     pleasure-loving; blacks as musical, aggressive, and
     straightforward; and the Japanese as industrious,
     ambitious, loyal to family, and quiet.

455. LaManna, Richard. "Ecological Correlates of Attitudes
     toward School Desegregation," AMERICAN CATHOLIC
     SOCIOLOGICAL REVIEW, 22 (1961), 242-249.

     This ecological study reveals that areas of low
     urbanization tend to contain more people in favor of
     desegregation and fewer segregationists - an unusual
     result.

456. Levy, Sheldon G. "Polarization and Racial Attitudes,"
     PUBLIC OPINION QUARTERLY, 36 (1972), 221-234.

100

A national survey of 7,000 respondents finds little
white-non-white agreement on changes in race relations,
including the young and better educated.

457. Liu, William T. "The Community Reference System,
Religiosity, and Race Attitudes," SOCIAL FORCES,
39 (1961), 324-328.

196 northern Catholics in a southern town reveal the
importance of religion as well as their community
reference system to desegregation attitudes.

458. Lyman, Stanford M. and William A. Douglass. "Ethnicity: Strategies of Collective and Individual
Impression-Management," SOCIAL RESEARCH, 40 (1973),
344-365.

A phenomenological analysis of ethnic relations,
focusing on ethnic cues and clues involved in
impression-management.

459. Middleton, Russell. "Negro and White Reactions to
Racial Humor," SOCIOMETRY, 2 (1959), 175-183.

50 Negro and white college students are found to
react more favorably to jokes against the other racial
group rather than their own. Middle-class Negroes,
however, favored both types of joke.

460. Miller, Ruth and Paul J. Dolan, eds. RACE AWARENESS.
New York: Oxford University Press, 1971.

A reader which focuses on the nightmare of racism,
factors behind its development, and minority responses
to it.

461. Morriss, David C. "Racial Attitudes of White
Residents in Integrated and Segregated Neighborhoods," SOCIOLOGICAL FOCUS, 6 (1973), 74-94.

White racial attitudes among both integrated and segregated neighborhood residents reveal no significant differences, highlighting the relevance of class perception, school concerns, residential preference, and contact.

462. O'Gorman, Hubert J. and Stephen L. Garry. "Pluralistic Ignorance - A Replication and Extension," PUBLIC OPINION QUARTERLY, 40 (1976), 449-458.

A replication of a previous study indicating how whites misperceive the racial values of other whites.

463. Orbell, John and Eugene K. Sherrill. "Racial Attitudes and the Social Context," PUBLIC OPINION QUARTERLY, 33 (1969), 46-54.

Census tract data reveal that anti-Negro attitudes predominate in low income areas with a high Negro percentage while suburban high status residents are more intolerant than low status residents.

464. Pettigrew, Thomas F. "Personality and Sociocultural Factors in Intergroup Attitudes: A Cross-National Comparison," JOURNAL OF CONFLICT RESOLUTION, 2 (1958), 29-42.

Racial attitudes among white South Africans and American Southerners are compared with respect to the relative importance of psychological and sociocultural factors to prejudice, highlighting the relevance of the latter.

465. Poskocil, Art. "Encounters between Black and White Liberals: The Collision of Stereotypes," SOCIAL FORCES, 55 (1977), 715-727.

Black distrust of white liberals as hypocritical and implicitly racist tends to impair interracial communication.

466. Rodgers, Harold R. and Charles S. Bullock, III. "Political and Racial Attitudes: Black versus White," JOURNAL OF BLACK STUDIES, 4 (1974), 463-485.

A review of changing racial attitudes during the last fifteen years, concluding that blacks have become more impatient, more negative towards whites, and less trusting of the political system.

467. Schuman, Howard and Barry Gruenberg. "The Impact of City on Racial Attitudes," AMERICAN JOURNAL OF SOCIOLOGY, 76 (1970), 213-261.

City of residence is shown to account for a wide range of racial attitudes, reflecting different demographic distributions with respect to minority size and educational levels.

468. Stephan, Walter G. "Cognitive Differentiation and Intergroup Perception," SOCIOMETRY, 40 (1977), 50-58.

750 fifth-grade and sixth-grade black, Chicano, and Anglo students from segregated and integrated schools indicated that ingroup members perceived their own group as less differentiated than outgroups , with little school type effect.

469. Sterne, Richard S. A STUDY OF ATTITUDES TOWARDS JEWS. Fallsington: William Penn Center, 1962.

Anti-Semitic responses to Jewish suburban migration appear relatively rare in Lower Bucks County, Pennsylvania.

470. Sue, Stanley and Harry L. Kitano. "Stereotypes as a Measure of Success," JOURNAL OF SOCIAL ISSUES, 29 (1973), 83-98.

103

A discussion of the shift from negative to positive stereotyping of the Chinese and Japanese as models of success.

471. Triandis, Harry C. and Vasso Vassiliou. "Frequency of Contact and Stereotyping," JOURNAL OF PERSON-ALITY AND SOCIAL PSYCHOLOGY, 7 (1967), 316-328.

A study of the effects of degree of contact between U.S. and Greek culture on stereotyping, revealing mixed results.

472. Weissbach, Theodore and J. Briggam, eds. RACIAL ATTITUDES IN AMERICA: ANALYSES AND FINDINGS OF SOCIAL PSYCHOLOGY. New York: Harper and Row, 1972.

A reader which deals with the current racial climate and racial attitudes in particular - their development, measurement, correlates, content, relationship to behavior, and attempted change.

473. Woodmansee, John J. and Stuart W. Cook. "Dimensions of Verbal Racial Attitudes: Their Identification and Measurement," JOURNAL OF PERSONALITY AND SOCIAL PSYCHOLOGY, 7 (1967), 240-250.

An empirical study of racial attitudes towards Negroes, producing dimensions such as private rights, derogatory beliefs, local autonomy, and acceptance of integration.

MINORITY GROUP IDENTITY

474. Blake, Robert R. and Jane S. Mouton. "Loyalty of Representatives to Ingroup Positions During Intergroup Competition," SOCIOMETRY, 28 (1961), 177-183.

A laboratory study of intergroup negotiation, revealing that ingroup loyalty tends to produce deadlocks, thereby negating the effectiveness of such interaction.

475. Burgess, M. Elaine. "The Resurgence of Ethnicity: Myth or Reality?" ETHNIC AND RACIAL STUDIES, 1 (1978), 265-285.

The resurgence of ethnicity is explained in terms of institutional change and the consequences of modernization.

476. Caditz, Judith. "Ethnic Identification, Interethnic Impact and Belief in Integration," SOCIAL FORCES, 54 (1976), 632-645.

A study of ambivalence towards ethnic integration under conditions when status concerns and ethnic values are threatened.

477. Lambert, Wallace E. and Yosh Taguchi. "Ethnic Cleavage among Young Children," JOURNAL OF ABNORMAL SOCIAL PSYCHOLOGY, 53 (1956), 380-382.

A study of ethnic cleavage among pre-school children, documenting its existence at an early age.

478. Lincoln, C. Eric. "Color and Group Identity in the United States," DAEDALUS, 96 (1967), 527-541.

A critique of race and color consciousness as inadequate in unifying Negroes in their attempt to enter the American mainstream.

479. Stoll, Clairace. "Games and Socialization: An Exploratory Study of Race Differences," SOCIOLOGICAL QUARTERLY, 11 (1970), 374-380.

Sixth-grade student games are examined for their socializing effects, finding differential effects by race.

480. Bagley, Christopher. "Self-Esteem as a Pivotal
     Concept in Race and Ethnic Relations," RESEARCH
     IN RACE AND ETHNIC RELATIONS, 1 (1979), 127-167.

     A study of 300 English adolescents confirms the
     relationship between low self-esteem and prejudice
     against ethnic minorities.

481. Barbero, Fred. "Ethnic Resentment," TRANSACTION, 11
     (1974), 67-75.

     Argues that minorities need to reduce their differ-
     ences and mobilize their resources in order to maxi-
     mize their political interests.

482. Barnham, Kenneth, John F. Connors, III, et al.
     "Racial Prejudice in Relation to Education,
     Sex and Religion," JOURNAL FOR THE SCIENTIFIC
     STUDY OF RELIGION, 8 (1969), 318.

     A study of 1,000 white college students, confirming
     previous findings regarding the relationship of
     sex, religion, and socioeconomic status to racial
     prejudice.

483. Brewer, David L. UTAH ELITES AND UTAH RACIAL NORMS.
     Diss. Univ. of Utah, 1965.

     82 members of the Utah elite (political, religious,
     economic, academic, medical, and legal) are inter-
     viewed, revealing a positive relationship between
     support for civil rights and liberalizing church
     policy.

484. Byrne, Don and Terry J. Wong. "Racial Prejudice,
     Interpersonal Attraction, and Assumed Dissimilar-
     ity of Attitudes," JOURNAL OF ABNORMAL SOCIAL
     PSYCHOLOGY, 65 (1962), 246-253.

High levels of racial prejudice are found to be correlated with assumed attitude dissimilarity between one's self and Negroes.

485. Clark, Kenneth B. PREJUDICE AND YOUR CHILD. Boston: Beacon, 1963.

Deals with the problem of prejudice and how children learn it, along with a specific program for action.

486. Cox, John A. and John D. Crumholtz. "Racial Bias in Peer Ratings of Basic Airmen," SOCIOMETRY, 21 (1958), 292-299.

Leadership ratings among Negro and white airmen tend to reflect racial ethnocentrism but to a limited degree only as reflected in the predominant significance of ability rather than race.

487. Cummings, Cott. "Racial Prejudice and Political Orientations among Blue Collar Workers," SOCIAL SCIENCE QUARTERLY, 57 (1977), 907-920.

Using 1972 Survey Research Center data, the relationship between left-wing political movements and racial prejudice is found to be ambiguous at best.

488. Ditz, Gerhart. "Outgroup and Ingroup Prejudice among Members of Minority Groups," ALPHA KAPPA DELTA, 29 (1959), 26-31.

A study of ingroup as well as outgroup prejudice, in contrast to the usual studies of ethnic prejudice.

489. Ehrlich, Howard J. "The Study of Prejudice in American Social Science," JOURNAL OF INTERGROUP RELATIONS, 3 (1962), 117-125.

A discussion of stereotyping as conceptualization and its relationship to types of family structure and other social situations.

490. Ehrlich, Howard J. "Instrument Error and the Study of Prejudice," SOCIAL FORCES, 43 (1964), 197-206.

Critiques the forced response format used in many prejudice studies for possibly inflating the degree of acceptance of prejudicial statements.

491. Eye, Kenneth E. INDICATORS OF WHITE RACISM. Diss. Ohio State Univ., 1973.

A study which finds that white racism in America is universal, varying only in degree, and requiring immediate and imperative change.

492. Feagin, Joe R. "Prejudice, Orthodoxy and the Social Situation," SOCIAL FORCES, 44 (1965), 46-56.

A study of 166 Southern Baptists which finds a significant, positive correlation between ortho-doxy and racial prejudice.

493. Fischer, Donald and Brendan G. Rule. "Anti-Semitism, Stress, and Anchor Effects on Interpersonal Judgements," JOURNAL OF PERSONALITY AND SOCIAL PSYCHOLOGY, 6 (1967), 447-450.

A study of personality and situational factors influencing evaluations of neutral by-standers following stress, using a homogeneous sample of 96 students.

494. Hargett, Sheila L. SOME DETERMINANTS OF WHITE RACIAL ATTITUDES: A MULTIVARIATE ANALYSIS. Diss. Univ. of North Carolina at Chapel Hill, 1976.

While region and education were found to be the best
predictors of white attitudes towards blacks, a large
number of other variables analyzed together in a
multivariate model could account for less than 25%
of the variance in such attitudes.

495. Herman, Redge. "Power and Prejudice: A Survey and
     a Hypothesis," JOURNAL OF HUMAN RELATIONS, 17
     (1969), 1-11.

A discussion of the importance of authoritarianism
and conformity as they relate to the sanctioning of
ethnic prejudice by the upper class.

496. Holloway, Robert C. AN INVESTIGATION OF THE RELATION-
     SHIP OF SELECTED STRUCTURAL VARIABLES AND
     RACIAL PREJUDICE: A CAUSAL MODEL APPROACH. Diss.
     Case Western Reserve Univ., 1976.

A multivariate model consisting of early and adult
socialization, adult attitudes, and racial prejudice
measures was found to explain a substantial amount
of variance in racial prejudice and tolerance.

497. Hotopf, W.H.N. "Psychological Studies of Race
     Prejudice," POLITICAL QUARTERLY, 32 (1961), 328-
     340.

A survey of attitude studies, finding they highlight
that prejudice tends to be social, relatively uni-
form and consistent, involves ethnocentrism and
general stereotypes, linked to authoritarianism,
and directed towards low status minorities.

498. Jeffries, Vincent. "Cultural Forces of Solidarity
     and Antagonism towards Blacks," SOCIAL SCIENCE
     QUARTERLY, 55 (1971), 860-872.

583 Los Angeles whites reveal that self-centeredness
is associated with antagonism while solidarity is
more a product of other-centeredness.

499. Jones, James M. PREJUDICE AND RACISM. Reading: Addison-Wesley, 1969.

A study of the problem of the "color line," including its history, attitudes and stereotypes, and racist dimensions.

500. King, Larry L. CONFESSIONS OF A WHITE RACIST. New York: Viking, 1969.

An autobiographical account of a white racist and his lifetime experience of race.

501. Kogan, Nathan and James F. Downey. "Scaling Norm Conflicts in the Area of Prejudice and Discrimination," JOURNAL OF ABNORMAL PSYCHOLOGY, 53 (1956), 292-295.

A study of anti-discrimination tendencies among a sample of New England high school students.

502. Kovel, Joel. WHITE RACISM: A PSYCHOHISTORY. New York: Vintage, 1971.

White racism is analyzed from a psycho-historical perspective, particularly within the individual personality structure, with prejudice viewed as a form of psychological compensation or outlet for inner frustration.

503. LaFarge, John. "American Catholics and the Negro, 1962," SOCIAL ORDER, 12 (1962), 153-163.

A statement of Catholic views of the race problem as indicated in an interview with the Chaplain of the National Catholic Conference on Interracial Justice.

504. Levin, Jack. THE FUNCTIONS OF PREJUDICE. New York: Harper and Row, 1975.

An analysis of prejudice in terms of its nature, personality and social functions for the majority, minority functions, and relationship to American society.

505. Mann, John H. "The Relationship between Cognitive, Affective, and Behavioral Aspects of Racial Prejudice," JOURNAL OF SOCIAL PSYCHOLOGY, 49 (1959), 223-228.

102 graduate students reveal that among Negroes cognitive, affective, and behavioral aspects of prejudice are positively related while for whites, affective and behavioral factors are negatively associated.

506. Maranell, Gary M. "An Examination of Some Religious and Political Correlates of Bigotry," SOCIAL FORCES, 45 (1967), 356-361.

A study of college students reveals that both political conservatism and religiosity tend to be correlated with bigotry.

507. Martin, James G. "Intergroup Tolerance - Prejudice," JOURNAL OF HUMAN RELATIONS, 10 (1962), 197-204.

A discussion of the ethical and empirical dimensions of prejudice, particularly the inconsistencies in each case.

508. Monti, Daniel J. "Biased and Unbiased News: Reporting Racial Controversies in THE NEW YORK TIMES, 1960-1964," THE SOCIOLOGICAL QUARTERLY, 20 (1979), 399-409.

Media coverage of racial controversies is found to be relatively lacking in bias, permitting minorities to successfully present their case to the public.

111

509. Noel, Donald L. and Alphonso Pinkney. "Correlates
of Prejudice: Some Racial Differences and
Similarities," AMERICAN JOURNAL OF SOCIOLOGY,
69 (1964), 609-622.

A study of 2,000 whites and Negroes in four cities
indicates that among both prejudice is correlated
with education, interracial contact, authoritarianism,
sex, and marital status.

510. Peek, Charles W. and Sharon Brown. "Sex Prejudice
among White Protestants: Like or Unlike Ethnic
Prejudices?" SOCIAL FORCES, 59 (1980), 169-185.

Data on 1,000 white Protestants indicate that
religious affiliation is correlated with prejudice
toward women as well as racial-ethnic minorities.

511. Petersen, William. "Prejudice in American Society,"
COMMENTARY, 26 (1958), 343-348.

A critique of the shift from sociological to more
psychological concerns in the study of prejudice,
as reflected in the focus on authoritarianism.

512. Pettigrew, Thomas F. "Regional Differences in Anti-
Negro Prejudice," JOURNAL OF ABNORMAL SOCIAL
PSYCHOLOGY, 59 (1959), 28-36.

366 Northern and Southern respondents reveal that
while personality factors are related to prejudice
in both areas, sociocultural and adjustment factors
are more important among the latter.

513. Pinkney, Alphonso. "Prejudice toward Mexican and
Negro Americans: A Comparison," PHYLON, 24
(1963), 353-359.

Interviews of 319 urban whites reveal greater
tolerance of Mexican rather than Negro Americans
and acceptance of local rather than general minority
rights.

514. Pinkney, Alphonso. "A Quantitative Factor in Prejudice," SOCIOLOGY AND SOCIAL RESEARCH, 47 (1963), 161-168.

A study of the racial attitudes of 319 urban whites finds that prejudice is not correlated with the percentage of the minority in the population.

515. Rainwater, Lee and William L. Yancey. THE MOYNIHAN REPORT AND THE POLITICS OF CONTROVERSY. Cambridge: MIT Press, 1967.

A study of the Moynihan Report and consequent reactions of the government, civil rights leaders, and academics.

516. Riedesel, Paul L. and T. Gene Blocker. "Prejudice and Socioeconomic Status," SOCIOLOGY AND SOCIAL RESEARCH, 62 (1978), 558-571.

Interviews with 312 whites and 37 mixed white-Indians indicate that among high status respondents class is more salient than race in attitudes towards minorities.

517. Rose, Arnold M. "On an Empirical Test of AN AMERICAN DILEMMA," AMERICAN SOCIOLOGICAL REVIEW, 31 (1966), 103.

A critique of categorical questions used in prejudice research for obscuring the ambiguous and inconsistent nature of such attitudes.

518. Ryan, William. BLAMING THE VICTIM. New York: Vintage, 1971.

An analysis of the process by which minorities are blamed for their negative position in society and how this operates in all its major institutions.

519. Stryker, Sheldon. "Social Structure and Prejudice," SOCIAL PROBLEMS, 6 (1958-59), 340-354.

An historical discussion of middleman trader minorities, concluding that they are not always subject to systematic prejudice unless particular structural conditions are present.

520. Suelzle, Hilda M.F. SOCIAL INDICATORS OF WHITE RACIAL ATTITUDES. Diss. Univ. of California at Berkeley, 1977.

A study of racial attitudes towards black-white inequalities in terms of a respondent's objective social location, using data collected in San Francisco.

521. Surlin, Stuart H. "Authoritarian Advertising Executives and the Use of Black Models in Advertising: Implications for Racial Relations," JOURNAL OF BLACK STUDIES, 8 (1977), 105-116.

A study of advertising executives which confirms the positive association between authoritarian values and racist economic practices.

522. Treiman, Donald J. "Status Discrepancies and Prejudice," AMERICAN JOURNAL OF SOCIOLOGY, 71 (1966), 651-654.

A national sample of whites reveals that status discrepancy per se appears to have no effect on prejudice when analyzed in relation to an additive model.

523. Westie, Frank R. "THE AMERICAN DILEMMA: An Empirical Test," AMERICAN SOCIOLOGICAL REVIEW, 30 (1965), 527-538.

An empirical test of Myrdal's assertions, indicating that a dilemma exists but its resolution is different from those assumed by Myrdal.

114

524. Works, Ernest. "Role Violation and Intergroup
        Prejudice," PACIFIC SOCIOLOGICAL REVIEW, 3
        (1972), 327-344.

   Prejudice is accounted for in terms of violating
   group expectations, producing stereotypes of the
   Japanese as opportunistic, Negroes and Mexicans as
   immoral, and hippies as unfaithful.

SOCIAL DISTANCE

525. Allen, Ben P. "Race and Physical Attractiveness as
        Criteria for White Subjects' Dating Choices,"
        SOCIAL BEHAVIOR AND PERSONALITY, 4 (1976), 289-
        296.

   An experimental study of dating choices, revealing
   that females gave more weight to race than attractiveness while the reverse applied to males.

526. Ansari, A. "A Study of the Relations between Group
        Stereotypes and Social Distances," JOURNAL OF
        EDUCATION AND PSYCHOLOGY, 14 (1956), 28-35.

   300 subjects confirmed the close relation between
   stereotypes and social distance reflected in their
   positive correlation.

527. Banton, Michael. "Social Distance: A New Appreci-
        ation,' SOCIOLOGICAL REVIEW, 8 (1960), 169-183.

   Advocates further application and elaboration of the
   Bogardus Test in the study of attitudes towards
   outgroups.

528. Bogardus, Emory S. "Racial Distance Changes in the
        United States During the Past Thirty Years,"
        SOCIOLOGY AND SOCIAL RESEARCH, 43 (1958), 127-135.

Studies conducted in 1926, 1946, and 1956 indicate decreased racial distances over time unless competition emerges, arousing insecurity, fear, or loss of status.

529.   Bogardus, Emory S.   "Race Reactions by Sexes,"
          SOCIOLOGY AND SOCIAL RESEARCH,42 (1958), 439-441.

A study of 2,000 college students reveals that racial distance reactions of women were significantly greater than those of men.

530.   Bogardus, Emory S.   "Racial Reactions by Regions,"
          SOCIOLOGY AND SOCIAL RESEARCH, 43 (1959), 286-
          290.

A national study of 2,000 subjects found that racial reactions in each of the geographic regions were similar, with some variations according to acquaintance and competition with particular groups.

531.   Bogardus, Emory S.   "Comparing Racial Distance in
          Ethiopia, South Africa, and the United States,"
          SOCIOLOGY AND SOCIAL RESEARCH, 52 (1968), 149-156.

Racial distance studies in Ethiopia, South Africa, and the U.S. indicate that such distance is lowest in the U.S. and illustrate the wide applicability of the scale.

532.   Brown, Robert L.   "Social Distance Perception as a
          Function of Mexican American and Other Ethnic
          Identity," SOCIOLOGY AND SOCIAL RESEARCH, 57
          (1973), 273-287.

Administration of the Bogardus Social Distance Scale to 430 students in Texas reveals high self-rankings and placement of other groups in relation to one's own group.

533. Crull, Sue R. and Brent T. Bruton. "Bogardus Social
     Distance in the 1970's," SOCIOLOGY AND SOCIAL
     RESEARCH, 63 (1979), 771-783.

     1,000 Introductory Sociology students completed the
     Social Distance Scale, indicating slightly higher
     scores than previous studies (1950's and 1960's) as
     well as high rejection of new groups added to the
     Scale - Arabs, hippies, and homosexuals.

534. Davidson, Chandler and Charles M. Gaitz. "Ethnic
     Attitudes as a Basis for Minority Cooperation
     in a Southwestern Metropolis," SOCIAL SCIENCE
     QUARTERLY, 53 (1973), 738-748.

     Blacks, Mexican Americans, and Anglos in Houston,
     administered a social distance scale, revealed that
     Mexican Americans and blacks were more tolerant of
     each other, more likely to perceive discrimination,
     and favored equality more than Anglos.

535. DeFleur, Melvin L. and Frank R. Westie. "The
     Interpretation of Interracial Situations,"
     SOCIAL FORCES, 38 (1959), 17-23.

     A study which finds that prejudiced whites perceive
     Negro females in interracial situations as lower in
     morals and mental ability.

536. Fennell, V. "International Atlanta and Ethnic Group
     Relations," URBAN ANTHROPOLOGY, 6 (1977), 345-
     354.

     A study of the manner in which native Atlantans
     label foreigners with more inclusive terms than
     they initially accept as relevant to their identities.

537. Greenfield, Robert W. "Factors Associated with
     Attitudes towards Desegregation in a Florida
     Residential Suburb," SOCIAL FORCES, 40 (1961),
     31-42.

Attitudes towards desegregation among 309 whites
indicate the relevance of occupation, education,
region of birth and socialization, as well as
regional identity. In general, Northerners favored
desegregation more than Southerners.

538. Jacobson, Cardell K. "Separatism, Integrationism,
and Avoidance among Black, White, and Latin
Adolescents," SOCIAL FORCES, 55 (1977), 1011-1027.

A study of racial avoidance among black, white, and
Latin junior and senior high school students in
Milwaukee.

539. Jacobson, Cardell K. "School Racial Position Effects
on Avoidance, Separatism, and Integrationist
Attitudes of Adolescents," SOCIOLOGICAL QUARTERLY,
20 (1979), 223-235.

A study which finds that students in segregated
schools tended to be high in racial avoidance and
separatism.

540. Jones, Sandra and Edward Diener. "Ethnic Preference
of College Students for Their Own and Other
Racial Groups," SOCIAL BEHAVIOR AND PERSONALITY,
4 (1976), 225-231.

Ethnic preferences of black and white college
students are measured in reference to ratings of
employment application, finding each group preferred
applications of its own race.

541. Mabe, Paul A. and John E. Williams. "Relation of
Racial Attitudes to Sociometric Choices among
Second Grade Children, " PSYCHOLOGICAL REPORTS,
37 (1975), 547-554.

A study of 50 Euro and Afro-American second-grade
children in an integrated public school indicated
lower racial bias and ethnocentric choices in
racially-balanced classrooms.

542. Mann, John H. "The Influence of Racial Prejudice on Sociometric Choices and Perceptions," SOCIOMETRY, 21 (1958), 150-158.

Sociometric choices are found to be racially homogeneous and influenced by age and regional background.

543. Miller, James, Jr. "A Comparison of Racial Preference in Young Black and Mexican American Children: A Preliminary View," SOCIOLOGICAL SYMPOSIUM, 7 (1971), 37-48.

The Doll Test was applied to 238 black and Mexican American children, revealing that preference for white dolls decreased with age and was influenced by sex.

544. Seigel, Arthur I. and Loyal F. Greer. "A Variation of the Bogardus Technique as a Measure of Perceived Prejudice," JOURNAL OF SOCIAL PSYCHOLOGY, 43 (1956), 275-281.

A variation of the Bogardus Scale was administered to 200 Puerto Ricans and found to be a valid measure of perceived prejudice.

545. Skeen, J.T. "Status and Ethnic Relations," PSYCHOLOGICAL REPORTS, 35 (1974), 123-126.

A field experiment confirming that minority groups exhibit avoidance and/or rejection of majority members on the basis of perceived status dissimilarity.

546. Smith, Arthur L. TRANSRACIAL COMMUNICATION. Englewood Cliffs: Prentice-Hall, 1973.

An analysis of the process of transracial communication with particular reference to symbols, stereotypes, and determinants of normalization.

547. Triandis, Harry C., Shin-Ichi Takezawa, et al.
      "Some Determinants of Social Distance among
      American, German, and Japanese Students," JOURNAL
      OF PERSONNEL AND SOCIAL PSYCHOLOGY, 2 (1965),
      540-551.

      Social distance studies conducted in Germany, the
      U.S., and Japan indicated the relevance of race,
      occupation, religion, and nationality in all three
      cases.

ATTITUDINAL CHANGE

548. Baker, Therese L. "The Weakening of Authoritarianism
      in Black and White College Students," SOCIOLOGY
      AND SOCIAL RESEARCH, 60 (1976), 440-460.

      Black students attending a predominantly white
      college who lack dependent relationships with faculty
      and have a greater number of student friends tend
      to experience greater change toward nonauthoritarian
      attitudes.

549. Caditz, Judith. "Ambivalence toward Integration:
      The Sequence of Response to Six Interracial
      Situations," SOCIOLOGICAL QUARTERLY, 16 (1975),
      16-32.

      White liberals were found to accept interracial
      situations from high to low as follows: quota,
      busing, residence, apartment, hiring, and occupation-
      al.

550. Campbell, John D., Leon J. Yarrow, et al. "A Study
      of Adaptation toward a New Social Situation,"
      JOURNAL OF SOCIAL ISSUES, 14 (1958), 3-7.

      Negro and white adjustment in an integrated camp
      setting is accounted for in terms of a controlled,
      imposed situation.

551. Geyer, Frances. "A Study of Prejudice Reduction," SOCIOLOGICAL FOCUS, 6 (1973), 23-41.

A study which finds that education, socioeconomic status, and urban residence are most crucial in reducing prejudice.

552. Glenn, Norvell D. "Recent Trends in White-Nonwhite Attitudinal Differences," PUBLIC OPINION QUARTERLY, 38 (1974-75), 596-604.

1950-1960 white-nonwhite attitudinal changes indicate increasing divergence with regard to racially-oriented issues (e.g., death penalty) and convergence with respect to non-racial issues (e.g., world affairs).

553. Halle, Robert A. THE EFFECTS OF A TEACHING RESOURCE UNIT ON THE ATTITUDES OF SEGREGATED WHITE FIFTH-GRADE STUDENTS. Diss. Michigan State Univ., 1970.

A study of the effects of a teaching resource unit on the American Negro on the racial attitudes of segregated white fifth-grade students, finding little positive outcomes.

554. Paige, Jeffrey. "Changing Patterns of Anti-White Attitudes among Blacks," JOURNAL OF SOCIAL ISSUES, 26 (1970), 69-86.

A study of 236 black males in Newark indicates increased anti-white sentiment among young blacks most receptive to new strategies while traditional blacks appear less anti-white than previously.

555. Sampson, William A. and Vera Milam. "The Inter-racial Attitudes of the Middle Class: Have They Changed?" SOCIAL PROBLEMS, 2 (1975), 153-165.

Middle-class blacks are found to be racially conscious, proud, in-group oriented, and feel that they are not doing enough for less fortunate blacks.

121

556. Siegel, Alberta E. and Sidney Siegel. "Reference Groups, Membership Groups, and Attitude Change," JOURNAL OF ABNORMAL SOCIAL PSYCHOLOGY, 3 (1957), 360-364.

Among students in a small, church-related college varying relationships among prejudice, authoritarianism, conservatism, and attitude change were found, depending on student status (lower or upper division).

557. Stroup, Atlee L. and Joseph Landis. "Change in Race Prejudice Attitude as Related to Changes in Authoritarianism and Conservatism in the College Population," SOUTHWESTERN SOCIAL SCIENCE QUARTERLY, 46 (1965), 255-263.

Greatest attitude change was found among students who changed their reference groups.

558. Wilson, Warner and Norman Miller. "Shifts in Evaluations of Participants following Intergroup Participation," JOURNAL OF ABNORMAL PSYCHOLOGY, 63 (1961), 428-431.

A study which finds that positive interaction tends to increase interpersonal liking and in-group solidarity.

559. Young, Robert K. "Change in Attitudes toward the Negro in a Southern University," JOURNAL OF ABNORMAL PSYCHOLOGY, 60 (1960), 131-133.

Student attitudes towards Negroes at the University of Texas did not appear to change between 1955 and 1958 - a period of social tension.

RACIAL AND ETHNIC DISCRIMINATION/SEGREGATION

SOCIAL AND ATTITUDINAL DISCRIMINATION

560. Butsch, Richard J. "Some Dynamics of Racial Stratification in the United States," INTERNATIONAL REVIEW OF MODERN SOCIOLOGY, 8 (1978), 167-178.

An analysis of racial stratification which highlights the organizational structure of institutionalized racism, designed to exclude blacks from upward mobility.

561. Campbell, Ernest Q. "Moral Discomfort and Racial Segregation - An Examination of the Myrdal Hypothesis," SOCIAL FORCES, 39 (1961), 228-234.

275 Southern college students were studied for the incidence and correlates of racial guilt, revealing the counter-norms of a segregated system.

562. Hamblin, Robert L. "The Dynamics of Racial Discrimination," SOCIAL PROBLEMS, 10 (1962), 103-121.

A study of 100 adults which finds that support for discrimination varies with anomia, competition, status fear, as well as family and friend pressure to discriminate.

563. Linn, Lawrence S., "Verbal Attitudes and Overt Behavior: A Study of Racial Discrimination," SOCIAL FORCES, 43 (1965), 353-364.

Discrepancies between verbal attitudes and overt behavior were found in 59% of the cases in this study, implying that attitudinal measurements have little predictive behavioral value.

564. McConahay, John B. and Joseph C. Hough, Jr. "Symbolic Racism," THE JOURNAL OF SOCIAL ISSUES, 32 (1976), 23-45.

Symbolic racism - rejection of black demands for change as illegitimate - is found to be correlated with conventionalism, low sympathy for blacks, and Republican Party identification.

565. Wilcox, Roger C. THE PSYCHOLOGICAL CONSEQUENCES OF BEING A BLACK AMERICAN. New York: Wiley, 1971.

A collection of research by black psychologists dealing with the effects of cultural disadvantage, racial integration, intelligence and achievement, higher education, educational psychology, personality factors, and psychology as a profession.

566. Works, Ernest. "Types of Racial Discrimination," PHYLON, 30 (1969), 223-233.

Focusing on role relations, four patterns of discrimination are outlined: categorical rejection, prejudgement, situational, and interpersonal discrimination.

ECONOMIC AND OCCUPATIONAL DISCRIMINATION

567. Antonovsky, Aaron and Lewis Lorwin, eds. DISCRIMINATION AND LOW INCOMES: SOCIAL AND ECONOMIC DISCRIMINATION AGAINST MINORITY GROUPS IN RELATION TO LOW INCOMES IN NEW YORK STATE. New York: New School for Social Research, 1959.

A symposium on economic discrimination as it affects minorities with respect to income, occupational distributions, childhood experiences, hiring practices, and employment situations.

568. Bacon, Emery F. "Race Relations in an Industrial
     Society," RACE, 4 (1963), 32-38.

     A discussion of union policies on civil rights,
     particularly within the steel industry.

569. Becker, Henry J. "Racial Segregation among Places
     of Employment," SOCIAL FORCES, 58 (1980), 761-
     776.

     Employment indexes of segregation for black and non-
     Hispanic white workers are presented, showing that
     laborers and service workers are the most segre-
     gated while females are more segregated than males.

570. Boyce, Richard J. "Racial Discrimination and the
     National Labor Relations Act," NORTHWESTERN
     UNIVERSITY LAW REVIEW, 65 (1970), 232-258.

     Argues that the National Labor Relations Board could
     become a major medium for redress of racial discrimi-
     nation in employment, whether by union or employer.

571. Bullock, Charles S. and Harold R. Rodgers, Jr.
     "Institutional Racism: Prerequisites, Freezing
     and Mapping," PHYLON, 37 (1976), 212-223.

     A discussion of subtle discrimination, including
     black exclusion, application of rigorous standards,
     and mapping - use of geographical lines to concentr-
     ate blacks in one area.

572. Carey, Phillip. "Crisis in the Environment: A
     Sociological Perspective," AMERICAN JOURNAL OF
     ECONOMICS AND SOCIOLOGY, 36 (1977), 263-273.

     Contends that racial, sexual, and ethnic discrim-
     ination is as great a threat as nuclear war,
     threatening social survival. Education is viewed as
     an important path to equality.

573. Cutright, Phillip. "Region, Migration, and the
      Earnings of White and Black Men," SOCIAL FORCES,
      53 (1974), 297-305.

      A study which finds that at every level, white and
      black migrants from the South earn more than those
      who remain in the South.

574. Donnerstein, Edward, et al. "Racial Discrimination
      in Apartment Rentals: A Replication," JOURNAL
      OF SOCIAL PSYCHOLOGY, 96 (1975), 37-38.

      18 apartment block managers reveal no white-black
      discrimination with respect to rents and fees but
      do discriminate when it comes to apartment availa-
      bility.

575. Feagin, Joe R. and Clairece B. Feagin. DISCRIMINATION
      AMERICAN STYLE. Englewood Cliffs: Prentice-
      Hall, 1978.

      Analyzes institutional racism and sexism with respect
      to employment, housing, education, health, social
      services, politics, and the courts.

576. Fleischaker, Marc L., Steven Garfinkel, et al.
      "Racial Discrimination in the Federal Civil
      Service," GEORGE WASHINGTON LAW REVIEW, 38 (1968),
      265-304.

      The relative ineffectiveness of the Civil Service
      Commission in dealing with career discrimination is
      discussed as well as relevant theories of jurisdiction.

577. Fox, William S. and John R. Faine. "Trends in White-
      Nonwhite Income Equality," SOCIOLOGY AND SOCIAL
      RESEARCH, 57 (1973), 288-299.

      An Equality Index is applied to racial income
      differences, indicating that during the past two
      decades substantial progress towards equality has
      been attained.

126

578. Frisbie, W. Parker and Eliza Neidert. "Inequality in the Relative Size of Minority Population: A Comparative Analysis," AMERICAN JOURNAL OF SOCIOLOGY, 82 (1977), 1007-1030.

   1970 Census data for 40 Southwestern S.M.S.A.'s, including whites, Mexican Americans, and blacks indicate the majority-minority income and occupational disparities tend to grow as relative minority size increases.

579. Geschwender, James A. RACIAL STRATIFICATION IN AMERICA. Dubuque: Brown, 1978.

   An analysis of racial stratification with respect to basic models, the history of the "black experience" in America, and discussion of the notion of "nation-class" as a model for analysis.

580. Glenn, Norvell D. "White Gains from Negro Subordination," SOCIAL PROBLEMS, 15 (1966), 159-178.

   The relationship between percentage of nonwhites in an ecological unit and the economic characteristics of whites is examined using 1960 Census data and a generally positive correlation is found.

581. Kain, John F., ed. RACE AND POVERTY: THE ECONOMICS OF DISCRIMINATION. Englewood Cliffs: Prentice-Hall, 1969.

   A reader which focuses on the economic condition of the Negro, the labor market, the housing market, white and black attitudes, and various policy alternatives.

582. Kaplan, H. Roy, ed. AMERICAN MINORITIES AND ECONOMIC OPPORTUNITY. Itasca: Peacock, 1977.

   A collection of papers focusing on the work situation of American blacks, Mexicans, Puerto Ricans, Indians, women, and those over 45.

583. Katzman, N.T. "Discrimination, Subculture, and
     Economic Performance of Minority Groups,"
     AMERICAN JOURNAL OF ECONOMICS AND SOCIOLOGY,
     27 (1968), 371-376.

     1950 and 1960 Census data highlight the differential
     economic performance of U.S.-born Negroes, Puerto
     Ricans, West Indians and Latin Americans, under-
     lining the possible relevance of subcultural factors
     as well as discrimination.

584. Kluegel, James R. "The Causes and Costs of Racial
     Exclusion from Job Authority," AMERICAN SOCIO-
     LOGICAL REVIEW, 43 (1978), 285-310.

     A study of economic discrimination which focuses on
     exclusion of blacks from job authority positions
     as a central factor in such discrimination.

585. Leggett, John C. RACE, CLASS, AND POLITICAL
     CONSCIOUSNESS. Cambridge: Schenkman, 1972.

     A case study of public attitudes toward a proposal
     to ban housing discrimination in Berkeley, California,
     in the early 1960's.

586. Lindley, James T. and Edward B. Selby, Jr. "Differ-
     ences between Blacks and Whites in the Use of
     Selected Services," AMERICAN JOURNAL OF ECONOMICS
     AND SOCIOLOGY, 36 (1977), 393-399.

     Blacks and whites in Atlanta reveal that race is
     significantly related to the use of bank loans,
     checking accounts, and bank credit cards, with white
     differences due to education and black variation
     explained by income.

587. Long, Elton, James Long, et al. AMERICAN MINORITIES,
     THE JUSTICE ISSUE. Englewood Cliffs: Prentice-
     Hall, 1975.

An analysis of the problem of minority group victims of prejudice and discrimination, including the civil rights struggle, violent conflict, political trials, and the criminal justice system.

588. Long, James E. "Productivity, Employment Discrimination, and the Relative Economic Status of Spanish Males," SOCIAL SCIENCE QUARTERLY, 58 (1977), 357-375.

Compared with whites, Spanish-origin males more often tend to be laborers or service workers, earn 34% less, and tend to be lower in educational attainment.

589. Mindeiola, Tatcho, Jr. "Age and Income Discrimination against Mexican Americans and Blacks in Texas, 1960-1970," SOCIAL PROBLEMS, 27 (1975), 196-208.

During 1960-1970 the young appeared to experience less discrimination than the aged, blacks experienced more discrimination than Mexican Americans, black discrimination declined, and Mexican discrimination increased.

590. Parsel, Toby L. "Race, Regional Labor Markets and Earnings," AMERICAN SOCIOLOGICAL REVIEW, 44 (1979), 262-269.

1,400 blacks and whites in Michigan in a 1972 study revealed that black earnings were hindered by racial competition and segregation while white earnings were also hindered by segregation but facilitated by competition.

591. Pettigrew, Thomas F., ed. RACIAL DISCRIMINATION IN THE UNITED STATES. New York: Harper and Row, 1975.

A reader focusing on housing, employment, education, criminal, and political discrimination along with human costs and personal remedies.

592. Ponder, Henry. "An Example of the Alternative Costs
     Doctrine Applied to Racial Discrimination,"
     JOURNAL OF NEGRO EDUCATION, 35 (1966), 42-47.

     A study of income loss experienced by Virginian
     merchants subject to a Negro boycott in response to
     segregation.

593. Rosenberg, Bernard. "Ethnic Liberalism and Employ-
     ment Discrimination in the North," AMERICAN
     JOURNAL OF ECONOMICS AND SOCIOLOGY, 26 (1967),
     387-398.

     Northern liberal employers are found to stereotype
     Negroes negatively and tend to prefer to hire whites,
     thereby confirming the existence of de facto discrim-
     ination in the North.

594. Sorenson, A.B. and Sara Fuerst. "Black-White
     Differences in the Occurrence of Job Shifts,"
     SOCIOLOGY AND SOCIAL RESEARCH, 62 (1978), 537-
     557.

     2,400 black and white male workers are studied with
     respect to job changes, revealing very different
     mechanisms behind actual quits and layoffs by race.

595. Sowell, Thomas. RACE AND ECONOMICS. New York:
     McKay, 1975.

     A discussion of American slavery, the economic
     evolution of blacks, the characteristics of immi-
     grant minorities, and the relationship between race,
     the market, and government.

596. Spreitzer, Elmer A. and Saad Z. Nagi. "Race and
     Equality of Opportunity: A Controlled Study,"
     PHYLON, 34 (1973), 248-255.

     Applicants for Social Security disability benefits
     during the period 1961-1964 indicated that blacks
     were consistently disadvantaged in terms of occupation

130

job satisfaction, income, indebtedness, and housing.

597. Stewart, James B. and Thomas Hyclak. "Ethnicity and Economic Opportunity," AMERICAN JOURNAL OF ECONOMICS AND SOCIOLOGY, 38 (1979), 319-335.

1970 Census data highlight group discrimination as a major factor behind differential economic performance despite other factors.

598. Stolzenberg, Ross M. "Education, Occupation, and Wage Differences between White and Black Men," AMERICAN JOURNAL OF SOCIOLOGY, 81 (1975), 299-323.

A study which confirms the hypothesis that years of schooling and labor force experience have joint, nonadditive effects on white-black earnings.

599. Szymanski, Albert. "Racial Discrimination and White Gain," AMERICAN SOCIOLOGICAL REVIEW, 41 (1976), 403-414.

1970 Census data are used to test whether whites gain economically from economic discrimination against Third World people, finding that working class whites lose everywhere, including the most racist areas.

600. Thurow, Lester. "Not Making It in America: The Economic Progress of Minority Groups," SOCIAL POLICY, 6 (1976), 5-11.

A study which concludes that while blacks and Native Americans have not experienced significant economic gains, Spanish Americans have.

601. Wilcox, Jerry and Wade C. Roof. "Percent Black and Black/White Status Inequality: Southern versus Non-Southern Patterns," SOCIAL SCIENCE QUARTERLY, 59 (1978), 421-434.

Black-white disadvantages with respect to education,
occupation, and income are found to be higher in
the South compared with the non-South.

EDUCATIONAL SEGREGATION

602. Daniel, Phillip B. "A History of the Segregation-
Discrimination Dilemma: The Chicago Experience,"
PHYLON, 41 (1980), 126-136.

An historical analysis which documents the deliberate
attempts made by school officials, parents, legis-
lators, and others to deprive blacks of secondary
school facilities or ensure their segregation.

603. Pettigrew, Thomas F. and Robert L. Green. "The
Legitimizing of Racial Segregation?" NEW SOCIETY,
35 (1976), 214-216.

A critique of Coleman's conclusions that court-
ordered school desegregation has produced significant
white flight from these districts and his notion
that racial change should be based on community will.

604. St. John, Nancy H. "The Effect of Segregation on the
Aspirations of Negro Youth," HARVARD EDUCATIONAL
REVIEW, 36 (1966), 284-294.

A study which finds that the hypothesized negative
relationship between percent Negro school population
and educational aspirations does not hold.

605. St. John, Nancy H. "De Facto Segregation and Interracial Association in High School," SOCIOLOGY
OF EDUCATION, 37 (1964), 326-344.

Negro students in predominantly white elementary
schools participate and hold offices in non-academic
organizations but self-preference increases with more
intimate relationships.

606. Sly, David F. and Louis G. Pol. "The Demographic
    Context of School Segregation and Desegregation,"
    SOCIAL FORCES, 56 (1978), 1072-1086.

    In this analysis the white-flight model is not
    confirmed and, in fact, the process is found to
    decline. Furthermore, school segregation is expl-
    ained in terms of black-white reproductive different-
    ials.

607. Wolff, Max. "Segergation in Schools of Gary, Indiana,
    JOURNAL OF EDUCATIONAL SOCIOLOGY, 36 (1963),
    251-261.

    A delineation of educational segregation in Gary,
    outlining its history, conflict, and attempts to
    maintain it.

EDUCATIONAL DISCRIMINATION

608. Carrouthers, Iva E. "Centennials of Black Mis-
    education: A Study of White Educational Manage-
    ment," JOURNAL OF NEGRO EDUCATION, 46 (1977),
    291-304.

    Advocates an Afrocentric view of history and educat-
    ion in contrast to white management of the educat-
    ional system for their own racist purposes.

609. Higginbotham, Elizabeth. "Ensuring Tolerance of
    Critical Perspectives," BLACK SOCIOLOGIST, 6
    (1977), 10-18.

    A discussion of major problems blacks experience
    in graduate school, including the denial of credi-
    bility of ethnic studies, distrust of white faculty,
    and conflict over research topics.

610. Loxley, William A. THE HOUSEHOLD PRODUCTION AND THE
     DISTRIBUTION OF COGNITIVE SKILLS WITHIN SIX
     RACIAL-ETHNIC CULTURES. Diss. Univ. of Chicago,
     1979.

     A study which finds that in the case of Jewish,
     white, and black families, mother's education has
     significant effects on offspring cognition.

611. Luetgert, M.J. "The Ethnic Student: Academic
     Social Problems," ADOLESCENCE, 12 (1977), 321-
     327.

     The problems encountered by the ethnic student are
     discussed with reference to communication, reaction
     to criticism, independence, identity, and intimacy.

612. Mieme, Albert W., Jr. "Occupational/Educational
     Discrimination against Black Males," JOURNAL OF
     BLACK STUDIES, 9 (1978), 87-92.

     Racial discrimination is examined in terms of the
     relationship between educational and occupational
     levels, comparing whites and blacks. At all levels,
     blacks are relatively disadvantaged, greatest in the
     south and least in the northeast.

613. Thomas, Gail E. RACE AND SEX EFFECTS IN THE PROCESS
     OF EDUCATIONAL ACHIEVEMENT. Diss. Univ. of North
     Carolina at Chapel Hill, 1975.

     A national survey of high school seniors reveals
     that racial and sexual differences in educational
     attainment tend to reflect socioeconomic and ability
     differences.

134

RESIDENTIAL SEGREGATION

614. Bleda, Sharon E. "Intergenerational Differences in
     Patterns and Bases of Ethnic Residential Dis-
     similarity," ETHNICITY, 5 (1978), 91-107.

     An analysis of the relative contributions of socio-
     economic, cultural, and demographic differentials
     to patterns of residential segregation by ethnicity.

615. Bleda, Sharon E. "Socioeconomic, Demographic, and
     Cultural Bases of Ethnic Residential Segre-
     gation," ETHNICITY, 6 (1979), 147-167.

     1970 data reveal the importance of mother tongue
     differences to ethnic residential segregation while
     social class and ethnic class models do not reveal
     clear trends.

616. Byuarm, Samuel W. COMMUNITY ACTION: A CASE STUDY
     IN RACIAL CLEAVAGE. Diss. Univ. of Illinois,
     1962.

     Community development in a small, segregated town
     was found to be generally unsuccessful with regard
     to improving economic and racial conditions.

617. Farley, Reynolds, Suzanne Bianchi, et al. "Barriers
     to Racial Integration of Neighborhoods: The
     Detroit Case," ANNALS OF THE AMERICAN ACADEMY
     OF POLITICAL AND SOCIAL SCIENCE, 441 (1979),
     97-113.

     Ignorance among whites and blacks of each other's
     changing values is discussed as a major barrier to
     residential integration.

618. Ginzberg, Eli. "Segregation and Manpower Waste,"
     PHYLON, 21 (1960), 311-316.

135

A discussion of the manner in which segregation in
the south discourages Negroes from fully developing
their educational and occupational potential, conse-
quently reinforcing the under-development of the area
as a whole.

619. Kantrowitz, Nathan. "Racial and Ethnic Residential
Segregation in Boston: 1830-1970," ANNALS OF
THE AMERICAN ACADEMY OF POLITICAL AND SOCIAL
SCIENCE, 441 (1979), 41-54.

Ethnic residential segregation in Boston this century
appears to have declined little and racial segregation may be viewed as its extension.

620. Killian, Lewis M. and Charles M. Grigg. "Rank Orders
of Discrimination of Negroes and Whites in a
Southern City," SOCIAL FORCES, 39 (1961), 235-
239.

A study of the manner in which Negroes and whites
rank order discrimination, finding some racial
similarities which counter those suggested by
Myrdal.

621. Larson, Calvin J. and Richard J. Hill. "Segregation,
Community Consciousness, and Black Power,"
JOURNAL OF BLACK STUDIES, 3 (1972), 263-276.

A study of two black neighborhoods, revealing that
while segregation appears to be associated with
community consciousness, it is not correlated with
support for black power.

622. Lieberson, Stanley. "The Impact of Residential
Segregation on Ethnic Assimilation," SOCIAL
FORCES, 40 (1961), 52-58.

The relationship between residential segregation and
ethnic assimilation is used, based on Census data
for 1930 and 1950. Language, citizenship, intermarriage, and occupations of ethnic groups are all
found to be partially affected.

623. Lopez, David E. and Georges Sabagh. "Untangling
Structural and Normative Aspects of the Minority
Status-Fertility Hypothesis," AMERICAN JOURNAL
OF SOCIOLOGY, 83 (1978), 1491-1497.

Minority status fertility is found to be positively
associated with occupational and residential segregation.

624. Marston, Wolword G. and Thomas L. VanValey. "The
Role of Residential Segregation in the Assimilation Process," ANNALS OF THE AMERICAN ACADEMY
OF POLITICAL AND SOCIAL SCIENCE, 441 (1979), 13-
25.

Assimilation is viewed as a sequential process,
defined by segregation, that begins with the
cultural dimension, proceeds with the socioeconomic,
and ends with the structural.

625. Mitchell, Robert E. and Richard A. Smith. "Race and
Housing: A Review and Comments on the Content
and Effects of Federal Policy," ANNALS OF THE
AMERICAN ACADEMY OF POLITICAL AND SOCIAL SCIENCE,
441 (1979), 168-185.

Accomplishment of stable interracial residential
environments is viewed as a function of demand-and-
supply strategies, federal enforcement, broad
strategies, and socioeconomic trends.

626. O'Connell, George E. RESIDENTIAL SEGREGATION BY
RACIAL-ETHNIC BACKGROUND AND SOCIOECONOMIC STATUS
IN FOUR STANDARD METROPOLITAN STATISTICAL AREAS,
1970. Diss. Univ. of Minnesota, 1974.

A demographic study of residential segregation, revealing that while Negro-white segregation is high, Spanish-white and Spanish-Negro levels of segregation are even higher.

627. Pearce, Dianna M. "Gatekeepers and Homeseekers: Institutional Patterns in Racial Steering," SOCIAL PROBLEMS, 26 (1979), 325-342.

An experimental study of the attitudes of real estate agents towards black and white homeseekers with similar background and economic characteristics. Fewer, less expensive, and more segregated homes tended to be shown to blacks.

628. Pettigrew, Thomas M. RACIALLY SEPARATE OR TOGETHER? New York: McGraw-Hill, 1971.

A book which advocates integration as the major means of combatting white racism and discusses relevant issues such as the police, housing, employment, education, desegregation, racial attitudes, politics, and future racial contact.

629. Roof, Wade C. "Southern Birth and Racial Residential Segregation: The Case of Northern Cities," AMERICAN JOURNAL OF SOCIOLOGY, 86 (1980), 350-358.

A study of the effects of region of birth, finding that segregation levels in northern cities are increased by southern birth of both blacks and whites.

630. Spain, Daphne. "Race Relations and Residential Segregation in New Orleans: Two Centuries of Paradox," ANNALS OF THE AMERICAN ACADEMY OF POLITICAL AND SOCIAL SCIENCE, 441 (1979), 82-96.

Delineates the shift from patriarchal to segregated
race relations in New Orleans history, with little
improvement in black status expected in the near
future.

631. Taeuber, Karl E. "Negro Residential Segregation:
Trends and Measurement," SOCIAL PROBLEMS, 12
(1964), 42-50.

Use of the Index of Dissimilarity to measure segregation in 109 cities for 1940, 1950, and 1960, revealing that racial segregation is pronounced in all
cities with large Negro populations, decreased in
northern cities during the 1950's but continued to
increase in the south.

632. Taeuber, Karl E. and Alma F. Taeuber. "The Negro
as an Immigrant Group: Recent Trends in Racial
and Ethnic Segregation in Chicago," AMERICAN
JOURNAL OF SOCIOLOGY, 69 (1964), 374-382.

An analysis of the distinct differences between
Negro and ethnic assimilation, highlighting the
greater success of the latter.

633. Taeuber, Karl E. "Racial Segregation: The Persisting
Dilemma," ANNALS OF THE AMERICAN ACADEMY OF
POLITICAL AND SOCIAL SCIENCE, 422 (1975), 87-96.

Argues that the demographic changes of the 1970's
and 1980's hold optimistic potential for change,
but significant reduction in housing discrimination
is vital to black integration.

634. Taylor, D. Garth. "Housing, Neighborhoods, and
Race Relations: Recent Survey Evidence,"
ANNALS OF THE AMERICAN ACADEMY OF POLITICAL
AND SOCIAL SCIENCE, 441 (1979), 26-40.

Accounts for changing patterns of residential segregation in terms of shifts in the housing market rather than racial attitudes.

635. van den Berghe, Pierre L. "Apartheid: A Sociological Interpretation of Racial Segregation," CAHIERS INTERNATIONAUX DE SOCIOLOGIE, 28 (1960), 47-56.

Jim Crowism and apartheid are analyzed as techniques designed to control intergroup relations following significant social and economic change.

636. Winship, Christopher. "A Revaluation of Indexes of Residential Segregation," SOCIAL FORCES, 55 (1977), 1058-1066.

Advocates using the eta-squared statistic, which is independent of the proportion black using the random segregation baseline, as an index of residential segregation.

637. Wright, Marian A. "Legal and Moral Aspects of Segregation," JOURNAL OF HUMAN RELATIONS, 8 (1959), 81-86.

Attacks segregation for its deprivation of personal rights and narrow, provincial views of the world and future.

638. Yinger, J. Milton and George E. Simpson, "Can Segregation Survive in an Industrial Society," ANTIOCH REVIEW, 18 (1958), 15-24.

Industrialization and consequent urbanization are viewed as reducing segregation in areas such as voting, income, and education but with residential segregation most resistant to change.

OTHER FORMS OF DISCRIMINATION

639. Butler, John S. and Kenneth L. Wilson. "THE AMERICAN
      SOLDIER Revisited: Race Relations in the
      Military," SOCIAL SCIENCE QUARTERLY, 59 (1978),
      451-467.

      A sample of 9,000 soldiers reveals that while educat-
      ion has a slightly negative effect on separatist
      attitudes, prior racial contact has the greatest
      influence on interracial contact.

640. David, Morris, Robert Seibert, et al. "Interracial
      Seating Patterns on New Orleans Public Transit,"
      SOCIAL PROBLEMS, 13 (1966), 298-306.

      A study of the effects of desegregation on behavior
      in New Orleans city buses, finding much of the
      usual segregation in operation.

641. Eitzen, D. Stanley and David C. Sanford. "The
      Segregating of Blacks by Playing Position in
      Football: Accident or Design?" SOCIAL SCIENCE
      QUARTERLY, 55 (1975), 948-959.

      Discrimination in professional football is studied
      in the careers of 387 athletes, highlighting the
      manner in which minority players are gradually
      shifted from crucial to peripheral positions.

642. Feagin, Joe R. "White Separatist and Black Separatist:
      A Comparative Analysis," SOCIAL PROBLEMS, 19
      (1971), 167-180.

      The degree to which whites support separatism is
      used to question Parsons' view of ongoing inclusion
      in the larger society.

643. Martin, James G. "Group Discrimination and Organi-
          zational Membership Selection," PHYLON, 20
          (1959), 186-192.

      Discrimination is discussed in terms of the logical
      and ethical dimensions of organizational membership
      selection.

644. Murray, Paul T. "A Local Draft Board Composition
          and Institutional Racism," SOCIAL PROBLEMS, 19
          (1971), 129-137.

      A study which finds that increases in black represen-
      tation on local draft boards do not reduce the
      proportion of black draftees.

645. Pride, Richard A. and Daniel H. Clarke. "Race
          Relations in Television News: A Content Analysis
          of the Networks," JOURNALISM QUARTERLY, 50 (1973),
          319-328.

      A study which finds consistently negative treatment
      of "white society" and "black militancy" in network
      T.V. news but generally balanced coverage of race
      relations in the media.

646. Schubert, Frank N. "Black Soldiers on the White
          Frontier: Some Factors Influencing Race
          Relations," PHYLON, 32 (1971), 410-415.

      Community response to black troops is found to be
      most positive in areas with significant black or
      Indian populations.

647. Wright, Gerald C., Jr. "Racism and the Availability
          of Family Planning Services in the U.S.,"
          SOCIAL FORCES, 56 (1978), 1087-1098.

County-provided family planning services are interpreted as reflecting racist motives while services
facilitated by more general agencies are viewed neither as racist nor altruistic in intent.

RACIAL AND ETHNIC CONFLICT

SOCIAL MOVEMENTS

648. Borden, Karen W. "Black Rhetoric in the 1960's:
     Sociohistorical Perspectives," JOURNAL OF BLACK
     STUDIES, 3 (1973), 423-431.

     Major events of the 1960's are discussed to clarify
     changes in black rhetoric and life, including the
     emergence of black power and response of law-enforce-
     ment agencies.

649. Dumond, Dwight L. ANTI-SLAVERY: THE CRUSADE FOR
     FREEDOM IN AMERICA. Ann Arbor: University of
     Michigan Press, 1961.

     An historical study of the anti-slavery struggle,
     highlighting various movements, both religious
     and secular.

650. Ehrlich, Howard J. "The Swastika Epidemic of 1959-
     1960: Anti-Semitism and Community Characterist-
     ics," SOCIAL PROBLEMS, 9 (1962), 197-212.

     A demographic study of the swastika epidemic which
     finds that such anti-Jewish acts tend to occur in
     locations and strata which Jews primarily occupy.

651. Eynon, Thomas G. "Black Equality: Revolution from
     the Movement?" SOCIOLOGICAL FOCUS, 3 (1970), 23-
     31.

Outlines a progression of four types of white-black
situations during this century, beginning with white
mobs, moving through black-white mob battles, to black
riots and battles with the forces of order.

652. Goering, John M. "The Emergence of Ethnic Interests,"
SOCIAL FORCES, 49 (1971), 379-384.

A study of ethnic interests among 100 Irish and
Italian Catholics in Providence concludes that the
declining importance of ethnic constraints creates
more ideological ethnic interests rather than
complete assimilation.

653. Hadden, Jeffrey K. and Raymond C. Rymph. "Social
Structure and Civil Rights Involvement: A Case
Study of Protestant Ministers," SOCIAL FORCES,
45 (1966), 51-60.

25 of 48 Protestant clergymen who chose to be
arrested in a civil rights demonstration tended to
be younger, without all-white congregations, and
came from denominations which favored integration.

654. Helmreich, William B. THE BLACK CRUSADERS. New
York: Harper and Row, 1973.

A case study of the life history of an urban black
militant organization from its foundation in 1968
through its demise in 1969.

655. Hicks, John H. "Negroes and African Nationalism,"
SOCIAL ORDER, 11 (1961), 150-155.

African nationalism and the Negro struggle for civil
rights are seen as interrelated in the worldwide
struggle for colored freedom and independence.

656. Horowitz, Donald L. "Cultural Movements and Ethnic Change," ANNALS OF THE AMERICAN ACADEMY OF POLITICAL AND SOCIAL SCIENCE, 433 (1977), 6-18.

A discussion of the manner in which ethnic groups often assimilate with or differentiate themselves from previous group origins, producing associated cultural movements.

657. Kapel, William C. "Cognitive Dissonance, Reconstruction and Negro Civil Rights: Applications of a Theory," JOURNAL OF HUMAN RELATIONS, 20 (1971), 225-238.

Accounts for the failure of Reconstruction in terms of the failure of measures to create dissonance and consequent extension of civil rights to Negroes.

658. Killian, Lewis M. THE IMPOSSIBLE REVOLUTION. New York: Random House, 1968.

An analysis of the Negro movement for change, focusing on revolutionary pressures, leaders, protest strategies, government reaction, and black power.

659. Laue, James H. "A Contemporary Revitalization Movement in American Race Relations: The 'Black Muslims,'" SOCIAL FORCES, 42 (1964), 315-323.

An analysis of the Black Muslim movement as a case of this-worldly activism motivated by religiously sanctioned asceticism.

660. Lomax, Louis E. THE NEGRO REVOLT. New York: Harper and Row, 1962.

A study of the historical background and characteristics of major Negro movements, their leadership problems and relationship to both national and international contexts.

145

661. Louis, Debbie. AND WE ARE NOT SAVED. Garden City: Doubleday, 1970.

A detailed study of the civil rights movement as it developed between 1959 and 1965.

662. Mack, Raymond W. "Of White Racism and Black Mobilization," SOCIAL SCIENCE QUARTERLY, 49 (1968), 444-447.

Delineates a number of conditions viewed as relatively unique to contemporary blacks - upward mobility, increased expectations, organized reaction to discrimination, and the effects of massive migration to the north.

663. Meier, August and Elliot Rudwick, eds. BLACK PROTEST IN THE SIXTIES. Chicago: Quadrangle, 1970.

A reader which deals with nonviolent direct action and the emergence of black power as forms of black protest in the 1960's.

664. Meier, August and Elliot Rudwick. "Attorneys Black and White: A Case Study of Race Relations Within," JOURNAL OF AMERICAN HISTORY, 62 (1976), 913-946.

A discussion of the declining utility of white counsel to the NAACP as the movement gained strength and was accorded greater external legitimacy.

665. Morsell, John A. "Black Nationalism," JOURNAL OF INTERGROUP RELATIONS, 3 (1961-62), 5-11.

The historical background to black nationalism is depicted in terms of Negro rebellion against low status, slum life, and the positive influence of spiritual regeneration.

146

666. Noel, Donald L. "Minority Responses to Intergroup Situations," PHYLON, 30 (1969), 367-374.

Data collected from 655 Negroes indicates that protest or aggression is normative but assimilation is approved provided any discrimination experienced is protested.

667. Peck, Sidney M. "White Ethnics and Black Liberation," SOCIAL THEORY AND PRACTICE, 1 (1970), 12-16.

Advocates a radical reform movement to cope with the growing danger of civil war in the U.S. Such a movement would be based on the schools, churches, unions, and health-welfare services.

668. Roucek, Jospeh S. and Bernard Eisenberg, eds. AMERICA'S ETHNIC POLITICS. Westport: Greenwood, 1982.

A collection of wide-ranging essays on the political activities of America's major European ethnic groups and racial minorities.

669. Saltman, Juliet Z. OPEN HOUSING AS A SOCIAL MOVE-MENT: A SOCIOLOGICAL STUDY OF CHALLENGE, CONFLICT, AND CHANGE. Diss. Case Western Reserve Univ., 1971.

A study of the institutionalization of open housing as a social movement, revealing that such a process does not lead to its decline; rather, external factors and internal leadership are more important.

670. Stone, John. "Black Nationalism and Apartheid: Two Variations on a Separatist Theme," SOCIAL DYNAMICS, 2 (1976), 19-30.

An exploration of the separatist ideology as espoused by blacks in the U.S. and white South Africans.

671. Tucker, Sterling. FOR BLACKS ONLY. Grand Rapids: Eerdmans Publishing, 1971.

An overview of the civil rights movement and why it failed, along with an analysis of realistic strategies.

672. Wax, Murray L. "Indian Protest: Romance and Reality," NEW SOCIETY, 25 (1973), 135-137.

A comparison of Indian tribal movements (often dominated by whites) and the American Indian Movement in relation to the Indian occupation of Wounded Knee.

673. Wildavsky, Aaron. "The Empty Head Blues: Black Rebellion and White Reaction," PUBLIC INTEREST, 11 (1968), 3-16.

Economic inequality has driven blacks to rebellion and whites to frustration, underlining the need for occupational, educational, and political development at the national and neighborhood level.

674. Vander Zanden, James W. "The Klan Revival," THE AMERICAN JOURNAL OF SOCIOLOGY, 65 (1960), 456-462.

An analysis of the Klan revival as atypical, particularly in terms of Klansmen positions in the social structure.

675. Vander Zanden, James W. "The Nonviolent Resistance Movement against Segregation," AMERICAN JOURNAL OF SOCIOLOGY, 68 (1963), 544-559.

Nonviolent resistance movements among southern Negroes are interpreted as attempts to mediate between accommodating and emerging militant Negroes.

676. Zangrando, Johanna S. and Robert L. Zangrando. "Black Protest: A Rejection of the American Dream," JOURNAL OF BLACK STUDIES, 1 (1970), 1-41.

Since blacks have been largely excluded from full assimilation in U.S. society, some of them have urged rejection of the "American Dream," searching instead for a sense of self-identity coupled with group commitment.

CONFLICT AND PROTEST

677. Anderson, William A. "The Reorganization of Protest: Civil Disturbances and Social Change in the Black Community," AMERICAN BEHAVIORAL SCIENTIST, 16 (1973), 426-439.

The 1960's race riots caused some black leaders and groups to assume new roles in order to politicize rioter demands along with other attempts at reconstruction.

678. Back, Kurt W. "Sociology Encounters the Protest Movement for Desegregation," PHYLON, 24 (1963), 232-239.

Critiques sociology for neglecting the proponents of change in race relations and discusses the conditions necessary for action.

679. Byor, Ronald H. "Italians, Jews, and Ethnic Conflict, INTERNATIONAL MIGRATION REVIEW, 6 (1972), 377-391.

An historical study of Italian-Jewish conflict in the U.S. during the 1930's, focusing on internal conflict as well as conflict over foreign affairs, resulting eventually in intergroup accommodation.

680. Conforti, Joseph M. "Racial Conflict in Central
     Cities: The Newark Teachers' Strikes," TRANS-
     ACTION, 12 (1974), 22-33.

     A case study of white suburban-black city resident
     conflict over central city jobs as illustrated in
     the Newark teachers' strike.

681. Elder, Glenn H., Jr. "Racial Conflict and Learning,"
     SOCIOMETRY, 34 (1971), 151-173.

     A survey of Negro and white high school students with
     respect to racial conflict indicates that negative
     feelings rather than actual conflict experience
     was prevalent among whites while the reverse was
     true for Negroes.

682. Geschwender, James A. "Social Structure and the
     Negro Revolt: An Examination of Some Hypotheses,
     SOCIAL FORCES, 43 (1964), 248-256.

     An empirical study of the 'Negro Revolt' which
     explains rebellion in terms of objective conditions
     producing relative deprivation.

683. Gluckman, Max. "New Dimensions of Change, Conflict
     and Settlement," INTERNATIONAL SOCIAL SCIENCE
     JOURNAL, 23 (1971), 548-563.

     Separate group identities are seen to be countered
     by an international economic interdependence and
     increasing resentment against racial and ethnic
     discrimination.

684. Hare, Nathan. "The Sociological Study of Racial
     Conflict," PHYLON, 33 (1972), 27-31.

     Critiques sociology as victimology which views
     minority behavior as sick and pathological, thereby
     neglecting the sickness of the general society.

685. Himes, Joseph S. "The Functions of Racial Conflict,"
     SOCIAL FORCES, 45 (1966), 1-10.

     Views the Negro struggle as realistic conflict which
     increases social communication, solidarity, and
     personal identity in the larger society.

686. Katz, Daniel. "Consistent Reactive Participation of
     Group Members and Reduction of Intergroup
     Conflict," JOURNAL OF CONFLICT RESOLUTION, 3
     (1959), 28-40.

     Delineates four major types of conflict outcome
     as stalemate, conquest, compromise, and conflict
     solution (based on group participation in decision-
     making). The last of these is the most important.

687. Killian, Lewis and Charles M. Grigg. RACIAL CRISIS
     IN AMERICA. Englewood Cliffs: Prentice-Hall,
     1964.

     An analysis of white-Negro conflict with specific
     reference to various models of race relations, the
     community biracial committee, Negro protest leaders,
     the role of white liberals, tokenism, and possible
     future developments.

688. LaManna, Richard. "Lunch-Counter Protests,"
     THE COMMONWEAL, 71 (1960), 653-654.

     Views the lunch-counter protest as influential and
     significant in terms of its spontaneity, grass-roots
     leadership, mass participation, moral tone, and
     positive images of Negroes.

689. Marx, Gary T., ed. RACIAL CONFLICT. Boston: Little,
     Brown, 1971.

     A reader dealing with perspectives on conflict, the
     relationship between social structure and racial
     conflict, ideology and strategy, and the consequences
     of such conflict.

690. Meier, August, Elliot Rudwick, et al., eds. BLACK
      PROTEST THOUGHT IN THE TWENTIETH CENTURY.
      Indianapolis: Bobbs-Merrill, 1971.

      An edited collection of documents dealing with the
      black shift from accommodation to protest, the era
      of legalism, nonviolent action, and black power.

691. Morsell, John A. "Ethnic Relations of the Future."
      ANNALS OF THE AMERICAN ACADEMY OF POLITICAL
      AND SOCIAL SCIENCE, 408 (1973), 83-93.

      Argues that the recent increase in ethnic awareness
      and its relationship to black power means that
      serious sources of social tension exist which require
      careful handling.

692. Powledge, Fred. BLACK POWER - WHITE RESISTANCE.
      NOTES ON THE NEW CIVIL WAR. New York: World
      Publishing, 1967.

      Race relations in the U.S. north and south are
      analyzed with respect to major Negro and white
      movements for change.

693. Rousseve, Ronald J. DISCORD IN BROWN AND WHITE.
      New York: Vantage, 1961.

      A Negro's view of racial tensions and challenges in
      the U.S., emphasizing that the Negro's enforced
      acculturation represents the basis of psychological
      tension and unrest.

694. Searles, Ruth and J. Allen Williams, Jr. "Negro
      College Students' Participation in Sit-Ins,"
      SOCIAL FORCES, 40 (1962), 215-220.

      A questionnaire study of 827 Negroes suggests that
      anti-segregation protests reflect identification
      with rather than alienation from American society.

695. Shreiner, Scott C. RACIAL CONFLICT IN THE SOUTHERN
     UNITED STATES, 1954-1964: SYSTEMIC AND MATHE-
     MATICAL MODELS OF CONFLICT ESCALATION AND
     DIFFUSION PROCESSES. Diss. Univ. of Massachus-
     etts, 1977.

     A study of attitudinal diffusion types of tactic,
     tactic modification, and conflict continuity using
     time series, quasi-experimental designs, and
     regression techniques of analysis.

696. Smith, Carles U. "The Sit-Ins and the New Negro
     Student," JOURNAL OF INTERGROUP RELATIONS, 2
     (1961), 223-229.

     The "new" Negro student is seen as more active in
     self-image and participation in attempted social
     change, particularly civil rights than in past
     years, disturbing both whites and older Negroes.

697. Vander Zanden, James W. "The Impact of Little
     Rock," JOURNAL OF EDUCATIONAL SOCIOLOGY, 36
     (1962), 381-384.

     A case study of the impact of Little Rock on school
     desegregation given federal government intervention,
     the power of law and order forces, and clarification
     of control.

698. Williams, Robin M.,Jr. "Social Change and Social
     Conflict: Race Relations in the United States,
     1944-1964," SOCIOLOGICAL INQUIRY, 35 (1965),
     8-25.

     A discussion of the manner in which partial assimi-
     lation has produced structural pluralism, increasing
     racial protest and conflict.

153

699. Wojniusz, Helen K. DIMENSIONS OF RACIAL HOSTILITY:
AN EMPIRICAL TEST OF THE THEORIES OF WILLIAMS
AND WILSON. Diss. Univ. of Chicago, 1976.

300 blacks and whites in Chicago were interviewed,
indicating that white hostility was most associated
with feelings of claims to neighborhood while for
blacks perceived job discrimination was most crucial.

RIOTS AND DISTURBANCES

700. Bellisfield, Gwynn. "White Attitudes toward Racial
Integration and the Urban Riots of the 1960's,"
PUBLIC OPINION QUARTERLY, 36 (1972-73), 579-584.

Five nationwide surveys do not support the existence
of white backlash in response to urban riots
although there is evidence of riot effects in
immediately adjacent areas.

701. Boesel, David, Richard Burk, et al. "White Institutions and Black Rage," TRANSACTION, 6 (1969),
24-31.

A survey of white managers reveals highly negative
views of Negroes as employees while a study of Negro
political workers highlights the inadequacies of
urban politics and the emergence of an increasingly
militant black population.

702. DeFronzo, James. "Commentary on the Causes of
Racial Disturbances: A Comparison of Alternative
Explanations," AMERICAN SOCIOLOGICAL REVIEW,
36 (1971), 515-516.

A critique of Spilerman's predominantly demographic
explanation of black disturbances, instead pointing
to the importance of social psychological and
structural factors.

154

703. Feagin, Joe R. and Paul B. Sheatsley. "Ghetto
          Resident Appraisals of a Riot," PUBLIC OPINION
          QUARTERLY, 32 (1968), 352-362.

      A study of 200 ghetto residents who identified the
      "real cause" of an area riot as deprivation and
      discrimination, with little perception of extremist
      agitators as precipitant elements.

704. Fogelson, R.M. "From Resentment to Confrontation:
          The Police, the Negroes, and the Outbreak of the
          1960's Riots," POLITICAL SCIENCE QUARTERLY, 83
          (1968), 217-247.

      Police harassment is identified as the major irri-
      tant in Negro community relations, with the latter
      powerless to protest and remedy their grievances.

705. Glazer, Nathan. "The Detroit Riots," NEW SOCIETY,
          10 (1967), 148-150.

      Discusses the continuing impact of the Detroit riots
      on the level of violence and non-ghetto type cities.

706. Gooding, Earl N. URBAN RACE RIOTS AND SOCIAL CHANGE:
          AN ANALYSIS OF TWO CITIES. Diss. Vanderbilt
          Univ., 1977.

      Post-riot Detroit and Washington, D.C. are studied
      with respect to riot effects, concluding that social
      change is not inevitable but depends on rioter and
      power group characteristics.

707. Gregor, A. James. "Race Relations, Frustration,
          and Aggression," REVISTA INTERNACIONAL DE
          SOCIOLOGICA, 2 (1965), 90-112.

A discussion of the social factors related to Negro aggression, including exposure to prejudice, high visibility in society, and the urban context.

708. Grimshaw, Allen D. "Lawlessness and Violence in America and the Special Manifestations in Changing Negro and White Relationships," JOURNAL OF NEGRO HISTORY, 54 (1959), 62-72.

Attributes Negro-white conflict to the breakdown of an unstable accommodative pattern due to Negro refusal to accept its subordinate status and possession of power to challenge it.

709. Grimshaw, Allen D. "Relationships between Prejudice, Discrimination, Social Tension, and Social Violence," JOURNAL OF INTERGROUP RELATIONS, 2 (1961), 302-310.

A consideration of the possible relations among prejudice, discrimination, tension, and violence in relation to external control factors.

710. Grimshaw, Allen D. "Police Agencies and the Prevention of Racial Violence," JOURNAL OF CRIMINAL LAW, CRIMINOLOGY AND POLICE SCIENCE, 4 (1963), 110-113.

Discussion of different approaches to improving the role of police agencies in the event of racial violence, arguing for an immediate rather than belated show of force.

711. Grimshaw, Allen D. "The Major Causes of Color Violence in the United States," RACE, 5 (1963), 76-86.

A comparative analysis of northern versus southern style race riots with respect to precipitating events, minority response, and outcomes.

712. Grimshaw, Allen D., ed. RACIAL VIOLENCE IN THE
     UNITED STATES. Chicago: Aldine, 1969.

     A reader which deals with the history of Negro-white
     violence in America, patterns in such violence,
     their causes, and changing nature.

713. Jeffries, Vincent and H.E. Ransford. "Interracial
     Social Contact and Middle Class White Reactions
     to the Watt's Riot," SOCIAL PROBLEMS, 16 (1969),
     312-324.

     A post-Watts study of the racial attitudes of
     white, middle-class respondents, highlighting the
     importance of previous racial contacts on such
     reactions.

714. Lieberson, Stanley and Arnold Silverman. "The
     Precipitants and Underlying Conditions of Race
     Riots," AMERICAN SOCIOLOGICAL REVIEW, 30 (1965),
     887-898.

     A study which finds that riots are most likely to
     occur in cities which are unable to resolve racial
     problems and are precipitated by violations of one
     racial group by another.

715. Lieberson, Stanley. "The Meaning of Race Riots,"
     RACE, 7 (1966), 371-378.

     A study of the social conditions behind race riots,
     including the reduction of intergroup accommodation,
     low earnings, rising expectations, and lack of
     minority participation in the police force.

716. Mack, Raymond W. "Riot, Revolt, or Responsible
     Revolution? On Reference Groups and Racism,"
     SOCIOLOGICAL QUARTERLY, 10 (1969), 147-156.

     Argues that the present racial conflict stems from
     recent Negro gains in social mobility, resulting in
     rising expectations.
                           157

717. Masotti, Louis H., Jeffrey K. Hadden, et al. A
     TIME TO BURN? Chicago: McNally, 1970.

     An attempt to understand the broader implications
     of racial violence in reference to the future of
     the nation.

718. Mazur, Allen. "The Causes of Black Riots," AMERICAN
     SOCIOLOGICAL REVIEW, 37 (1972), 490-493.

     A reanalysis of Spilerman's data confirms a relation-
     ship between size of Negro population and proximity
     to other black communities, thereby reinforcing the
     geographic contagion explanation of black riots.

719. Paige, Jeffrey M. "Political Orientation and Riot
     Participation," AMERICAN SOCIOLOGICAL REVIEW,
     36 (1971), 810-820.

     A sample of black males in Newark, surveyed six
     months after the 1967 disorders occurred, indicates
     that rioters tend to be highly distrustful of
     political institutions rather than simply alienated.

720. Reed, John S. "A Note on the Control of Lynching,"
     PUBLIC OPINION QUARTERLY, 33 (1969), 268-271.

     Historical statistics on lynching and their attempted
     prevention between 1914 and 1939 are examined,
     revealing fluctuations and the effects of adverse
     non-Southern opinion.

721. Reed, John S. "Percent Black and Lynching: A Test
     of Blalock's Theory," SOCIAL FORCES, 50 (1972),
     356-360.

     A model of random interracial interaction is presented
     which, when applied to Mississippi for the period
     1889-1930, suggests that proportion of black popul-
     ation is positively related to lynching.

722. Rudwick, Elliot M. RACE RIOT IN EAST ST. LOUIS:
JULY 2, 1917. Carbondale: Southern Illinois
University Press, 1964.

A detailed case study of the East St. Louis riot,
focusing on political and economic conditions, as
well as the role of the media, Negro migration, and
law enforcement agencies.

723. Spilerman, Seymour. "The Causes of Racial Disturbances: A Comparison of Alternative Explanations,"
AMERICAN SOCIOLOGICAL REVIEW, 35 (1970), 627-650.

A study of the location of the 1960 racial disorders
which concludes that such disturbances were responses
to general frustrations experienced by Negroes,
regardless of community situation.

724. Spilerman, Seymour. "The Causes of Racial Disturbances: Tests of an Explanation," AMERICAN
SOCIOLOGICAL REVIEW, 36 (1971), 427-442.

South-non-South distributions of disorders are found
to decline, indicating the decreasing importance of
regional cultures to black solidarity.

725. Warren, Donald I. "Suburban Isolation and Race
Tension," SOCIAL PROBLEMS, 17 (1970), 324-339.

A sample of 788 white suburbanites surrounding
Detroit indicates the relevance of socioeconomic
status and neighborhood tension to racial perceptions.

726. Waskow, Arthur I. FROM RACE RIOT TO SIT-IN. Garden
City: Doubleday, 1966.

A study of two major crises of racial conflict that
occurred in America in 1919 and the early 1960's.

727. Weinberg, Carl. "Education Level and Perceptions
      of Los Angeles Negroes of Educational Condition
      in a Riot Area," JOURNAL OF NEGRO EDUCATION,
      36 (1967), 377-384.

      A sample of 106 Los Angeles Negroes revealed that
      education tended to mediate the respondents' hostility
      toward white power and discrimination.

MAJOR CHANGES IN RACE AND ETHNIC RELATIONS

GENERAL SOCIAL CHANGE

728. Caditz, Judith. "Coping with the AMERICAN DILEMMA:
      Dissonance Reduction among White Liberals,"
      PACIFIC SOCIOLOGICAL REVIEW, 20 (1977), 21-42.

      204 white liberals were confronted with six hypo-
      thetical interracial situations, eliciting a number
      of dissonance reduction mechanisms, including
      refusal to answer, minimization, specification of
      groups, and attacking the questioner.

729. Campbell, John D. and Marion R. Yarrow. "Personal
      and Situational Variables and Adaptation to
      Change," JOURNAL OF SOCIAL ISSUES, 14 (1958),
      29-46.

      A study which shows that desegregation is more
      difficult for Negro females than males, given
      greater tolerance of the latter's aggression.

730. Carey, Phillip and Stephen McLaughlin. "Selection
      without Discrimination: An Analysis of the
      A.S.A. Minority Fellowship Program," SOCIOLOGY
      OF EDUCATION, 50 (1977), 144-150.

A description of the distribution of the American
Sociological Association's minority fellowships
and the demographic characteristics of recipients,
most being black but with Indians, and Puerto Ricans
receiving higher proportions than other minorities.

731. Clark, Dennis. "Leadership Education in an All-
      White Neighborhood," JOURNAL OF INTERGROUP
      RELATIONS, 3 (1961-1962), 38-44.

      A description of the Philadelphia Commission on
      Human Rights' educational program for community
      leaders in all-white neighborhoods to assist them
      in dealing with racial change.

732. Coleman, A. Lee. "Race Relations and Developmental
      Change," SOCIAL FORCES, 46 (1967), 1-7.

      Argues that developmental change in race relations
      is feasible if conceived as a planning process
      readjusted to changing conditions.

733. Cross, Delores E., Margo A. Long, et al. "Minority
      Cultures and Education in the United States,"
      EDUCATION AND URBAN SOCIETY, 10 (1978), 263-
      276.

      A discussion of the need to train professionals
      adequately to act fairly to all children.

734. Danowitz, Ronald M. "Racial Succession in New York
      City, 1960-1970," SOCIAL FORCES, 59 (1980), 440-
      455.

      A study of 103 tracts in New York City which experi-
      enced racial succession during the 1960-70 decade,
      reveals blacks with above average education and
      median family income.

735. Dixon, Vernon J. and Badi Foster. BEYOND BLACK OR
     WHITE. Boston: Little, Brown, 1971.

     A collection of essays focusing on black referents,
     black-white relations, black artists, economic
     issues, black liberation, and an alternate America.

736. Elder, Glenn H., Jr. "Group Orientations and
     Strategy in Racial Change," SOCIAL FORCES, 48
     (1970), 445-460.

     1,800 Negro and white 7 through 12 year-olds were
     studied for their responses to racial change and
     protests in the 1960's, and revealed that limited
     opportunity produces high interracial distance among
     both races.

737. Farley, Reynolds. "Trends in Racial Inequalities:
     Have the Gains of the 1960's Disappeared in the
     1970's?" AMERICAN SOCIOLOGICAL REVIEW, 42 (1977),
     189-218.

     An analysis of Census data indicates that the
     recession of the 1970's has not destroyed the gains
     made by blacks during the 1960's, although racial
     differences remain large.

738. Fishman, Joshua. "Some Social and Psychological
     Determinants of Intergroup Relations in Changing
     Neighborhoods: An Introduction to the Bridge-
     view Study ," SOCIAL FORCES, 40 (1976), 42-51.

     Attitudes and behavior among both Negroes and whites
     in racially changing neighborhoods appear inconsistent
     although status needs are found to regulate such
     contradictions.

739. Gentry, Joe E. and J. Foster Watkins. "Organizational
     Training for Improving Race Relations," EDUCATION
     AND URBAN SOCIETY, 6 (1974), 269-283.

A study which shows that race as a major factor of concern in schools undergoing desegregation can be significantly decreased by organizational training activities.

740. Giles, Harry H. and S.J. Velarde. "Intergroup Relations and Education," JOURNAL OF INTERGROUP RELATIONS, 2 (1961), 219-222.

66 members of the National Association of Intergroup Relations highlight the importance of race and religious group relations with mixed attitudes toward integration.

741. Glenn, Norvell D. "Some Changes in the Relative Stages of American Nonwhites to 1960," PHYLON, 24 (1963), 109-122.

The occupational and educational status of nonwhites relative to whites between 1940 and 1960 are found to experience significant gains, despite increased unemployment, primarily due to their northern migration and the society's high rate of economic development.

742. Gordon, Milton M. ASSIMILATION IN AMERICAN LIFE. New York: Oxford University Press, 1964.

A classic study of the role of race, religion, and national origins on the process of assimilation in American society.

743. Grigg, Carles M. and Lewis M. Killian. "The Bi-racial Committee as a Response to Racial Tensions in Southern Cities," PHYLON, 23 (1962), 370-382.

A survey of 366 southern communities indicated that only 55 had appointed bi-racial committees and tended to do so when community crises alerted them to the possibility of militant minority action.

744. Guest, Avery M. "Changing Racial Composition of
      Suburbs: 1950-1970," URBAN AFFAIRS QUARTERLY,
      14 (1978), 195-206.

      1,363 suburbs were analyzed for changes in racial
      composition between 1950 and 1970, indicating growth
      in both black and white suburban populations,
      particularly in southern communities.

745. Kahalis, Harvey and David R. Grove. "Racial Equality
      and Justice: A Constitutional and Sociological
      View," INTERNATIONAL JOURNAL OF CONTEMPORARY
      SOCIOLOGY, 12 (1975), 217-231.

      Argues that racial justice can only be obtained within
      the boundaries of legal rationality through consti-
      tutionalism instead of political rationality.

746. Katz, Irwin and Melvin Cohen. "The Effects of
      Training Negroes upon Cooperative Problem-Solving
      in Biracial Teams," JOURNAL OF ABNORMAL PSYCHO-
      LOGY, 64 (1962), 319-325.

      An experimental study of assertion training using 36
      Negro-white dyads, finding that Negro influence
      increased with such training.

747. Keyes, Charles F. ETHNIC CHANGE. Seattle: Univer-
      sity of Washington Press, 1981.

      A set of papers dealing with the process of ethnic
      change as it operates world-wide, illustrated with
      specific case studies.

748. Lipset, Seymour M. and William Schneider. "Racial
      Equality in America," NEW SOCIETY, 44 (1978),
      128-131.

      A discussion of the Bakke case in light of poll data
      indicating that white Americans distinguish between
      compensatory action and preferential treatment which

164

violates the traditional value of equality of
opportunity.

749. Loye, David. THE HEALING OF A NATION. New York:
Delta, 1971.

An analysis of America's racial "sickness" and
varying prescriptions for its remedy.

750. Mathews, Donald R. and James W. Prothro. "Southern
Racial Attitudes: Conflict, Awareness, and
Political Change," ANNALS OF THE AMERICAN ACADEMY
OF POLITICAL AND SOCIAL SCIENCE, 344 (1962), 108-
121.

Discusses the intensity of southern white-Negro
differences in racial attitudes on the one hand,
and the gradual change in white attitudes, on the
other.

751. McAllister, Ronald J., Edward J. Kaiser, et al.
"Residential Mobility of Blacks and Whites:
A National Longitudinal Survey," AMERICAN JOURNAL
OF SOCIOLOGY, 77 (1971), 445-456.

A study of 1,500 households with respect to residential mobility, revealing the relatively higher mobility
of blacks within their own neighborhoods or communities partially due to their rental rates.

752. McKee, James B. "Community Power and Strategies in
Race Relations: Some Critical Observations,"
SOCIAL PROBLEMS, 59 (1958), 195-203.

A critique of the community power approach to intergroup relations strategy as conservative, arguing
for expanding the role of sociologist to social
critic and analyst.

165

753. Morsell, John A. "Ethnic Relations of the Future,"
     ANNALS OF THE AMERICAN ACADEMY OF POLITICAL AND
     SOCIAL SCIENCE, 408 (1973), 83-93.

     Argues that the Negro revolution of the 1960's has
     stimulated interethnic competition for resources,
     resulting in sources of social tension which threatens
     the "social fabric."

754. Moss, James A. "Currents of Change in American Race
     Relations," BRITISH JOURNAL OF SOCIOLOGY, 11
     (1960), 232-243.

     Delineates major factors behind changing race relat-
     ions, including white attitudes, methods of and
     commitments to change, and degree of integration.

755. Palmore, Erdman and Frank M. Whittington, "Differ-
     ential Trends toward Equality between Whites and
     Nonwhites," SOCIAL FORCES, 49 (1970), 108-116.

     An equality index is applied to white-nonwhite
     differences since 1940, revealing substantial non-
     white progress in income, education, occupation,
     and housing but with increasing difference in
     mortality and marital status.

756. Patchen, Martin, James D. Davidson, et al. "Determi-
     nants of Student Interracial Behavior and Opinion
     Change," SOCIOLOGY OF EDUCATION, 50 (1977), 55-
     75.

     4,000 white and black high school students reveal that
     negative interracial orientations tend to be a funct-
     ion of personal aggression, initial racial attitudes,
     and family and peer racial attitudes rather than
     interracial contact.

757. Patterson, Orlando. "Toward a Future that Has No
     Past: Reflection on the Fate of Blacks in America,"
     PUBLIC INTEREST, 27 (1972), 25-62.

Argues that the New World black experience is highly
diverse and differs from the American black experience
who instead need to face the challenge of the present.

758. Pettigrew, Thomas F. "Complexity and Change in
     American Racial Patterns: A Social Psychological
     View," DAEDALUS, 94 (1965), 974-1008.

     Views racial patterns as changing in contact, pro-
     tection, and the law, although de facto Negro segre-
     gation appears to be increasing.

759. Record, Jane C. and Wilson Record. "Ethnic Studies
     and Affirmative Action: Ideological Routes and
     Implications for the Quality of American Life,"
     SOCIAL SCIENCE QUARTERLY, 55 (1974), 502-519.

     A discussion of the tension between ethnic studies
     and affirmative action--between civil rights and
     civil liberties--and its implications.

760. Reed, Rodney J. "Increasing the Opportunities for
     Black Students in Higher Education," JOURNAL OF
     NEGRO EDUCATION, 47 (1978), 143-150.

     A number of techniques are outlined, designed to
     develop black feelings of self-confidence and
     belonging within institutions of higher education.

761. Roof, Wade C. "Race and Residence: The Shifting
     Basis of American Race Relations," ANNALS OF THE
     AMERICAN ACADEMY OF POLITICAL AND SOCIAL SCIENCE,
     441 (1979), 1-12.

     Unlike European immigrants, blacks have not experi-
     enced reduced segregation with economic progress
     and greater black-white tension is predicted for
     the future.

762. Rose, Arnold M. "The American Negro Problem in the
     Context of Social Change," ANNALS OF THE AMERICAN
     ACADEMY OF POLITICAL AND SOCIAL SCIENCE, 357
     (1965), 1-17.

     Traditional race relations are seen as significantly
     affected by industrialization, urbanization, economic
     prosperity, the decline of cotton, increased federal
     control, and the role of the U.S. as a world power.

763. Rothman, Jack, ed. ISSUES IN RACE AND ETHNIC
     RELATIONS. Itasca: Peacock, 1977.

     A reader focusing on the major issues of equality
     of opportunity versus preferential treatment,
     integration versus community control, coalitions
     versus independent action, the white ethnic as
     oppressor or victim, and conflict versus consensus
     as group relations strategy.

764. Shin, Eui H. "Trends and Variations in Efficiency
     of Black Interregional Migration Streams,"
     SOCIOLOGY AND SOCIAL RESEARCH, 62 (1978), 228-
     245.

     1955-60 and 1965-70 migration intervals are studied,
     revealing the declining efficiency of South-North-
     East and South-West streams and increased efficiency
     between the South and North-Central.

765. Smith, Charles U. "Race, Human Relations and a
     Changing South," PHYLON, 23 (1962), 66-72.

     Argues that institutional trends in the South have
     provided the Negro with a self-concept and social
     milieu conducive to civil rights militancy.

766. Sowell, Thomas. "Ethnicity in a Changing America,"
     DAEDALUS, 107 (1978), 213-237.

     Views American pluralism as based on the need for
     cooperation with assimilation as a two-way process.

168

767. Stone, John, ed. RACE, ETHNICITY, AND SOCIAL CHANGE.
N. Scituate: Duxbury, 1977.

A reader dealing with theories and typologies of
race relations, perspectives on social change including migration, industrialization, riots, de-coloni-
zation, value conflicts, group boundary maintenance,
and the debate over harmony or conflict.

768. Terry, Robert W. FOR WHITES ONLY. Grand Rapids:
Eerdmann Publishing, 1970.

A discussion of the new white consciousness, focusing
on changing race relations, ethics, relevant strategies, and personal styles.

769. Tillman, James A. Jr. "Rationalization, Residential
Mobility and Social Change," JOURNAL OF INTER-
GROUP RELATIONS, 3 (1961-1962), 28-37.

Argues that segregation relieves as well as increases
majority feelings of anxiety, hostility, and insecurity, putting significant social change primarily in
their hands.

770. Tumin, Melvin M. and Robert Rotberg. "Leaders,
the Led, and the Law: A Case Study in Social
Change," PUBLIC OPINION QUARTERLY, 21 (1957),
355-370.

A study of 23 urban leaders finds that the majority
favor school desegregation and tend to be moderate
both in the content and expression of their opinions.

771. van den Berghe, Pierre L. "The Benign Quota: Panacea
or Pandora's Box?" THE AMERICAN SOCIOLOGIST, 6
(1971), 40-43.

Rejects caste and racial quotas as self-defeating
since they reinforce the ascriptive assumptions
underlying them as legitimate.

772. Villemez, Wayne K. and Candace H. Wiswell. "The
        Impact of Diminishing Discrimination on the
        Internal Side of Distribution of Black Income:
        1954-1974," SOCIAL FORCES, 56 (1978), 1019-
        1034.

Male income for the years 1954-1974 indicates that
in the industrial non-South, decreasing black-white
inequality has included increasing inequality among
blacks with most economic gains accomplished at the
top of black income distributions.

773. Watkins, Alfred J. "Inter-Metropolitan Migration
        and the Rise of the Sunbelt," SOCIAL SCIENCE
        QUARTERLY, 59 (1978), 553-561.

Sunbelt cities are found to experience either inertial
or explosive growth between 1940 and 1974, with
possible ethnic and class polarization due to outside
sources of immigration.

774. Weaver, Robert C. "The Changing Status of Racial
        Groups," JOURNAL OF INTERGROUP RELATIONS, 2
        (1961), 6-17.

The social, economic, and residential mobility of
recent immigrants is shown to be limited, underlining the need for reduced middle class righteous-
ness and chauvinism to deal with this problem.

775. Wilkerson, Doxey A. "Conscious and Impersonal
        Forces in Recent Trends toward Negro-White
        School Equality in Virginia," JOURNAL OF EDUCAT-
        IONAL SOCIOLOGY, 32 (1959), 402-408.

A study designed to examine the changing status of
white and Negro schools in the South during recent
years.

776. Wilson, William J. "The Declining Significance
of Race," SOCIETY, 15 (1978), 56-62.

Argues that recent changes in race relations,
particularly in regard to black economic position,
have reduced traditional racial oppression, instead
increasing class subordination within the society.

777. Youmans, E. Grant, S.E. Grigsby, et al. "Social
Change, Generation, and Race," RURAL SOCIOLOGY,
34 (1969), 305-312.

A study which finds that generational differences
in values, achievement, anomia, and family identification are higher among Negroes than whites, reflecting changes in race relations.

778. Zachin, Elliot. "The Progress of Black Americans in
Civil Rights: The Past Two Decades Assessed,
DAEDALUS, 107 (1978), 239-262.

An evaluation of black progress in civil rights,
concluding that while some gains have been made,
significant problems with respect to school and
residential segregation, political power, occupational
mobility, and adequate housing remain.

DESEGREGATION

779. Alston, John P. and Ben M. Crouch. "White Acceptance
of Three Degrees of School Desegregation,"
PHYLON, 39 (1978), 216-224.

A 1974 national survey of whites indicated that while
the greater majority, both north and south, accepted
some form of school desegregation, only token levels
of less than 50% were involved.

780. Breed, Warren. "Group Structure and Resistance to
      Desegregation in the Deep South," SOCIAL PROBLEMS,
      10 (1962), 84-94.

      The resistance to desegregation in the Deep South is
      accounted for in terms of the region's lack of
      political, religious, ethnic, and economic pluralism.

781. Campbell, Bruce A. "The Impact of School Desegre-
      gation: An Investigation of Three Mediating
      Factors," YOUTH AND SOCIETY, 9 (1977), 79-111.

      A study of the effects of family, peer group, and
      school environment on racial attitudes and self-
      concept among Atlanta high school seniors highlights
      the utility of deprivation theory in contrast to
      contact and socialization theory.

782. Campbell, Ernest Q. "On Desegregation and Matters
      Sociological," PHYLON, 22 (1961), 135-145.

      A discussion of the southern moderate, white adult,
      and student attitudes, and Negro aspirations,
      emphasizing the need to understand cultural expec-
      tations, the effects of interracial contact, and
      Negro socialization.

783. Canty, Donald. A SINGLE SOCIETY: ALTERNATIVES TO
      URBAN APARTHEID. New York: Praeger, 1969.

      A review of the civil disorders of the 1960's and
      warns that the present state of de facto apartheid
      could become de juro unless significant changes in
      laws and practices are forthcoming.

784. Cohen, Elizabeth G. "The Effects of Desegregation
      on Race Relations," LAW AND CONTEMPORARY PROBLEMS,
      39 (1975), 271-299.

      A critique of desegregation research as ambiguous
      and ignoring informal social segregation in integr-
      ated settings.

785. Coleman, James S. "Liberty and Equality and School Desegregation," SOCIAL POLICY, 6 (1976), 14-29.

Discusses policy options implied by the discovery that while within school district segregation has decreased, between district segregation has increased.

786. Cramer, Richard M. "School Desegregation and New Industry: The Southern Community Leader's Viewpoint," SOCIAL FORCES, 41 (1963), 384-389.

80 white leaders in five southern communities revealed little connection between support for school desegregation and favorableness to new industry.

787. Dickinson, George E. "Dating Behavior of Black and White Adolescents Before and After Desegregation," JOURNAL OF MARRIAGE AND THE FAMILY, 37 (1975), 602-608.

Adolescent dating prior to and after desegregation indicates that black dating today is similar to that of whites prior to desegregation while white dating has changed little in a decade.

788. Dwyer, Robert J. "The Administrative Role in Desegregation," SOCIOLOGY AND SOCIAL RESEARCH, 43 (1959), 183-188.

Argues that if a school administrator is a leader who is firm and direct in the early stages of desegregation, and has community support, he can be a positive element in implementing integration.

789. Giles, Michael W. "White Enrollment Stability and School Desegregation: A Two-Level Analysis," AMERICAN SOCIOLOGICAL REVIEW, 43 (1978), 848-864.

The relationship between white enrollment and school desegregation is examined in 1,600 southern schools, indicating a curvilinear relationship between percent black enrollments and the rate of white withdrawal.

790. Jones, Faustine C. "Ironies of School Desegregation," THE JOURNAL OF NEGRO EDUCATION, 47 (1978), 2-27.

An analysis of desegregation policies, problems, and issues spanning three and a half centuries from 1619 to 1977.

791. Johnson, Guy B. "Progress in the Desegregation of Education," JOURNAL OF EDUCATIONAL SOCIOLOGY, 32 (1959), 254-259.

A discussion of desegregation in higher education, including Negro enrollment, accommodation, campus activities, interpersonal contacts, academic adjustment, and social change.

792. Killian, Lewis M. and Charles M. Grigg. "Community Resistance and Acceptance of Desegregation," JOURNAL OF NEGRO EDUCATION, 34 (1965), 268-277.

Argues that racial tension will decrease significantly only if state and local governments implement civil rights, otherwise tokenism, quotas, segregation, and the Negro revolt will continue.

793. Levine, Daniel U. and Genie K. Meyer. "Level and Rate of Desegregation and White Enrollment Decline in a Big City School District," SOCIAL PROBLEMS, 24 (1977), 451-462.

1956-1974 enrollment data in Kansas City public schools indicate that white enrollment declines rapidly in schools with a 30% or higher black enrollment or rapid black increase.

794. Morris, David C. WHITE RACIAL ORIENTATIONS TOWARDS
     NEGROES IN AN URBAN CONTEXT. Diss. Ohio State
     Univ., 1969.

     White attitudes towards Negroes are found not to
     vary significantly by level of neighborhood integr-
     ation, length of residence, or social class;
     perceived class of blacks, however, was significant.

795. Muir, Donal E. and C.D. McGlamery. "The Evolution
     of Desegregation Attitudes of Southern University
     Students," PHYLON, 29 (1968), 105-118.

     Surveys of white students at the University of Alab-
     ama are interpreted as reflecting increased percent-
     ages perceiving Negroes as acceptable student peers.

796. Narot, Ruth E. THE EFFECTS OF INSTITUTIONAL CHARAC-
     TERISTICS ON THE RACIAL CLIMATE IN 194 DESEGRE-
     GATED HIGH SCHOOLS. Diss. John Hopkins Univ.,
     1975.

     Positive racial climates in a sample of 194 southern
     schools are found to be associated with staff
     attitudes and white male school participation.

797. Pettigrew, Thomas F. "Social Psychology and Desegre-
     gation Research," AMERICAN PSYCHOLOGIST, 16 (1961)
     105-112.

     Emphasizes the importance of psychology to desegre-
     gation, particularly research on the Negro personal-
     ity, desegregation attitudes, and before-after
     studies.

798. Puryear, Paul L. "Equity Power and the School
     Desegregation Cases," HARVARD EDUCATIONAL REVIEW,
     33 (1963), 421-438.

A study of legal defenses against desegregation
as they evolve around state police powers, court
decisions, de facto desegregation, school assignment,
and the support of private schools.

799. Silverman, Irwin and Marvin E. Shaw. "Effects of
Sudden Mass Desegregation on Interracial Inter-
action and Attitudes in One Southern City,"
JOURNAL OF SOUTHERN ISSUES, 29 (1973), 133-142.

Interracial interaction among southern high school
students during the first semester of total desegregation is found to be sparse although attitudes
appeared to become more tolerant.

800. Sizemore, Barbara A. "Educational Research and
Desegregation: Significance for the Black
Community," JOURNAL OF NEGRO EDUCATION, 47
(1978), 58-68.

The conflicting effects of desegregation on achievement and equal opportunity are discussed, particularly loss of black jobs, continuing prejudice,
and the denial of respect to black students.

801. Stock, John F., Jr. "Ethnicity, Racism and Bussing
in Boston: The Boston-Irish and School Desegregation," ETHNICITY, 6 (1979), 21-28.

The 1974-76 Boston school desegregation crisis is
examined in terms of ethnic and racial differences
in interests.

802. Tillman, James A., Jr. "The Quest for Identity and
Status: Facets of the Desegregation Process in
the Upper Midwest," PHYLON, 22 (1961), 329-339.

A discussion of the manner in which majority group
discrimination provides its members with unearned
identity and status and therefore becomes a compul-
sion.

176

803. Tumin, Melvin. "Readiness and Resistance to Segregation: A Social Portrait of the Hard Core," SOCIAL FORCES, 36 (1958), 256-263.

Those willing to use force to maintain segregation (the 'hard core') tend to be at the bottom of southern society in terms of education, income, occupation, and exposure to the urban milieu.

804. Vander Zanden, James W. RACE RELATIONS IN TRANSITION: THE SEGREGATION CRISIS IN THE SOUTH. New York: Random House, 1965.

A discussion of changing race relations in the south, focusing on status strain and collective behavior, as well as crisis situations and resistance to desegregation.

805. Vanfossen, Beth E. "Variables Related to Resistance to Desegregation in the South," SOCIAL FORCES, 47 (1968), 39-44.

A study which reveals that percent of nonwhites in a state and their class composition are closely related to desegregation in southern states.

806. Weinstein, Eugene A. and Paul N. Geisel. "Family Decision-Making over Desegregation," SOCIOMETRY, 25 (1962), 21-29.

88 Negro families in Nashville reveal that families with higher socioeconomic status tend more often to send their children to desegregated schools.

807. Yarrow, Marianne R, John D. Campbell, et al. "Acquisition of New Norms: A Study of Racial Desegregation," JOURNAL OF SOCIAL ISSUES, 14 (1958),8-28.

A two-week integrated camp is found to have a positive influence on personal self-esteem and the encouragement of interracial friendships.

177

808. Yinger, J. Milton. "Desegregation in American
     Society: The Record of a Generation of Change,"
     SOCIOLOGY AND SOCIAL RESEARCH, 37 (1963), 428-445.

     Significant desegregation forces and effects are
     delineated with respect to judicial, political,
     military, employment, housing, educational, and
     receational institutions.

809. Zion, Carol L. THE DESEGREGATION OF A PUBLIC JUNIOR
     COLLEGE: A CASE STUDY OF ITS NEGRO FACULTY.
     Diss. Florida State Univ., 1965.

     Negro faculty felt that lack of role clarity was
     the greatest problem in college desegregation while
     the administration viewed this as the greatest
     strength in the process.

ASSIMILATION

810. Alba, Richard D. "Social Assimilation among American
     Catholic National Origin Groups," AMERICAN
     SOCIOLOGICAL REVIEW, 41 (1976), 1030-1046.

     A 1963 national sample of 2,000 Catholics indicates
     little support for the notion of increased ethnic
     vitality with respect to intermarriage and friendship
     patterns.

811. Bugelski, B.R. "Assimilation through Marriage,"
     SOCIAL FORCES, 40 (1961), 148-153.

     Polish and Italian marital trends for the period
     1930 through 1960 were computed, indicating a
     significant decline in endogamy for both groups,
     with the prediction that exogamy will predominate
     by 1975.

812. Fong, Stanley L.M. "Assimilation and Changing Social
     Roles of Chinese Americans," JOURNAL OF SOCIAL
     ISSUES, 29 (1973), 115-127.

A study which concludes that Chinese distance from parental culture varies highly, with a number of disparate groups, while ethnic consciousness among Chinese youth appears to be on the rise.

813. Gaymon, William A. and John R. Garrett. "A Blueprint for a Pluralistic Society," JOURNAL OF ETHNIC STUDIES, 3 (1975), 57-69.

Discusses the importance of urban changes which involve minority participation in its problems, the development of coalitions to effect social change, and the emergence of an eventual urban utopia.

814. Gleason, Philip. "Confusion Compounded: Melting Pot in the 1960's and 1970's," ETHNICITY, 6 (1979), 10-20.

A critical discussion of the terms "melting pot" and "pluralism," highlighting their general ambiguity and non-exclusive character.

815. Gordon, Milton M. "Assimilation in America: Theory and Reality," DAEDALUS, 90 (1961), 263-285.

A discussion of the Anglo-conformity melting pot, and cultural pluralism models of assimilation, concluding that structural rather than behavioral assimilation has occurred.

816. Himmelfarb, Harold S. "Patterns of Assimilation-Identification among American Jews," ETHNICITY, 6 (1979), 249-267.

A study of 1,000 Jewish adults in Chicago fails to support the notion of continuing assimilation, indicating that such a process is more complex than it first appears.

817. Hunt, Janet G. "Assimilation or Marginality? Some
     School Integration Effects Reconsidered,"
     SOCIAL FORCES, 56 (1977), 604-610.

     7th through 12th-grade students reveal that comparing
     integrated blacks and whites, as well as segregated
     blacks, makes the consequences of integration
     difficult to interpret.

818. Levin, Jack and William J. Leong. "Comparative
     Reference Group Behavior and Assimilation,"
     PHYLON, 34 (1973), 289-294.

     A study of 200 Chinese American high school and
     college students reveals that cultural and structural
     assimilation involves reference group comparisons
     with majority group members.

819. Marshall, Harvey and Deborah Mayer. "Assimilation
     and the Election of Minority Candidates: The
     Case of Black Mayors," SOCIOLOGY AND SOCIAL
     RESEARCH, 60 (1975), 1-21.

     Data on 149 cities indicate that socioeconomic
     differentiation is inversely associated with the
     possibility of a city electing a black mayor.

820. Monahan, Thomas P. "Interracial Marriage and Divorce
     in Kansas and the Question of Instability in
     Mixed Marriages," JOURNAL OF COMPARATIVE FAMILY
     STUDIES, 2 (1971), 107-120.

     Interracial marriage and divorce in Kansas between
     1947 and 1969 is examined, revealing a rise in the
     former with most wives being white, while mixed
     marriage divorce appears underrepresented.

821. Monahan, Thomas P. "Interracial Marriage in a
     Southern Area: Maryland, Virginia, and the
     District of Columbia," JOURNAL OF COMPARATIVE
     FAMILY STUDIES, 8 (1977), 217-241.

Interracial marriage data indicate that it occurred
since colonial times, fewer tend to occur in the
District of Columbia, with interracial marriages
of other races being much higher.

822. Morris, Raymond N. "The Assimilation of Strangers
      in a Small Residential Community," SOCIOLOGICAL
      REVIEW, 11 (1963), 5-17.

      30 stranger families are found to assimilate into
      a hostile group of 40 local families by establishing
      positive relationships with their immediate neighbors.

823. Muguia, Edward and W. Parker Frisbie. "Trends in
      Mexican American Intermarriage: Recent Findings
      in Perspective," SOCIAL SCIENCE QUARTERLY, 58
      (1977), 374-389.

      Trends in Mexican American exogamy reveal very little
      increases in this direction, suggesting their
      continuing existence as a sociocultural minority.

824. Rubin, Israel. "Ethnicity and Cultural Pluralism,"
      PHYLON, 36 (1975), 140-148.

      Suggests that external hostility maintains ethnic
      diversity and decline in the former will accordingly
      reduce the need for the latter.

825. Triandis, Harry C. "The Future of Pluralism,"
      THE JOURNAL OF SOCIAL ISSUES, 32 (1976), 179-208.

      Advocates the development of interdependence,
      appreciation, and skills necessary to intercultural
      interaction as necessary prerequisites for the
      development of multiculturalism.

INTEGRATION

826. Brown, William R. EXPERIENCES PRIOR TO AND OUTSIDE
OF HIGH SCHOOL AS THESE AFFECT THE INTER-RACIAL
PERCEPTIONS AND BEHAVIOR OF HIGH SCHOOL STUDENTS.
Diss. Purdue Univ., 1974.

A study which highlights the importance of extra-
curricular positive cross-racial contacts on the
racial perceptions and behavior of black and white
high school students in Indianapolis.

827. Conant, Ralph W., Sheldon Levy, et al. "Mass
Polarization: Negro and White Attitudes on
the Pace of Integration," AMERICAN BEHAVIORAL
SCIENTIST, 13 (1969), 247-264.

A Roper survey of whites and blacks in six cities
finds that while the former feel the pace of integration is about right, the latter view it as far
too slow.

828. Crain, Robert L. "School Integration and the
Academic Achievement of Negroes," SOCIOLOGY OF
EDUCATION, 44 (1971), 1-26.

A study of 1,600 adult Negroes which finds that
those who attended integrated schools are more
likely to have graduated from high school, attend
college, and score higher on verbal tests than those
who attended segregated schools.

829. Davidson, James D., Gerhart Hoffman, et al. "Measuring and Explaining High School Interracial
Climates," SOCIAL PROBLEMS, 26 (1978), 50-70.

A method for measuring a school's interracial climate
is presented and applied to 5,000 Indianapolis high
school students, concluding that rate of racial
change, rather than racial composition, appears to
have most effect.

830. Ford, W. Scott. "Interracial Public Housing in
     a Border City: Another Look at the Contact
     Hypothesis," AMERICAN JOURNAL OF SOCIOLOGY, 78
     (1973), 1426-1447.

     168 black and white housewives in Lexington reveal
     that the contact hypothesis applies to lower-income
     white housewives but not to their black counterparts.

831. Elshorst, Hansjorg. "Two Years after Integration:
     Race Relations at a Deep South University,"
     PHYLON, 28 (1967), 41-51.

     A study of the effects of racial integration on
     Louisiana State University, finding significant
     reduction in insults and open discrimination.

832. Foster, Gerald A. SOCIAL PLANNING AND RACIAL
     INTEGRATION IN THE PUBLIC SCHOOLS. Diss.
     Columbia Univ., 1978.

     A planning approach to racial integration in public
     schools, highlighting planning instigators, definition
     of tasks, policy formulation, community input, and
     outcomes.

833. Gamberg, Herbert V. WHITE PERCEPTIONS OF NEGRO RACE
     AND CLASS AS FACTORS IN THE RACIAL RESIDENTIAL
     PROCESS. Diss. Princeton Univ., 1964.

     A study which finds a significant degree of white
     acceptance of interracial housing among whites with
     similar socioeconomic backgrounds living in planned
     projects, suggesting that segregation may decline
     in middle-class neighborhoods.

834. Glazer, Nathan. "Is Integration Possible in the
     New York Schools?" COMMENTARY, 30 (1960), 185-
     193.

Economic, educational, and cultural conditions affecting the condition and integration of New York schools
are discussed.

835. Goddjin, Walter. "Catholic Minorities and School
     Integration," SOCIAL COMPASS, 7 (1960), 161-
     176.

     Sociological and social psychological factors
     defining Catholic-Protestant differences are identi-
     fied and discussed with reference to minority
     group status.

836. Gordon, Leonard. AN ACCULTURATION ANALYSIS OF NEGRO
     AND WHITE HIGH SCHOOL STUDENTS: THE EFFECTS ON
     SOCIAL AND ACADEMIC BEHAVIOR OF INITIAL CLOSE
     INTERRACIAL ASSOCIATION AT THE SECONDARY SCHOOL
     LEVEL. Diss. Wayne State Univ., 1966.

     Negro-white relationships in a desegregated high
     school reveal lower Negro participation and leadership
     roles in extra-curricular activities, except for
     sports, but were lower also in the tendency toward
     self-preference of friends and leaders than white
     students.

837. Grabb, Edward J. "Class, Authoritarianism, and
     Racial Contact: Recent Trends," SOCIOLOGY AND
     SOCIAL RESEARCH, 64 (1980), 208-220.

     A national study of 1,300 adults in 1976 reveals
     increased acceptance of integration since the
     1960's with such tolerance positively associated
     with class background.

838. Handlin, Oscar. "The Goals of Integration,"
     DAEDALUS, 95 (1966), 268-284.

A discussion of major facets of integration, concluding that group interests and experience make the
insistence on integration an exercise in frustration.

839. Hauser, Philip M. "Demographic Factors in the
Integration of the Negro," DAEDALUS, 94 (1965),
847-877.

Deals with the demographic characteristics of the
Negro population in historical perspective and their
implications for potential integration.

840. Herman, Barry E. THE EFFECT OF NEIGHBORHOOD UPON THE
ATTITUDES OF NEGRO AND WHITE SIXTH-GRADE CHILDREN
TOWARD DIFFERENT RACIAL GROUPS. Diss. Univ.
of Connecticut, 1967.

Interracial attitudes, specifically social distance,
among Negro and white school children are found
not to differ significantly with respect to level
of neighborhood integration.

841. Iskander, Michel G. "The Neighborhood Approach in
Intergroup Relations," JOURNAL OF INTERGROUP
RELATIONS, 3 (1961-1962), 80-86.

A discussion of the important role neighborhood
organizations can play in community action and
development.

842. Johnson, David C. "White Resistance to Racial
Integration," DIALOGUE, 3 (1964), 112-117.

A discussion of white resistance to integration
which concludes that many segregationists will
change if led by the law and formal agencies of
social control generally.

843. Kelley, Joseph B. RACIAL INTEGRATION POLICIES OF
     THE NEW YORK CITY HOUSING AUTHORITY: 1958-1961.
     Diss. Columbia Univ., 1963.

     A study of the manner in which the New York City
     Housing Authority attempted to bring about de facto
     racial integration in conjunction with its other
     objectives.

844. Lincoln, Eric C. "Anxiety, Fear, and Integration,"
     PHYLON, 21 (1960), 278-285.

     Major types of social anxiety behind the rejection
     of integration are outlined, in an era of fear,
     tension, loneliness, and anxiety.

845. McDowell, Sophia F. "White Intermarriage in the
     United States," INTERNATIONAL JOURNAL OF THE
     SOCIOLOGY OF THE FAMILY, 1 (1971), 49-58.

     It is found that recent studies concur that inter-
     racial spouses tend to be similar in socioeconomic
     background, are more mature than average, highly
     conscientious, and subject to high status.

846. McMillan, Joseph H. THE INFLUENCE OF CAUCASIAN
     TEACHERS ON NEGRO AND CAUCASIAN STUDENTS IN
     SEGREGATED AND RACIALLY-MIXED SCHOOLS. Diss.
     Michigan State Univ., 1967.

     A study which finds that the relationship between
     perceived teacher evaluations and self-defined level
     of academic ability is higher among Negro students
     with Caucasian teachers in racially-mixed inner-
     city schools than in predominantly white inner-city
     schools.

186

847. Mastroianni, Mike and Joe Khatena. "The Attitudes of
     Black and White High School Seniors toward
     Integration," SOCIOLOGY AND SOCIAL RESEARCH, 56
     (1972), 221-227.

     142 high school seniors from an integrated and all-
     white school revealed that blacks had a greater
     awareness of the race problem while whites were
     generally unaware of their own prejudices.

848. Meyers, Edmund D. EFFECTS OF SOCIAL AND EDUCATIONAL
     CLIMATE OF HIGH SCHOOLS UPON THE ACADEMIC PERFO-
     RMANCE OF NEGRO AND WHITE ADOLESCENTS. Diss.
     Johns Hopkins Univ., 1967.

     650 Negro and white high school students reveal
     that the former are more influenced by interpersonal
     variables than whites while the latter respond more
     to the social and educational climate of the school.

849. Molotch, Harvey. "Racial Integration in a Transition
     Community," AMERICAN SOCIOLOGICAL REVIEW, 34
     (1969), 878-893.

     Integration in the South Shore community of Chicago
     is studied, revealing that social life remains
     segregated except within the Baptist Church and
     integrated organizations.

850. Moskos, C.C. "Racial Integration in the Armed
     Forces," AMERICAN JOURNAL OF SOCIOLOGY, 72
     (1966), 132-148.

     Reports that with desegregation more favorable
     attitudes among whites toward integration have
     emerged, as well as improved performance of Negroes,
     while careers at enlisted levels have become avenues
     of Negro mobility. However, off-duty racial
     separatism remains high.

851. Motz, Annabelle B. and Elaine K. Hollander. "When Black and White College Students Meet--Experiences in Interracial Awareness," JOURNAL OF NEGRO EDUCATION, 44 (1975), 42-52.

A program involving students in interracial learning situations is described and found to result in increased awareness of the society's political and social characteristics.

852. Pettigrew, Thomas F. "Racially Separate or Together?" JOURNAL OF SOCIAL ISSUES, 25 (1969), 43-70.

The racial ideologies of white separatists and liberals are critiqued, advocating mixed strategies for change instead.

853. Piccagli, Georgio A. RACIAL TRANSITION IN CHICAGO PUBLIC SCHOOLS, 1963-1971, AN EXAMINATION OF THE TIPPING POINT HYPOTHESIS. Diss. Univ. of Chicago, 1975.

A study of racial data for Chicago public elementary schools for the period 1963 to 1971 do not indicate development of a tipping point nor racially motivated white flight.

854. Reed, John S. "Getting to Know You: The Contact Hypothesis Applied to the Sectional Beliefs and Attitudes of White Southerners," SOCIAL FORCES, 59 (1980), 123-135.

Survey data from a study of 734 whites in North Carolina indicate that the effect of non-South exposure on stereotyping is U-shaped, perhaps reflecting genuine cultural differences.

855. Reid, Ira. "Integration Reconsidered," HARVARD
EDUCATIONAL REVIEW, 27 (1957), 85-91.

Analyzes problems associated with integration in
relation to Negro tribalism and white marginality,
emphasizing the need to understand the societal
context in which school desegregation is taking
place.

856. Rent, George S. and J.D. Lord. "Neighborhood Racial
Transition and Property Values in a Southern
Community," SOCIAL SCIENCE QUARTERLY, 59 (1978),
51-59.

Property values in racially changing areas were
found to appreciate at a lower rate than those in
all-white areas but for the first and second years
only.

857. Roucek, Joseph S. "The Sociological Aspects of the
Progress of Integration of American Minorities,"
SOCIOLOGICA INTERNATIONALIS, 2 (1964), 143-156.

American sociologists' concern with the concepts of
acculturation, assimilation, amalgamation, desegregation, integration, and pluralism is discussed.

858. Sanow, Michael L. A CASE STUDY OF RACE RELATIONS
AMONG STUDENTS IN A TRANSITIONAL HIGH SCHOOL.
Diss. Ohio State Univ., 1972.

A high school which becomes increasingly black
indicates increasing white student and faculty withdrawal from extra-curricular activities in reaction
to black assertiveness but accompanied by passive
interracial acceptance and increased tolerance.

859. Schermerhorn, R.A. "Minorities and National Inte-
          gration," JOURNAL OF SOCIAL RESEARCH, 13 (1970),
          25-35.

      The cultural and structural factors involved in
      minority group situations are conceptualized in terms
      of centripetal and centrifugal tendencies, concluding
      that there can be no uniform policy for all minorities.

860. Schofield, Janet U. and H. Andrew Sagar. "Peer
          Interaction Patterns in an Integrated Middle
          School," SOCIOMETRY, 40 (1977), 130-138.

      A study of an integrated middle school which finds
      seventh-graders and males more integrated than
      eighth-graders or females.

861. Slavin, Robert E. and Eileen Dickle. "Effects of
          Cooperative Learning Teams on Student Achievement
          and Race Relations," SOCIOLOGY OF EDUCATION,
          54 (1981), 174-180.

      An experiment involving the use of cooperative
      learning methods among 230 students in grades 6
      through 8th indicates increased black academic
      achievement and white-black friendships.

862. Swanson, Austin D. "An International Perspective
          on Social Science Research and School Inte-
          gration," JOURNAL OF NEGRO EDUCATION, 48 (1979),
          57-66.

      A review which argues that integration does not
      ensure higher achievement for lower class children
      but does improve the life chance of many of them.

863. Tenhouten, Warren D. SOCIALIZATION, RACE, AND THE
          AMERICAN HIGH SCHOOL. Diss. Michigan State
          Univ., 1965.

Social personality growth in two segregated and
three integrated high schools is studied with
respect to child-reference group role relationships
involved in the socialization process.

864. Watts, Louis G. "Social Integration and the Use of
         Minority Leadership in Seattle, Washington,"
         PHYLON, 21 (1960), 136-143.

Argues that minority leadership is being under-
utilized in Seattle--a laboratory for studying
integration and the uses of minority leadership.

865. Weigel, Russell H., Patricia L. Wiser, et al. "The
         Impact of Cooperative Learning Experiences
         on Cross-Ethnic Relations and Attitudes."
         JOURNAL OF SOCIAL ISSUES, 31 (1975), 219-244.

An experiment in cooperative ethnic contact carried
out among white, black, and Mexican American high
school students revealed significantly higher
levels of cross-ethnic behavior and positivism.

866. Williams, J. Allen, Jr. "Reduction of Tension
         through Intergroup Contact: A Social Psycho-
         logical Interpretation," PACIFIC SOCIOLOGICAL
         REVIEW, 7 (1964), 81.

A reward-cost approach to intergroup contact,
delineating the conditions under which negative
attitudes will decrease.

867. Wilson, Kenneth L. "The Effects of Integration and
         Class on Black Educational Attainment,"
         SOCIOLOGY OF EDUCATION, 52 (1979), 84-98.

A national sample of 2,000 black and white high
school students documents the extremely positive
effects of school integration on black educational
achievement.

868. Wolf, Eleanor P.   CHANGING NEIGHBORHOOD: A STUDY OF
     RACIAL TRANSITION.   Diss. Wayne State Univ., 1959.

     A study of the racial invasion-succession sequence
     in private urban neighborhoods based on longitudinal
     interviews conducted with 670 Detroit middle-class
     residents.

869. Young, Whitney M., Jr.   BEYOND RACISM: BUILDING AN
     OPEN SOCIETY.   New York: McGraw-Hill, 1969.

     A book which deals with the nature of the open
     society, conditions in black and white America,
     and the need to effect an open society.

CHAPTER IV

RACE AND ETHNIC RELATIONS IN OTHER SOCIETIES

COMPARATIVE ANALYSIS

870. Bagley, Christopher. "Racialism and Pluralism: A
      Dimensional Analysis of Forty-Eight Countries,"
      RACE, 13 (1972), 347-354.

      In an empirical study of 48 countries, the author
      finds that racialism tends to be associated with
      relatively advanced economic development while
      highly pluralist, non-economically developed
      societies have experienced colonial domination.

871. Baker, Donald G. "Dominance Patterns in Anglo
      Fragment Societies," INTERNATIONAL REVIEW OF
      MODERN SOCIOLOGY, 4 (1974), 148-164.

      An extended study of intergroup relations in Anglo
      fragment societies (the U.S., Canada, New Zealand,
      Australia, South Africa, and Rhodesia), focusing on
      power resources, situational factors, and structural
      elements within the context of plural society theory.

872. Banton, Michael. RACE RELATIONS. London: Tavis-
      tock, 1967.

      A text which focuses on the study of race relations,
      the history of racial thought, slavery, white
      supremacy, and race relations in colonial Africa,
      Brazil, the U.S., and Great Britain.

873.   Baxter, Paul and Basil Sanson, eds. RACE AND
        SOCIAL DIFFERENCE. Middlesex: Penguin, 1972.

        A selection of readings on hereditary differences,
        race and social consciousness, race in western
        thought, literary and folk images, sex and color,
        power and domination, and race in the Caribbean,
        South America, Africa, America, and New Zealand.

874.   Beer, Samuel H. "Group Representation in Britain
        and the United States," ANNALS OF THE AMERICAN
        ACADEMY OF POLITICAL AND SOCIAL SCIENCE, 319
        (1958), 130-140.

        A comparison of group representation in Britain and
        the United States in terms of collectivist versus
        individualist, laissez-faire economic models.

875.   Das, Man S. "A Cross-National Study of Intercaste
        Conflict in India and the United States,
        INTERNATIONAL JOURNAL OF CONTEMPORARY SOCIOLOGY,
        13 (1976), 261-277.

        Whereas the Indian caste system originated in a non-
        conflictual manner, black-white conflict in the
        U.S. has existed since slavery, but in both cases
        the growth of democratic ideals has increased such
        conflict.

876.   Degler, Carl N. NEITHER BLACK NOR WHITE. New York:
        Macmillan, 1971.

        A comparative analysis of slavery in Brazil and the
        United States with particular reference to the
        manner in which a special place for the mulatto
        developed in the case of the former but not the
        latter.

877. Driedger, Leo and Glenn Church. "Residential Segregation and Institutional Completeness: A Comparison of Ethnic Minorities," CANADIAN REVIEW OF SOCIOLOGY AND ANTHROPOLOGY, 11 (1974), 30-52.

The residential segregation of six ethnic groups in Winnipeg is analyzed finding the French, Jews, and Ukrainians were more segregated than Scandinavians.

878. Ehrlich, Stanislaw and Graham Wootton, eds. THREE FACES OF PLURALISM. Westmead: Gower, 1980.

A collection of articles on ethnic, political, and religious pluralism on a world-wide basis, including critical discussion of the term and associated theories.

879. Eitzen, D.S. "Two Minorities: Jews of Poland and the Chinese of the Philippines," JEWISH JOURNAL OF SOCIOLOGY, 10 (1968), 221-240.

Two minorities in societies with similar histories of domination, Catholic majorities, and minority problems are found to possess many striking similarities.

880. Fredrickson, George M. WHITE SUPREMACY, A COMPARATIVE STUDY IN AMERICAN AND SOUTH AFRICAN HISTORY. New York: Oxford University Press, 1981.

A comparative study of the manner in which white supremacy has emerged historically in South Africa and the United States, with varying consequences in each case.

881. Gelfand, Donald E. and Russell D. Lee, eds. ETHNIC CONFLICTS AND POWER: A CROSS-NATIONAL PERSPECTIVE New York: Wiley, 1973.

A reader dealing with class and ethnic conflicts,
tensions and ethnic relations, boundary maintenance,
intergroup conflict, conflicts and alliances, and
social change.

882. Gist, Noel P. and Anthony G. Dworkin, eds. THE
      BLENDING OF RACES. New York: Wiley, 1972.

      A symposium of essays on racial intermixture and
      consequent marginality in a wide variety of situat-
      ions world-wide.

883. Grove, John D. "A Cross-National Examination of
      Cross-cutting and Reinforcing Cultural Cleavages,"
      INTERNATIONAL JOURNAL OF COMPARATIVE SOCIOLOGY,
      3-4 (1977), 217-227.

      A study of 45 multi-ethnic societies indicates the
      differential effects of cultural homogeneity and
      heterogeneity on intergroup conflict.

884. Grove, John D. "A Test of the Ethnic Equalization
      Hypothesis: A Cross-National Study," ETHNIC
      AND RACIAL STUDIES, 1 (1978), 175-195.

      Ethnic equalization in 9 countries with such policies
      was studied with respect to the effects of economic
      development, partially confirming the "inverted U
      hypothesis."

885. Guillemin, Jeanne. "The Politics of National Integ-
      ration: A Comparison of the United States and
      Canadian Indian Administrations," SOCIAL PROBLEMS,
      25 (1978), 319-332.

      The demographic, land rights, administrative, and
      ideological aspects of reservations in North America
      are outlined and compared.

886. Heisler, Marton O. "Ethnic Conflict in the World
     Today: An Introduction," ANNALS OF THE AMERICAN
     ACADEMY OF POLITICAL AND SOCIAL SCIENCE, 433
     (1977), 1-5.

     Discusses the need to build rules and institutions
     for ethnic coexistence in a single society, state,
     and economy.

887. Hunt, Chester L. and Lewis Walker. ETHNIC DYNAMICS.
     Homewood: Dorsey, 1974.

     A comparative analysis of ethnic dynamics in various
     societies, including Belgium, Northern Ireland,
     Switzerland, the Soviet Union, the Philippines,
     Africa, Mexico, Islamic States, Europe, and the
     United States.

888. Katznelson, Ira. BLACK MEN, WHITE CITIES. London:
     Oxford University Press, 1973.

     A comparative study of the political responses and
     relationships formed in the early periods of inter-
     racial contact in Northern U.S. cities, 1900-1930,
     and in Britain, 1948-1968.

889. Kinloch, Graham C. "Racial Prejudice in Highly and
     Less Racist Societies: Social Distance Prefer-
     ences among White College Students in South Africa
     and Hawaii," SOCIOLOGY AND SOCIAL RESEARCH, 59
     (1974), 1-13.

     A comparative analysis of white-black social distance
     preferences in South Africa and Hawaii, high-
     lighting the relevance of sex and interracial inter-
     action in the South African case, while religiosity
     and conformity were more important in Hawaii.

890. Kinloch, Graham C. "Comparative Race and Ethnic
     Relations," INTERNATIONAL JOURNAL OF COMPARATIVE
     SOCIOLOGY, 22 (1981), 257-271.

197

Societal and economic dimensions are used to explain varying minority group policies, institutions, majority attitudes and intergroup relations on a comparative basis.

891. Lauwagie, Beverley N. "Ethnic Boundaries in Modern States: Romano Lavo-Lil Revisited," AMERICAN JOURNAL OF SOCIOLOGY, 85 (1979), 310-337.

A comparison of ethnic groups which maximize their resource control with others who maximize their reproductive rate (e.g., gypsies and travelers).

892. Li, Win L. and Linda Yu. "Interpersonal Contact and Racial Prejudice: A Comparative Study of American and Chinese Students," THE SOCIOLOGICAL QUARTERLY, 4 (1974), 559-566.

Racial prejudice among both American and Chinese students (in Taiwan) was found to be associated with family socioeconomic status rather than interpersonal contact.

893. Makabe, Tomoko. "The Split Labor Market: A Comparison of the Japanese Experience in Brazil and Canada," SOCIAL FORCES, 59 (1981), 784.

While the Japanese experienced severe economic discrimination in Japan, this was not the case in Brazil.

894. Mason, Philip. PATTERNS OF DOMINANCE. London: Oxford University Press, 1970.

A study of major types of contact and conquest and consequent systems of inequality, including India, Southern Africa, Spanish America, Brazil, and the Caribbean.

895. Rose, Arnold M. "The Comparative Study of Inter-
     group Conflict," SOCIOLOGICAL QUARTERLY, 1 (1960),
     57-66.

     40 past and present societies with minorities are
     examined for the relationship between social
     structure and discrimination, highlighting the
     importance of monarchy, perceived political threat,
     and racist ideologies.

896. Stephen, David. "Race Relations after Bristol,"
     NEW SOCIETY, 52 (1980), 352-353.

     Highlights the possible parallels between racial
     violence in Britain and the United States, advocating
     a Kerner Commission-like inquiry into the former.

897. Toplin, Robert B. "Reinterpreting Comparative Race
     Relations: The United States and Brazil,"
     JOURNAL OF BLACK STUDIES, 2 (1971), 135-155.

     Rejects the notion that racial attitudes in Brazil
     are more tolerant and class-oriented than in the U.S.,
     suggesting instead that racial prejudice is signifi-
     cant in both settings.

898. Tumin, Melvin M., ed. COMPARATIVE PERSPECTIVES ON
     RACE RELATIONS. Boston: Little, Brown, 1969.

     A reader including analyses of race relations in
     Brazil, Great Britain, Hawaii, India, Japan, Malaya,
     New Zealand, Puerto Rico, South Africa, the West
     Indies, and the United States.

899. van den Berghe, Pierre L. "Integration and Conflict
     in Multinational States," SOCIAL DYNAMICS, 1
     (1975), 3-10.

     Argues that many multinational states have been held
     together by coercive, manipulative elites rather
     than through cultural pluralism.

900. van den Berghe, Pierre L. "The African Diaspora in
      Mexico, Brazil, and the United States," SOCIAL
      FORCES, 54 (1976), 530-545.

      Acculturation is found to be greater in Mexico and
      the U.S. than in Brazil; however, Mexico makes the
      least racial distinctions, the U.S. the most, with
      Brazil in between.

901. van den Berghe, Pierre L. "Nigeria and Peru: Two
      Contrasting Cases in Ethnic Pluralism," INTER-
      NATIONAL JOURNAL OF COMPARATIVE SOCIOLOGY, 20
      (1979), 174.

      Whereas ethnicity is more important than social class
      in Nigeria, Peru is dominated by Spanish culture
      with the Peruvian Indians occupying the society's
      lowest ranks.

902. Wilson, William J. POWER, RACISM, AND PRIVILEGE.
      New York: Macmillan, 1973.

      Discusses race, power, and the development of
      racial stratification, comparing such race relations
      in South Africa and the United States.

AFRICA-GENERAL

903. Bates, Robert H. "Ethnic Competition and Moderni-
      zation in Contemporary Africa," COMPARATIVE
      POLITICAL STUDIES, 6 (1974), 457-484.

      A discussion of the manner in which modernity causes
      stratification, leading to social, economic, and
      political competition among ethnic groups.

904. Francis, E.K. "The Ethnic Factor in Nation-Building,"
      SOCIAL FORCES, 46 (1968), 338-346.

Argues that post-colonial independence situations
result in a new awareness of ethnic bonds, producing
"secondary ethnic groups" which need to be acknowledged in the process of nation-building.

905. July, Robert W. A HISTORY OF THE AFRICAN PEOPLE.
New York: Scribners, 1970.

Deals with the history of ancient and modern Africa
during the last century and a half, highlighting
significant sociopolitical changes during that
period.

906. Kuper, Leo and M.G. Smith, eds. PLURALISM IN AFRICA.
Berkeley: University of California Press, 1969.

A collection of edited papers from an inter-disci-
plinary colloquium dealing with perspectives on
and related factors of pluralism, case studies in
African pluralism, and the consequences of such
pluralism.

907. Kuper, Leo. THE PITY OF IT ALL. Minneapolis:
University of Minnesota Press, 1977.

An analysis of racial and ethnic polarization which
has led to violence and genocide in the cases of
Algeria, Rwanda, Burundi, and Zanzibar.

908. Lee, Rose H. "Urbanization and Race Relations in
Africa," JOURNAL OF HUMAN RELATIONS, 8 (1960),
518-533.

Delineates racial discrimination in white-controlled
cities in Africa and its negative effects.

909. LeMelle, Tilden J. "Race, International Relations,
U.S. Foreign Policy, and the African Liberation
Struggle," JOURNAL OF BLACK STUDIES, 3 (1973),
95-109.

Explores the relationship between race and stratification at the international level, focusing on white and black transnational ties and their possible consequences.

910. Sithole, Ndabaningi. AFRICAN NATIONALISM. London: Oxford University Press, 1968.

An autobiographical analysis of African nationalism, its major problems, and reaction to the philosophy of white supremacy.

911. van den Berghe, Pierre L. "Racialism and Assimilation in Africa and the Americas," SOUTHWESTERN JOURNAL OF ANTHROPOLOGY, 19 (1963), 424-432.

Emphasizes that European colonial impact in Africa was considerably lower than in the Americas given lower levels of conquest, the absence of slavery, voluntary Christianization, and the maintenance of traditional structures.

912. van den Berghe, Pierre L., ed. AFRICA, SOCIAL PROBLEMS OF CHANGE AND CONFLICT. San Francisco: Chandler, 1965.

A general reader on Africa dealing with theoretical perspectives, family structure, social stratification, urbanization, social change, and political movements.

913. van den Berghe, Pierre L. "Ethnicity: The African Experience," INTERNATIONAL SOCIAL SCIENCE JOURNAL, 23 (1971), 507.

Discusses the manner in which post-independence ethnic disparities in power, education, and wealth combine to result in high levels of internal conflict.

914. Herman, Simon N. and Erling Schild. "Ethnic Role
     Conflict in A Cross-Cultural Situation," HUMAN
     RELATIONS, 13 (1960), 215-228.

     A study of American Jewish students training in
     Israel, examining their ethnic identities in varying
     roles, highlighting situational factors.

915. Hoffman, John E. "Readiness for Social Relations
     between Arabs and Jews in Israel," JOURNAL OF
     CONFLICT RESOLUTION, 16 (1972), 241-251.

     A questionnaire study of Arab and Jewish intergroup
     attitudes, concluding that the behavior of Israeli
     Arabs is more dependent on that of their Jewish
     counterparts than vice versa.

916. Nachmias, David and David H. Rosenbloom. "Bureauc-
     racy and Ethnicity," AMERICAN JOURNAL OF
     SOCIOLOGY, 83 (1978), 967-974.

     A study of 1,200 urban Israeli citizens and public
     bureaucrats finds that bureaucratic achievement does
     not reduce the effects of ethnicity upon attitudes.

917. Peres, Yochnan and Zipporah Levy. "Jews and Arabs:
     Ethnic Group Stereotypes in Israel," RACE, 10
     (1969), 479-492.

     Jewish and Arab stereotypes are found to involve
     the images of victor and vanquished as well as
     veteran and newcomer.

918. Poll, Solomon and Ernest Krausz, eds. ON ETHNIC
     AND RELIGIOUS DIVERSITY IN ISRAEL. Ramat-Gan:
     Bar-Ilan University Press, 1975.

A set of analyses of ethnicity in Israel, focusing on the integration of Oriental Jews, the religious factor, and religious zealotry.

919. Shuval, Judith T. "Emerging Patterns of Ethnic Strain in Israel," SOCIAL FORCES, 40 (1962), 323-330.

A study which documents the high rate of social rejection of North African immigrants in Israel, in particular Moroccans.

920. Zenner, Walter P. "Syrian Jews in Three Social Settings," JEWISH JOURNAL OF SOCIOLOGY, 10 (1968), 101-120.

An examination of the structural and cultural changes among Syrian Jews in Syria, New York, and Jerusalem, due to economic specialization, the growth of ethnic institutions, and the role of kinship.

WEST, EAST, AND CENTRAL AFRICA

921. Akiwowo, Akinsola. "The Sociology of Nigerian Tribalism," PHYLON, 25 (1964), 155-163.

A discussion of tribalism in Nigeria, highlighting the manner in which tribes represent status groups with unequal socioeconomic and political positions in the societal hierarchy as a whole.

922. Fordham, Paul and H.C. Wiltshire. "Some Tests of Prejudice in an East African Adult College," RACE, 5 (1963), 70-77.

A study of social distance among 333 East African college students, indicating that attitudes towards outgroups are not based rigidly on color or national origin.

204

923. Garrison, Howard H. "Ethnic Relations in Urban Zambia: The Case of Intergroup Friendship Choice," SOCIOLOGY AND SOCIAL RESEARCH, 64 (1979), 73-85.

A 1973 survey of respondents in three major Zambian cities reveals that residential propinquity is more important than social characteristics in determining patterns of ethnic friendship.

924. Hammond, Richard J. "Race Attitudes and Policies in Portuguese Africa in the Nineteenth and Twentieth Centuries," RACE, 9 (1967), 205-216.

Contemporary Portuguese racial policies of tolerance and multiracialism conflict with foregoing views of Africans as "savage" and deserving to work.

925. Perham, M. "White Minorities in Africa," FOREIGN AFFAIRS, 37 (1959), 637-648.

Predicts that British territories with smaller white elites will be subject to less racial conflict than in Central Africa with its solid block of European settlement.

926. Pocock, D. "Race and Racism in East Africa," ECON-OMICS WEEKLY, 10 (1958), 999-1004.

Delineates the race-class structure in East Africa as it applies to Europeans, Indians, and Africans, causing conflict and hostile judgements.

927. Proudfoot, L. and H.S. Wilson. "The Clubs in Crisis: Race Relations in the New West Africa," AMERICAN JOURNAL OF SOCIOLOGY, 66 (1961), 317-324.

The response of previously exclusive white clubs to contemporary pressures brought by younger Europeans who are identified with Africans is discussed.

928. Rogers, Cyril A. "A Study of Race Attitudes in Nigeria," RHODES-LIVINGSTON JOURNAL, 26 (1959), 51-64.

A study of the attitudes of African students in Nigeria towards Europeans, discovering a significant level of goodwill.

RHODESIA/ZIMBABWE

929. Burgess, M. Ealine. "Ethnic Scale and Intensity: The Zimbabwean Experience," SOCIAL FORCES, 59 (1981), 601-626.

A discussion of Zimbabwe, focusing on changing ethnic boundaries and factors related to ethnic intensity.

930. Dotson, Floyd and Lillian Dotson. "Indians and Coloreds in Rhodesia and Nyasaland," RACE, 5 (1963), 61-75.

Indians in British Central Africa were studied between 1959 and 1961, highlighting the dominant position of Europeans, the rejection of Indians by Coloureds, and vice versa.

931. Frantz, C. "Southern Rhodesia," INTERNATIONAL SOCIAL SCIENCE JOURNAL, 13 (1961), 215-224,

A sample of 500 Europeans indicates their desire to maintain the racial status quo as well as the influence of political pressure groups.

932. Hodder-Williams, Richard. "Afrikaners in Rhodesia: A Partial Portrait," AFRICAN SOCIAL RESEARCH, 18 (1974), 611-642.

Delineates the historical background of Afrikaners in Rhodesia, their group cohesion, and emerging political significance.

206

933. Kinloch, Graham C. "Social Types and Race Relations in a Colonial Setting: A Case Study of Rhodesia," PHYLON, 33 (1972), 276-289.

A case study of Rhodesia, applying the concepts of racial frontier, social types, and the race relations frontier to changing racial attitudes as indicated in newspaper editorials published between 1893 and 1968.

934. Kinloch, Graham C. "Changing Rhodesian Race Relations: A Study of Demographic and Economic Factors," PROCEEDINGS OF THE AMERICAN PHILO-SOPHICAL SOCIETY, 122 (1978), 18-24.

An empirical study of changing race relations in Rhodesia, based on the proposition that as the dominant elite grows in size and the society's level of economic differentiation increases, higher rates of racial competition and conflict result.

935. Kinloch, Graham C. RACIAL CONFLICT IN RHODESIA: A SOCIOHISTORICAL STUDY. Washington: University Press of America, 1978.

A case study of Rhodesian race relations from the 1890's through the 1970's, based on a wide range of demographic and attitudinal data, interpreted within an integrated conceptual framework.

SOUTH AFRICA

936. Adam, Heribert. "The Rise of Black Consciousness in South Africa," RACE, 15 (1973), 149-165.

Outlines the emergence of black consciousness in South Africa, its desire for liberation, rejection of Western values, and experience of Indian fear.

937. Adam, Heribert. "Ideologies of Dedication versus
      Blueprints of Experience," SOCIAL DYNAMICS, 2
      (1976), 83-91.

      Describes the flexible nature of white South African
      racial ideology, including its ability to accommodate
      to pressures and new situations.

938. Adam, Heribert. "When the Chips are Down: Confron-
      tation and Accommodation in South Africa,"
      CONTEMPORARY CRISES, 1 (1977), 417-435.

      An analysis of white and black options in South
      Africa, highlighting the costs, flexible adaptation,
      and maintenance of Afrikaner power.

939. Adam, Heribert. "Interests behind Afrikaner Power,"
      SOCIAL DYNAMICS, 4 (1978), 93-100.

      The interests of businessmen, farmers, unions,
      and civil servants are viewed as behind Afrikaner
      power and its maintenance.

940. Alverson, Hoyt S. "Minority Group Autonomy and the
      Rejection of Dominant Group Radical Mythologies:
      The Zulu of South Africa," AFRICAN STUDIES, 33
      (1974), 3-24.

      Documents the degree to which urban Zulus in South
      Africa feel a sense of power and resist negative
      white stereotypes of them.

941. Archibald, Drew. "The Afrikaners as an Emergent
      Minority," BRITISH JOURNAL OF SOCIOLOGY, 20
      (1969), 416-426.

      Depicts Afrikaners as an economic and social minority
      despite their political dominance, both historically
      and during the present era.

942. Attwell, Michael. "Crossroads: A Violent End to
     Conciliation?" NEW SOCIETY, 44 (1978), 592-594.

     Predicts that if a black-occupied shanty town,
     Crossroads, is destroyed by the South African
     government, new racial violence will result.

943. Bailanger, M. "South Africa: A Problem in Race
     Relations Challenge and Response," AUSTRALIAN
     OUTLOOK, 15 (1961), 5-28.

     Highlights the problems involved in implementing
     apartheid and the consequences of the oppposition
     this policy is engendering.

944. Bloom, L. "The Colored People of South Africa,"
     PHYLON, 28 (1967), 139-150.

     Depicts the Coloreds of South Africa as a marginal
     group both racially and psychologically, with
     increasing political isolation but significant
     cultural assimilation in relation to the Afrikaners.

945. Bonacich, Edna. "Capitalism and Race Relations in
     South Africa: A Split Labor Market Analysis,"
     POLITICAL POWER AND SOCIAL THEORY, 2 (1981),
     239-277.

     Views the South African racial system as a split
     labor market in which white labor attempts to
     prevent capital from replacing it with cheaper black
     labor through its racial policies.

946. Brett, E.A. "African Attitudes to South African
     Society," RACE, 6 (1974), 52-62.

     A questionnaire study of the attitudes of middle
     class Africans indicates relatively high acceptance
     of western values, the importance of education,
     material benefits, security, and Christianity, and
     and concern with economic and social integration.

947. Close, M.E., G.C. Kinloch, et al. "The Afrikaners
     as an Emergent Minority: An Alternative View,"
     BRITISH JOURNAL OF SOCIOLOGY, 22 (1971), 200-208.

     Disputes Archibald's view of the Afrikaners as a
     minority, highlighting the emergent differences
     within this group instead.

948. Danziger, K. "The Psychological Future of an
     Oppressed Group," SOCIAL FORCES, 42 (1963),
     31-39.

     A study of 162 African high school students through
     their projected autobiographies, indicating decreasing
     materialism and increased concern with political
     solutions over time.

949. De Ridder, J.C. THE PERSONALITY OF THE URBAN AFRICAN
     IN SOUTH AFRICA. London: Routledge and Kegan
     Paul, 1961.

     A study of the personality, motivations, frustrations,
     and ambitions of middle class blacks in South Africa,
     using the Thematic Apperception Test.

950. Dickie-Clark, H.F. THE MARGINAL SITUATION: A
     SOCIOLOGICAL STUDY OF A COLOURED GROUP. New York:
     Humanities Press, 1967.

     South African Coloreds are studied with respect to
     their marginal situation in the society and this
     situation, rather than psychological marginality, is
     found to define their perceptions.

951. Duncan, Patrick B. "Is Apartheid an Insoluable
     Problem?" RACE, 6 (1965), 263-266.

     Argues that it is no longer possible to conceive of
     a solution to apartheid based on the retention of
     most whites in the country.

952. Du Toit, J.B. "Key Facts of South Africa's Inter-
     group Problems," SOUTH AFRICAN JOURNAL OF
     SOCIOLOGY, 10 (1974), 9-14.

     Since South Africa will become increasingly black,
     traditional policies pertaining to housing as well
     as political and social institutions will have to
     be modified.

953. Feit, Edward and Randall G. Stokes. "Urbanization
     and the Afrikaner: Another Look," SOUTH AFRICAN
     JOURNAL OF SOCIOLOGY, 10 (1974), 1-8.

     A study of 1,000 white artisans finds that urban
     exposure is significantly related to lower levels
     of prejudice against nonwhites.

954. Fisher, John. THE AFRIKANERS. London: Cassell,
     1969.

     An historical study of the Afrikaners with respect
     to their origins, development as a minority, leader-
     ship, female roles, and relationship with the
     British.

955. Heaven, Patrick C.L. "A Historical Survey and
     Assessment of Research into Race Attitudes in
     South Africa: 1930-1975," SOUTH AFRICAN JOURNAL
     OF SOCIOLOGY, 16 (1977), 68-75.

     A review of research dealing with race relations
     during the periods 1930-49, 1950-59, 1960-1969, and
     1970-75, arguing for a higher level of indigeneous
     research.

956. Heaven, Patrick C.L. "Changes in Ethnic Attitudes
     among Some White South African Schoolboys,"
     PERCEPTUAL AND MOTOR SKILLS, 44 (1977), 986.

     Attitudes towards whites, blacks, Asians, and Coloreds
     among 111 English-speaking schoolboys are found to
     indicate a shift towards greater interracial contact.

957. Hugo, Pierre J. "Academic Dissent and Apartheid in South Africa," JOURNAL OF BLACK STUDIES, 7 (1977), 243-262.

Delineates the "apprehensive professor," "cautious activist," and "ivory-tower academic" in the context of South African politics.

958. Jubber, Ken. "The Persecution of Jehovah's Witnesses in Southern Africa," SOCIAL COMPASS, 24 (1977), 81-134.

Argues that Jehovah's Witnesses are persecuted in response to their politically neutral stand and predicts that such persecution will increase.

959. Kinloch, Graham C. "Intergroup Stereotypes and Social Distance among White College Students in Durban, South Africa," THE JOURNAL OF PSYCHOLOGY, 95 (1977), 17-23.

A study of 229 white South African college students which finds that their intergroup attitudes are defined by a stereotype and social distance hierarchy as well as background, personality, and experience factors.

960. Kuper, Leo. "The Heightening of Racial Tension," RACE, 2 (1960), 24-32.

Racial tension is increased by broadening of race consciousness, sanctions, racial stereotypes and ideologies, and the mutual reinforcement of prejudice and discrimination.

961. Kuper, Leo. "Racialism and Integration in South African Society," RACE, 4 (1963), 26-31.

Argues that apartheid has unleashed racialisms which threaten domination and encourage opposition.

962. Kuper, Leo. "The Problem of Violence in South Africa," INQUIRY, 7 (1964), 295-303.

A discussion of the factors contributing to and goals involved in the view that violence is unavoidable and perhaps desirable depending on long-term aims.

963. Legassick, Martin and Duncan Innis. "Capital Restructuring and Apartheid: A Critique of Constructive Engagement," AFRICAN AFFAIRS, 76 (1977), 437-482.

A critique of the view that South African blacks are gaining from economic growth in a manner which inhibits apartheid and results in limited occupational mobility.

964. Legum, Colin. "Color and Power in the South African Situation," DAEDALUS, 96 (1967), 483-495.

Given the high correlation between color and power in South Africa, it is argued that transfer of power will only result from the application of internal or external force.

965. Lewin, J. "Power and Race Relations in South Africa," POLITICAL QUARTERLY, 30 (1959), 389-399.

A discussion of the manner in which the Nationalist Party, since 1948, has used the State to further and promote Afrikaner interests despite legal and economic obstacles.

966. Lever, Henry. "An Experimental Modification of Social Distance in South Africa," HUMAN RELATIONS, 18 (1955), 149-154.

An experimental study of the effects of different media on racial attitudes, finding that the lecture method was most effective in reducing anti-African and Colored social distance.

967. Lever, Henry. "Ethnic Preferences of White Residents in Johannesburg," SOCIOLOGY AND SOCIAL RESEARCH, 52 (1968), 157-173.

A study of white attitudes towards fifteen ethnic groups suggests that ethnic preferences found in previous studies have become well-established.

968. Lever, Henry. "Changes in Ethnic Attitudes in South Africa," SOCIOLOGY AND SOCIAL RESEARCH, 56 (1972), 202-210.

Two Johannesburg surveys carried out in 1964 and 1968 indicate little change in ethnic attitudes although Afrikaners appear to reject Italians, Greeks, and the Portuguese more while non-Afrikaner whites reject the Chinese more.

969. Lever, Henry. "Some Problems in Race Relations Research in South Africa," SOCIAL DYNAMICS, 1 (1975), 31-44.

Advocates broader research on race relations, including topics such as disturbances, African attitudes, the consequences of discrimination, and content analysis of the media.

970. Lever, Henry. "Education and Ethnic Attitudes in South Africa," SOCIOLOGY AND SOCIAL RESEARCH, 64 (1979), 53-69.

Ethnic attitudes among 1,800 South African whites reveal that while education may be relevant, it may be overridden by in-group identity.

971. Lever, Henry. "Social Class and Ethnic Attitudes in Johannesburg," SOCIAL SCIENCE, 54 (1979), 35-44.

Survey data gathered in Johannesburg indicate the significant effects of social class on white ethnic attitudes.

972. Mann, J.W. "Group Relations in the Marginal
        Personality," HUMAN RELATIONS, 11 (1958), 77-92.

      A study of 50 Coloreds which reveals that degree
      of passibility (i.e., passing for white) is not
      related to psychological marginality.

973. Milkman, Ruth. "Apartheid, Economic Growth, and
        U.S. Foreign Policy in South Africa," BERKELEY
        JOURNAL OF SOCIOLOGY, 22 (1977-78), 45-100.

      An analysis of the crucial economic roles played by
      Great Britain and the U.S. in providing capital to
      develop South Africa's advanced capitalist economy,
      thereby reinforcing the apartheid policies which
      further such interests.

974. Mkele, Nimrod. "The Effects of Apartheid," NEW
        SOCIETY, 2 (1963), 6-7.

      The consequences of apartheid include high levels
      of African poverty, infantile mortality, disease,
      and crime.

975. Nieuwudt, J.M., C. Plug, et al. "White Ethnic
        Attitudes after Soweto: A Field Experiment,"
        THE SOUTH AFRICAN JOURNAL OF SOCIOLOGY, 16 (1977),
        1-12.

      The Soweto riots are found to have had a negative
      effect on Afrikaner attitudes towards blacks but a
      positive influence on English South African views
      of blacks and coloreds.

976. Orpen, Christopher. "Internal-External Control
        and Perceived Discrimination in a South African
        Minority Group," SOCIOLOGY AND SOCIAL RESEARCH,
        56 (1971), 44-48.

      A study of white and Colored attitudes which discovers
      a high correlation between external control and
      perception of discrimination.

977. Pettigrew, Thomas F. "Social Distance Attitudes of
      South African Students," SOCIAL FORCES, 38 (1960),
      246-253.

      627 white South African college students highlight
      Afrikaner rejection of nonwhites, Jewish tolerance,
      and the association between personality traits and
      social distance among the English.

978. Preston-Whyte, Eleanor. "Race Attitudes and
      Behavior: The Case of Domestic Employment in
      White South African Homes," AFRICAN STUDIES, 35
      (1976), 71-89.

      White employers of African domestic servants reveal
      little congruence between attitude and behavior while
      racial factors in general dominate master-servant
      relationships.

979. Pretorius, J.C. "Language and Sex as Factors in
      Social Distance involving Immigrants," SOUTH
      AFRICAN JOURNAL OF SOCIOLOGY, 3 (1971), 49-58.

      1,020 white respondents reveal that Afrikaners tend
      to express more social distance towards Britishers,
      Greeks, Italians, and the Portuguese while sexual
      differences were not significant.

980. Rex, John. "The Plural Society: The South African
      Case," RACE, 12 (1971), 401-413.

      Discusses the compound, reserve, and location
      institutions as the basis of the South African labor
      system, arguing that neither Marxist nor pluralist
      models are adequate for the society's analysis.

981. Rich, Paul. "Ideology in a Plural Society: The
      Case of Segregation," SOCIAL DYNAMICS, 1 (1975),
      167-180.

An analysis of the historical rise of segregationist ideology in South Africa during the present century.

982. Savage, Michael. "The Cost of Enforcing Apartheid and Problems of Change," AFRICAN AFFAIRS, 76 (1977), 287-302.

Argues that some of the costs of apartheid such as law and order enforcement, the pass system, and defense spending could be significantly reduced.

983. Schlemmer, Lawrence. "Homeland: A Study of Patterns of Identification among Africans and South Africa's Divided Society," SOCIAL FORCES, 51 (1972), 154-164.

Up to 50% and more of long-term African urban residents are found to maintain significant ties with the rural residents - a finding which is partially attributed to the effects of discrimination.

984. Staviulius, Kalvak. "Pluralist and Marxist Perspectives on Racial Discrimination in South Africa, THE BRITISH JOURNAL OF SOCIOLOGY, 31 (1980), 463-490.

A critique of the pluralist approach for obscuring racial domination, advocating a Marxist-oriented approach instead, linking discrimination with capitalist growth.

985. Stevens, Richard P. "Zionism, South Africa and Apartheid: The Paradoxical Triangle," PHYLON, 32 (1971), 123-142.

The compromise between Israel and South Africa in the international arena is described, allowing the former to develop and maintain ties with independent African states.

986. Swanson, M.W. "The Durban System: Roots of Urban Apartheid in Colonial Natal," AFRICAN STUDIES, 35 (1976), 159-176.

Apartheid in Natal is found to have emerged, not from Nationalist policies, but white colonial fear of African unrest in the wake of industrialization and urbanization.

987. van den Berghe, Pierre L. SOUTH AFRICA: A STUDY IN CONFLICT. Middletown: Wesleyan University Press, 1965.

Pluralism and conflict in South Africa, their historical evolution, structural mechanisms, and possible future developments are discussed.

988. Viljoen, H.G. "National Stereotypes and Social Distance among a Group of Afrikaans-Speaking Students," SOUTH AFRICAN JOURNAL OF SOCIOLOGY, 4 (1972), 61-67.

The close relationship between national stereotypes and racial/ethnic social distance among Afrikaner college students is documented.

989. Wilson, Monia. "South Africa," INTERNATIONAL SOCIAL SCIENCE JOURNAL, 13 (1961), 225-244.

A review of South African literature on race relations published during the past five years is presented, focusing on poverty, constitutional issues, education, and religion.

990. Wolheim, O.D. "The Colored People of South Africa," RACE, 5 (1963), 25-41.

Residential and industrial legislation which works to the advantage of whites and disadvantage of coloreds is discussed among with the demographic characteristics of this minority.

EUROPE

GREAT BRITAIN

991. Allen, Sheila. "The Institutionalization of Racism,"
RACE, 15 (1973), 99-106.

British race relations are examined with reference
to the immigrant-indigeneous situation, colonial-
metropolitan configuration, and the use of color
as an ascriptive criterion.

992. Bagley, Christopher. "Relation of Religion and
Racial Prejudice in Europe," JOURNAL FOR THE
SCIENTIFIC STUDY OF RELIGION, 9 (1970), 219-225.

Dutch and English surveys indicate that working class
Catholics tend to be most prejudiced among the
former while their English counterparts tend to be
members of the Church of England.

993. Bourne, Jenny. "Cheerleaders and Ombudsmen: The
Sociology of Race Relations in Britain," RACE
AND CLASS, 21 (1980), 331-352.

Outlines the history of race relations research in
Britain, including the contemporary emphasis on
racial prejudice as the major cause of intergroup
conflict.

994. Dummett, Ann. A PORTRAIT OF ENGLISH RACISM. Middle-
sex: Penguin, 1973.

An analysis of English values, self-concepts, and
reactions to the non-English, specifically coloured
immigrants in Britain.

995. Elkin, Stephen and William H. Panning. "Structural
Effects and Individual Attitudes: Racial
Prejudice in English Cities," PUBLIC OPINION
QUARTERLY, 39 (1975), 159-177.

Racial attitudes toward colored immigrants among
1,100 respondents are found to be closely related to
neighborhood opinion, an individual's level of
neighborhood identity, and external referents.

996. Gilroy, Paul. "Managing the 'Underclass:' A
Further Note on the Sociology of Race Relations
in Britain," RACE AND CLASS, 22 (1980), 47-62.

A critique of the colonial view of race relations
as too inflexible a picture of class competition
for power and dominance.

997. Gutpa, Y.P. "The Educational and Vocational Aspira-
tions of Asian Immigrants and English School-
Leavers: A Comparative Study," THE BRITISH
JOURNAL OF SOCIOLOGY, 28 (1977), 185-198.

A study which finds significantly higher educational
and vocational aspirations as well as higher
occupational mobility among Asian compared with
English high school students in London.

998. Holmes, Colin. "Violence and Race Relations in
Britain--1953-1968," PHYLON, 36 (1975), 113-
124.

Accounts for the lack of violence in British race
relations in terms of the absence of social
conditions causing organized group conflict.

999. Holton, James E. "The Status of the Coloured in
Britain," PHYLON, 22 (1961), 31-40.

An optimistic view of British race relations given
the relatively small percentage of coloreds, absence

of solidified white attitudes, the tolerant views
of opinion leaders, and the absence of legal barriers.

1000. Kawwa, Taysir. "Three Sociometric Studies of Ethnic
Relations in London Schools," RACE, 10 (1968),
173-180.

A study of racial ethnocentrism among British,
Cypriot, and West Indian schooldchildren in London.

1001. Kitzinger, Sheila. "Conditional Philanthropy
toward Coloured Students in Britain," PHYLON,
21 (1960), 167-172.

Critiques conditional philanthropy towards coloured
students as racist and a humiliating type of
prejudice which is difficult to resist.

1002. Kramer, Daniel C. "White versus Coloured in Britain:
An Explosive Confrontation?" SOCIAL RESEARCH,
36 (1969), 585-605.

A positive view of British race relations given low
minority numbers, ethnic differentiation, and
cultural differences; however, continuing discrimination may result in the emergence of minority
racial identity.

1003. Lee, Frank F. "Social Controls in British Race
Relations," SOCIOLOGY AND SOCIAL RESEARCH, 34
(1960), 326-334.

A study of West Indians and whites in Britain,
highlighting the lack of white pressure and anti-
coloured action with the former kept in place by
economic and cultural factors.

1004. Maddox, H. "The Assimilation of Negroes in Dockland
Areas in Britain," SOCIOLOGICAL REVIEW, 8 (1960),
5-15.

West Africans and West Indians are studied, with 29% found to be assimilative and social class closely correlated with group orientations.

1005. Marsh, Allen. "Race, Community, and Anxiety," NEW SOCIETY, 23 (1973), 406-418.

Community surveys indicate that racial hostility is highest in boroughs with high physical and housing proximity to immigrants as well as perceived unequal welfare benefits.

1006. Millner, David. "The Future of Race Relations Research in Britain: A Social Psychologist's View," RACE, 15 (1973), 91-99.

Argues that social scientists need to concentrate on behavior rather than attitudes, as well as power and action-oriented research if social science research is to produce more tangible results.

1007. Rex, John. "The Future of Race Relations Research in Britain--Sociological Research and the Politics of Racial Justice," RACE, 14 (1973), 481-488.

Advocates movement of race relations research away from policy concerns.

1008. Rex, John and Robert Moore. RACE, COMMUNITY, AND CONFLICT. London: Oxford University Press, 1967.

A study of racial conflict in Birmingham with respect to the characteristics of residents, immigrants, and consequent intergroup relations.

1009. Rex, John. RACE, COLONIALISM, AND THE CITY.
London: Routledge and Kegan Paul, 1973.

A collection of essays dealing with the general
topics of race and the city, colonial migration
to Britain, research on colonial migration, and
the relationship among pluralism, colonial conflict,
and black revolution.

1010. Schafer, Richard T. "Indians in Great Britain,"
INTERNATIONAL REVIEW OF MODERN SOCIOLOGY, 6
(1976), 305-327.

A study of the difficulties encountered by Indians
in Britain as they experience significant educational,
occupational, and attitudinal discrimination.

1011. Studlar, Donley T. "Social Context and Attitudes
toward Coloured Immigrants," BRITISH JOURNAL OF
SOCIOLOGY, 28 (1977), 168-184.

Contextual factors such as region, percent of immigrants, and economic competition are found to have
little effect on attitudes toward coloured immigrants.

1012. Studlar, Donley T. "Religion and White Racial
Attitudes in Britain," ETHNIC AND RACIAL STUDIES,
1 (1978), 306-315.

Religion and church attendance are found to be
significantly related to attitudes towards immigrants
with Anglicans most hostile, followed by Catholics,
other Protestants, and nonbelievers.

1013. Ward, Robin H. "Race Relations in Britain," BRITISH
JOURNAL OF SOCIOLOGY, 29 (1978), 464-480.

Argues that the political economy of British cities
must be understood in order to more fully account
for race relations.

1014. Boserp, Anders. "The Politics of Protracted Conflict,"
       TRANSACTION, 7 (1970), 22-31.

       A theory of political cohesion which attempts to
       understand the ruling groups of Ulster in their
       relation to the middle and lower middle classes.

1015. Giordan, Henri. "Ethnic Culture and Industrial
       Society," MAN AND SOCIETY, 9 (1968), 213-220.

       Examines the role of regional cultures in industrial
       society as a challenge to the future of Western
       civilization, particularly as a form of escape from
       the frustrations of consumer society.

1016. Harris, George S. "Ethnic Conflict and the Kurds,"
       ANNALS OF THE ACADEMY OF POLITICAL AND SOCIAL
       SCIENCE, 433 (1977), 112-124.

       Accounts for the lack of Kurdish independence in terms
       of their lack of linguistic, religious, and tribal
       unity as well as the Turkish government's denial of
       their existence as a separate group.

1017. Mayer, Kurt B. "The Jura Problem: Ethnic Conflict
       in Switzerland," SOCIAL RESEARCH, 35 (1968),
       707-741.

       The rise of a French separatist movement in Berne
       is accounted for empirically in terms of the degree
       to which religion and language are related to voting
       patterns.

1018. Moore, Robert. "Race Relations in the Six Counties:
       Colonialism, Industrialization, and Stratification
       in Ireland," RACE, 14 (1972), 21-42.

1019. Nielsen, Francois. "The Flemish Movement in Belgium after World War II: A Dynamic Analysis," AMERICAN SOCIOLOGICAL REVIEW, 45 (1980), 76-94.

The resurgence of Flemish ethnic solidarity is found to be explained best in terms of theories of solidarity based on group competition for resources.

1020. Rakowska-Harmstone, Teresa. "Ethnicity in the Soviet Union," ANNALS OF THE AMERICAN ACADEMY OF POLITICAL AND SOCIAL SCIENCE, 433 (1977), 73-87.

Depicts the Soviet Union as a multiethnic society in which the Russians represent the ruling majority and power is controlled by the Communists, with increasing ethnic forces which may bring about change.

1021. Roucek, Joseph S. "The Soviet Treatment of Minorities," PHYLON, 22 (1961), 15-23.

Examines the concept of "minorities," their general characteristics and treatment in the Soviet Union.

1022. Tentori, Tullio. "Prejudice towards Jews in a Group of Young Italians," REVISTA DE SOCIOLOGIA, 5 (1967), 67-78.

A survey of 120 young Catholics revealed little overt hostility toward Jews who were generally viewed within the context of church doctrine.

1023. Waughray, Vernon. "The French Racial Scene: North African Immigrants," RACE, 2 (1960), 60-70.

A discussion of French attitudes towards Algerian immigrants which, while somewhat tolerant in comparison to other societies, are generally negative as part of the problem of discrimination and economic deprivation.

1024.   Wheeler, Geoffrey.   RACIAL PROBLEMS IN SOVIET MUSLIM
        ASIA.   London: Oxford University Press, 1962.

        A brief study of the impact of Russian civilization
        on the Muslims of the eastern republics of the
        Soviet Union.

OTHER SOCIETIES

CANADA

1025.   Clairmont, D.H. and F.C. Wien.   "Race Relations in
        Canada," SOCIOLOGICAL FOCUS, 9 (1976), 185-197.

        Describes race relations in Canada as a vertical
        mosaic subject to declining English differences,
        increased nonwhite immigrants and Native peoples,
        changing types of immigration, and extension of
        citizenship rights.

1026.   Comeau, Larry R. and Leo Driedger.   "Ethnic Opening
        and Closing in an Open System: A Candian
        Example," SOCIAL FORCES, 57 (1978), 600-620.

        1,500 college students reveal that Poles and Germans
        experience considerable opening and limited closing
        of the social system, the French and Jews developed
        subsystems, while the British and Scandinavians
        opened up to the larger society.

1027.   Driedger, Leo.   "Ethnic Boundaries: A Comparison of
        Two Urban Neighborhoods," SOCIOLOGY AND SOCIAL
        RESEARCH, 62 (1978), 193-211.

        A comparison of two neighborhoods, one heterogeneous
        and experiencing invasion-succession, the other
        French which has maintained residential segregation
        and its own culture.

1028. Dutton, Donald G. "Tokenism, Reverse Discrimination, and Egalitarianism in Interracial Behavior," JOURNAL OF SOCIAL ISSUES, 32 (1976), 93-107.

A review of studies focusing on reverse discrimination and tokenism, finding that when subjects can monitor their own behavior, egalitarianism tends to result.

1029. Friederes, J.S. "British-Canadian Attitudes towards Minority Ethnic Groups in Canada," ETHNICITY, 5 (1978), 20-32.

A study of 184 British Canadians, revealing their favorable attitudes toward Native people and negative views of French Canadians and Asians.

1030. Goldstein, Jay E. and Rita M. Bienvenue, eds. ETHNICITY AND ETHNIC RELATIONS IN CANADA. Toronto: Butterworths, 1980.

A reader which focuses on ethnicity, ethnic group differences, and ethnic inequalities, attitudes, and conflict in Canada.

1031. Ireland, Ralph R. "The Role of Economic Motivation in Ethnic Relations," SOCIOLOGY AND SOCIAL RESEARCH, 43 (1958), 119-126.

Delineates changes in French-English Canadian relations brought about by industrialization.

1032. Renaud, Andre. "Ethnic Communities and Indian Settlements in Canada," RECHERCHES SOCIOGRAPHIQUES, 4 (1963), 91-106.

Suggests that Indians could be best integrated into Canadian society through the establishment of rural ethnic settlements designed to ease cultural adaptation.

1033. Aguilar, John L. "Shame, Acculturation and Ethnic Relations: A Psychological Process of Domination in Southern Mexico," JOURNAL OF PSYCHOANALYTIC ANTHROPOLOGY, 5 (1982), 155-171.

A study of a biethnic Ladino-Indian town in Mexico revealing how Ladinos induced shame among Indians, making them more compliant in interethnic relations.

1034. Bejar-Navarro, Raul. "Prejudice and Racial Discrimination in Mexico," REVISTA MEXICANA DE SOCIOLOGIA, 31 (1961), 417-434.

Finds that racial prejudice clearly operates in Mexico's rural areas while economic and occupational discrimination are dominant in urban settings.

1035. Colby, Benjamin and Pierre L. van den Berghe. "Ethnic Relations in Southeastern Mexico," AMERICAN ANTHROPOLOGIST, 63 (1961), 772-792.

Indian-Ladino relations are examined, highlighting cultural differences and the manner in which etiquette rules maintain social distance but segregation is minimal.

1036. Ruiz, Raymonde E. "Mexico: Indianismo and the Rural School," HARVARD EDUCATIONAL REVIEW, 28 (1958), 105-109.

Outlines two approaches to Mexican nationality (Europeanists versus Indianistas) and their varying views of the function of the school.

THE CARIBBEAN

1037. Dodge, Peter. "Comparative Racial Systems in the
Greater Caribbean," SOCIAL AND ECONOMIC STUDIES,
16 (1967), 249-261.

Deals with race relations in the Caribbean in terms
of demographic, market, cultural, religious, and
legal factors.

1038. Hoetink, H. CARIBBEAN RACE RELATIONS. London:
Oxford University Press, 1967.

A study of Caribbean race relations with respect to
major types, historical development, segmentation,
and orientations.

1039. Lowenthal, David. "Race and Color in the West
Indies," DAEDALUS, 96 (1967), 580-626.

While racial discrimination has no legal sanction
in the West Indies, color and associated status
distinctions clearly operate.

SOUTH AMERICA

1040. Comas, Juan. "Recent Research on Racial Relations
in Latin America," INTERNATIONAL SOCIAL SCIENCE
JOURNAL, 13 (1961), 271-299.

Even though prejudice and discrimination have never
been formalized in South America, non-whites have
always been dominated by whites, resulting in social
and economic discrimination.

1041. Dulfano, Maricio J. "Anti-Semitism in Argentina:
Patterns of Jewish Adaptations," JEWISH SOCIAL
STUDIES, 31 (1969), 122-144.

A study which indicates how Jews in Argentina have
adapted to rising anti-Semitism through their
insularity as a group.

1042. Harris, Marvin and Conrad Kottak. "The Structural
       Significance of Brazilian Racial Categories,"
       SOCIOLOGIA, 25 (1963), 203-208.

       The principle of descent, the basis of many systems
       of racial classification, was found to be absent
       in Brazil where the same individual was typed
       differently by different informants.

1043. Junior, Manuel D. "Ethnic and Cultural Pluralism in
       Brazil," REVISTA DE CIENCIAS SOCIALES, 1 (1963),
       389-397.

       A discussion of Brazil's ethnic and cultural
       pluralism, including a wide variety of native,
       European, and Asian immigrants with significant
       consequences for the larger society.

1044. Maeyama, Takashi. "Ethnicity, Secret Societies,
       and Associations: The Japanese in Brazil,"
       COMPARATIVE STUDIES IN SOCIETY AND HISTORY,
       21 (1979), 589-610.

       A discussion of voluntary associations among Japanese
       people in Brazil, their history, response to World
       War II, and high level of factionalism.

1045. Mason, Philip. "Gradualism in Peru: Some Impressions
       on the Future of Ethnic Group Relations," RACE,
       8 (1966), 43-62.

       Peruvian ethnic relations are outlined in terms of
       the society's elitist hierarchy and denial of
       discrimination.

1046. Oberg, Kalervo. "Race Relations in Brazil," SOCIOLOGIA, 20 (1958), 340-351.

Stratification in Brazil is found to be based on wealth, education, occupation, family, and color with a lack of overt discrimination and race consciousness.

1047. Schaden, Egon. "Acculturation of Germans and Japanese in Brazil," REV. ANTROP., 4 (1956), 41-46.

While Japanese acculturation has been relatively fast, the Germans were more isolated in the beginning but have been strongly affected by industrialization.

AUSTRALASIA

1048. Cox, David R. "Pluralism in Australia," AUSTRALIAN AND NEW ZEALAND JOURNAL OF SOCIOLOGY, 12 (1976), 112-117.

The distinction between cultural and structural pluralism is made and problems involved in effecting the second type are discussed.

1049. de Lepervanche, Marie. "From Race to Ethnicity," AUSTRALIAN AND NEW ZEALAND JOURNAL OF SOCIOLOGY, 16 (1980), 24-37.

Views ethnicity rather than racism as the predominant contemporary ideology, viewed as behind the attempt to proletarianize labor.

1050. Harre, John. "The Background to Race Relations in New Zealand," RACE, 5 (1963), 3-25.

A discussion of the historical and social background to New Zealand race relations, focusing on population, income, housing, Maori crime, health, education, and miscegenation.

1051. Harre, John. "The Interracial Mixing of a Group
      of Young New Zealand Adults," RACE, 7 (1966),
      271-288.

      Maori and white college students are interviewed
      with respect to interracial contact and while such
      contact appears acceptable, only 20% of whites had
      experienced close contact with Maoris.

1052. Lieberson, Stanley. "The Old-New Distinction and
      Immigrants in Australia," AMERICAN SOCIOLOGICAL
      REVIEW, 28 (1963), 550-564.

      The old-new theory as applied to Australian immi-
      grants is found to explain little, particularly
      when group length of residence and age distributions
      are taken into account.

1053. Tatz, Colin. "Aborigines, Law and Race Relations,"
      ETHNIC AND RACIAL STUDIES, 3 (1980), 281-302.

      Advocates legal organization of Australia's aborigines
      as the most successful method for gaining political
      visibility.

1054. Vaughan, Graham, ed. RACIAL ISSUES IN NEW ZEALAND.
      Auckland" Akarana Press, 1972.

      A set of essays dealing with racial intolerance,
      the position of Maoris, Polynesian crime, police-
      minority relations, linguistic diversity, ethnic
      awareness, and race relations and the law.

1055. Wild, R.A. "Social Stratification and Race Relations,"
      MANKIND, 11 (1977), 81-92.

      A symposium discussion of black-white relations in
      the context of Australian stratification and power,
      evolving around a modified Weberian model applied
      to such relations.

1056. Brown, Carolyn H. "Ethnic Politics in Fiji: Fijian-Indian Relations," JOURNAL OF ETHNIC STUDIES, 5 (1978), 1-17.

A case study of a Fijian attempt in 1975 to return Indian residents to their homeland and the politics which followed.

1057. Mamak, Alex and Ahmed Ali. RACE, CLASS, AND REBELLION IN THE SOUTH PACIFIC. Sydney: Allen and Unwin, 1979.

A discussion of five case studied of rebellion in the South Pacific, analyzed in terms of race, class, and ethnicity.

1058. Taylor, David M. and Robert C. Gardner. "The Role of Stereotypes in Communication between Ethnic Groups in the Philippines," SOCIAL FORCES, 49, (1970), 271-282.

Tagalog-Chinese communication was studied, finding that such intergroup interaction was not influenced by the ethnic combination of speaker and listener.

1059. Zobie, Arnold. "neo-Colonialism and Race Relations: New Guinea and the Pacific Rim," RACE, 14 (1973), 393-341.

Describes development of the Metaungan Association in New Guinea within the context of the dependency view of neocolonial race relations.

ASIA

1060. Dreyer, June T. "Ethnic Relations in China," ANNALS OF THE AMERICAN ACADEMY OF POLITICAL AND SOCIAL SCIENCE, 33 (1977), 100-111.

Outlines attempts by the Chinese Communist Party
to deal with the society's ethnic minorities (only
6% of the population), including the alternation
between tolerant and repressive policies.

1061. Eberhard, Wolfram. "Modern Tendencies in Islam in
Pakistan," SOCIOLOGUS, 10 (1960), 139-152.

Discusses conflict between the Sunni and Shil Muslims
in Pakistan, particularly as it has increased with
independence.

1062. Freedman, Morris and William E. Willmott. "Southeast
Asia with Special Reference to the Chinese,"
INTERNATIONAL SOCIAL SCIENCE JOURNAL, 15 (1961),
245-270.

A study of the socioeconomic position of the 'Overseas
Chinese' throughout Asia and the Pacific.

1063. Grimshaw, Allen D. "The Anglo-Indian Community:
The Integration of a Marginal Group," JOURNAL
OF ASIAN STUDIES, 18 (1959), 227-240.

An analysis of the stability and effectiveness of
the Anglo-Indian community in India, particularly in
Bombay.

1064. Kwong, Julia. "Theoretical Basis of China's Policies
toward her Minority Nationalities," ETHNICITY,
7 (1980), 203-217.

China's policies towards its minorities are outlined
as based on developing minority economics, political-
ization, political secession, and secession.

1065. Lee, Raymond, L.M. "Ethnic Relations in Interactionist
Perspective: A Case of Ethnic Conflict in West'
Malaysia," SYMBOLIC INTERACTION, 3 (1980), 89-104.

Ethnic conflict in West Malaysia is explored in terms
of the relationship between ethnic group interests,
power, and collective definitions of ethnic group
position.

1066. Schwarz, Henry G. "Ethnic Minorities and Ethnic
        Policies in China," INTERNATIONAL JOURNAL OF
        COMPARATIVE SOCIOLOGY, 20 (1979), 137-150.

Argues that while the Chinese encourage regional
autonomy, traditions which interfere with state plans
for economic and social development are discouraged.

1067. Smythe, Hugh H. "Thailand Minority Groups," PHYLON,
        25 (1964), 280-287.

A study of minority groups in Thailand, their inferior
position, ghettoization, and need for government
action.

1068. Tay, Alice, E.S. "The Chinese in Southeast Asia,"
        RACE, 4 (1962), 34-48.

Delineates the economic and political discrimination
experienced by Chinese minorities throughout Southeast Asia and the possibilities of their assimilation.

CHAPTER V:

RELEVANT PUBLICATIONS AND ADDRESSES

AMERICAN JOURNAL OF SOCIOLOGY:

Editor
University of Chicago
Chicago, Ill. 60637

Subscriptions
University of Chicago Press
P.O. Box 37005
Chicago, Ill. 60637

AMERICAN SOCIOLOGICAL REVIEW:

Editor
Institute for Social
Research
1022 E. 3rd Street
Bloomington, Ill. 47405

Subscriptions
American Sociological
Society
1722 N. Street, N.W.
Washington, D.C. 20036

ANNALS OF AMERICAN ACADEMY OF
POLITICAL & SOCIAL SCIENCE:

Editorial Office
3937 Chestnut Street
Philadelphia, Penn. 19104

Subscriptions
Sage Publications
275 S. Beverly Drive
Beverly Hills, Cal. 90212

JOURNAL OF SOCIAL ISSUES:

Editor
Psychology Department
University of Illinois
603 E. Daniel
Champaign, Ill. 61820

Subscriptions
Plenum Publishing Corp.
233 Spring Street
New York, N.Y. 10013

PHYLON:

    Editor   Subscriptions
    Atlanta University   Atlanta University
    Atlanta, Ga. 30314   Atlanta, Ga. 30314

RACE AND CLASS:

    Editor   Subscriptions
    Institute of Race Relations   Institute of Race Relations
    247-9 Pentonville Road   247-9 Pentonville Road
    London, N1 9NG   London, N1 9NG

SOCIAL FORCES:

    Editor   Subscriptions
    University of North   University of North
      Carolina   Carolina Press
    Chapel Hill, N.C. 27514   P.O. Box 2288
                             Chapel Hill, N.C. 27514

SOCIAL PROBLEMS:

    Editor   Subscriptions
    Department of Sociology   208 Rockwell Hall
    Florida State University   State University College
    Tallahassee, Fla. 32306   Buffalo, N.Y. 14222

SOCIAL SCIENCE QUARTERLY:

    Editor   Subscriptions
    University of Texas at   University of Texas Press
      Austin   P.O. Box 7819
    Austin, Tx. 78712   Austin, Tx. 78712

SOCIOLOGY & SOCIAL RESEARCH:

    Editor   Subscriptions
    Univ. of S. California   Univ. of S. California
    University Park   University Park
    Los Angeles, Cal. 90089   Los Angeles, Cal. 90089

238

AUTHOR INDEX

Abbot, C., 60
Abramson, H.J., 174
Adam, H., 936, 937, 938, 939
Aguilar, J.L., 1033
Akiwowo, A., 921
Alba, R.D., 810
Aldrich, H., 321
Alford, H.J., 403
Allen, S., 991
Alston, J.P., 779
Alverson, H.S., 940
Anderson, C.H., 231
Anderson, W., 314
Anderson, W.A., 677
Ansari, A., 526
Antonovsky, A., 567
Antunes, G., 404
Archibald, D., 941
Armstrong, E.G., 19, 162
Attwell, M., 942

Back, K.W., 678
Bacon, E.F., 342, 568
Bahr, H.M., 5
Bagley, C., 91, 480, 870, 992
Bahr, H.M., 175
Bailanger, M., 943
Baker, D.G., 92, 93, 94, 871
Baker, T.L., 548
Baldwin, C.H., 347
Banks, J.A., 165
Banton, M., 20, 37, 61, 527, 872
Barbero, F., 481
Barksdale, R.K., 232
Barnham, K.E., 482
Barron, M.L., 1

Barth, E.A.T., 21
Bates, R.H., 903
Baughman, E.E., 265
Baxter, P., 873
Becker, H.J., 569
Beer, S.H., 874
Bejar-Navarro, R., 1034
Bell, H., 331
Bellisfield, G., 700
Bellwig, D.J., 266
Bengston, V.L., 38
Benjamin, R., 267
Bennett, S.E., 431
Berg, P.L., 233
Bernard, S., 137
Berry, B., 176
Berwanger, E.H., 334
Beuf, A.H., 385
Binzen, P., 234
Black, M., 235
Blake, R.R., 432, 474
Blalock, H.M., 95, 96, 177
Blassingame, J.W., 332
Bleda, S.E., 614, 615
Bloom, L., 944
Blumer, H., 2
Boesel, D., 701
Bogardus, E.S., 138, 528, 529
Bonacich, E., 97, 295, 333, 945
Bond, H.M., 268
Bonilla, E.S., 425
Bonney, N., 178
Borden, K.W., 648
Boserp, A., 1014
Boskin, J., 62
Bourne, J., 993

239

Boyce, R.J., 570
Boyd, M., 368
Breed, W., 780
Breen, T.H., 179
Brett, E.A., 946
Brewer, D.L., 483
Brimmer, A.F., 296
Brink, W., 433
Bromley, D.G., 236
Broom, L., 180, 434
Brotz, H., 348
Brown, C.H., 1056
Brown, D., 386
Brown, W.R., 826
Bruening, W.H., 63
Brunswick, A.F., 181
Bullock, C.S., 139, 349, 571
Bugelski, B.R., 811
Burgess, M.E., 350, 475, 929
Burns, W.H., 351
Bush, L.F., 297
Butler, J.S., 639
Butsch, R.J., 560
Byor, R.H., 679
Byrne, D., 484
Byuarm, S.W., 616

Caditz, J., 476, 549, 728
Campbell, A., 435, 436
Campbell, B.A., 781
Campbell, E.Q., 561, 782
Campbell, J.D., 550, 729
Canty, D., 783
Cannon, J.A., 352
Carey, P., 572, 730
Carmichael, S., 353
Carrouthers, I.E., 608
Carter, B.L., 437
Castile, G.P., 182
Chace, W.M., 335
Chadwick, B.A., 387
Clairmont, D.H., 1025
Clark, D., 731
Clark, K.B., 322, 485
Clarke, J.H., 64

Cleaver, E., 269
Close, M.E., 947
Clute, W.T., 354
Cohen, E.G., 784
Cohen, P.S., 22
Cohen, S.M., 145
Colby, B.N., 1035
Coleman, A.L., 157, 732
Coleman, J.S., 785
Comeau, L.R., 1026
Conant, R.W., 827
Conforti, J.M., 680
Comas, J., 1040
Cook, T.J., 298
Cortese, C.F., 39
Cox, D.R., 1048
Cox, J.A., 486
Cox, O.C., 170
Crain, R.L., 828
Cramer, M.R., 237, 786
Cross, D.E., 733
Cross, G.J., 343
Cruse, H., 270, 355
Cummings, S., 238, 487
Cutright, P., 573

Daniel, P.B., 602
Daniels, D.H., 40
Daniels, R., 438
Danigelis, N.L., 356
Dann, M.E., 65
Danowitz, R.M., 734
Danzger, M.H., 41
Danziger, K., 948
Das, M.S., 875
David, J., 271, 388
Davidson, C., 534
Davidson, J.D., 829
David, D.B., 66
Davis, F.J., 183, 184
Davis, K.E., 299
Davis, M., 640
DeFleur, M.L., 535
DeFronzo, J., 702
De Lepervanche, M., 1049

Ginzberg, E., 359, 618
Giordan, H., 1015
Gist, N.P., 882
Glazer, N., 360, 705, 834
Gleason, P., 814
Glenn, N.D., 552, 580, 741
Gluckman, M., 683
Goddjin, W., 835
Goering, J.M., 652
Goldsby, R.A., 23
Goldstein, J.E., 1030
Gomez, R., 191
Gooding, E.N., 706
Gordon, D.N., 276
Gordon, L., 443, 836
Gordon, M.M., 3, 742, 815
Gottlieb, D., 158
Gould, J., 252
Gould, S.J., 72
Grabb, E.J., 837
Grebler, L., 408
Greeley, A.M., 240, 444
Greenfield, R.W., 537
Gregor, A.J., 707
Grier, W.H., 277
Griessman, B.E., 192
Grigg, C.M., 743
Grimshaw, A.D., 42, 708, 709, 710, 711, 712, 1063
Grossack, M.M., 278
Grove, J.D., 883, 884
Guest, A.M., 744
Guichard, C.P., 445
Guillemin, J., 885
Gupta, S.P., 370
Gurak, D.T., 193
Gutman, H.G., 73
Gutpa, Y.P., 997

Halle, R.A., 553
Halpern, B., 195
Hamblin, R.L., 446, 562
Hammond, R.J., 924
Handlin, O., 71, 194, 838
Hannen, J.K., 653

Hannerz, U., 6
Hare, N., 684
Hargett, S.L., 494
Harre, J., 1050, 1051
Harris, E.E., 196
Harris, G.S., 1016
Harris, M., 7, 43, 106, 1042
Harris, R.A., 163
Hatton, J.M., 279
Hauser, P.M., 839
Hawkins, D.F., 107
Heaven, P.C.L., 955, 956
Heisler, M.O., 886
Heller, C.S., 280
Helmreich, W.B., 654
Henderson, D., 108
Henderson, W.L., 303
Herman, B.E., 840
Herman, R., 495
Herman, S.N., 914
Hernandez, C.A., 409
Hernton, C.C., 197
Hershberg, T., 74
Hesselbart, S., 447
Hesslink, G.K., 281
Heyne, C.D., 448
Hicks, G.L., 198
Hicks, J.H., 655
Higginbotham, E., 609
Hildebrand, R.F., 24
Hill, R., 304
Hills, S.L., 337
Himes, J.S., 109, 685
Himmelfarb, H.S., 816
Himmelfarb, M., 449
Hodder-Williams, R., 932
Hodge, R.W., 110
Hoebel, E.A., 389
Hoetink, H., 1039
Hoffman, J.E., 915
Holden, M., 75
Holloway, R.C., 496
Holmes, C., 998
Holton, J.E., 999
Horowitz, D.L., 656

Hotopf, W.H.N., 497
Howard, D.R., 111
Howard, J.R., 199
Hough, R.L., 450
Howe, L.K., 241
Hughes, E.C., 25, 200
Hughes, H.M., 201
Hugo, P.J., 957
Hunt, C.L., 887
Hunt, J.G., 817
Hurst, C.E., 112

Insko, C.A., 451
Ireland, R.R., 1031
Iskander, M.G., 841

Jackson, J.D., 113
Jacobs, P., 76
Jacobson, C.K., 538, 539
Jeffries, V., 498, 713
Jiobu, R.M., 202
Johnson, D.C., 842
Johnson, D.W., 452
Johnson, G.B., 791
Johnson, N.E., 315
Jones, D.M., 371
Jones, F.C., 790
Jones, J.M., 499
Jones, R.S., 77, 203
Jones, S., 540
Jordan, W.D., 78
Josephy, A.M., 390
Jubber, K., 958
July, R.W., 905
Junior, M.D., 1043

Kahalis, H., 745
Kain, J.F., 581
Kantrowitz, N., 619
Kapel, W.C., 657
Kaplan, H.R., 582
Karnig, A.K., 306
Katz, D., 686
Katz, I., 26, 44, 746
Katzman, M.T., 242, 583

Katznelson, I., 888
Kawwa, T., 1000
Kelley, J.B., 843
Kelly, W.R., 305
Keyes, C.F., 747
Killian, L.M., 204, 282, 361,
    620, 658, 687, 792
King, L.L., 500
Kinloch, G.C., 114, 115, 379,
    889, 890, 933, 934, 935,
    959
Kitano, H.H.L., 205, 373, 374
Kitzinger, S., 1001
Klaff, V.Z., 159
Klobus-Edwards, P., 150
Klovus, P.A., 148
Kluegel, J.R., 584
Knowlton, C.S., 262
Kogan, N., 501
Kosa, J., 453
Kovel, J., 502
Kramer, D.C., 1002
Kramer, J.R., 253
Kren, G.M., 79
Kung, S.W., 372
Kuo, W.H., 375
Kuper, L., 27, 116, 906, 907,
    961, 962
Kurokawa, M., 206, 454
Kwong, J., 1064

Labovitz, S., 117
Lacy, L.A., 283
Ladner, J.A., 28
La Farge, J., 503
La Guerre, M.S., 325
Lake, R.W., 326
La Manna, R., 455, 688
Lambert, J.R., 8
Lambert, R.D., 208
Lampe, P.E., 410, 411
Larson, C.J., 621
Lash, J., 284
Laue, J.H., 659
Lauwagie, B.N., 891

243

Ledvinka, J., 45
Lee, F.F., 207, 1003
Lee, R.H., 376, 908
Lee, R.L.M., 1065
Legassick, M., 963
Leggett, J.C., 585
Leggon, C.B., 118
Legum, C., 964
Le Melle, T.J., 909
Lever, H., 966, 967, 968, 969, 970, 971
Levin, J.N., 46, 504, 818
Levine, D.U., 793
Levy, S.G., 456
Lewin, J., 965
Lewis, H.S., 243
Li, W.L., 892
Lieberson, S., 209, 622, 714, 715, 1052
Lincoln, C.E., 316, 362, 478, 844
Lind, A.W., 380, 381
Lindley, J.T., 586
Linn, L.S., 563
Lipset, S.M., 748
Liu, W.T., 457
Lomax, L.E., 660
Long, E., 587
Long, H.H., 9, 363
Long, J.E., 588
Lopez, D.E., 623
Louis, D., 661
Lowenthal, D., 1039
Loxley, W.A., 610
Loye, D., 749
Luetgert, M.J., 611
Luhman, R., 210
Lyman, S.M., 140, 458

Mabe, P.A., 541
Macisco, J.J., 429
Mack, R.W., 662, 716
Maddox, H., 1004
Maeyama, T., 1044
Makabe, T., 893

Makielski, S.J., 211
Maldonaldo-Denis, M., 430
Mamak, A., 1057
Manheim, H.L., 171
Mann, J.H., 505, 542, 972
Maranell, G.M., 506
Marden, C.F., 212
Margon, A., 391
Marrett, C.B., 412
Marriott, A., 392
Marsh, A., 1005
Marshall, H., 819
Marston, W.G., 624
Martin, J.G., 213, 507, 643
Martin, W.T., 244
Marx, G.T., 689
Mason, D., 119
Mason, P., 141, 894, 1045
Masotti, L.H., 717
Mastroianni, M., 847
Mathews, D.R., 750
Mayer, K.B., 1017
Maykovich, M.K., 47
Mazur, A., 718
McAllister, R.J., 751
McCarthy, J.D., 48, 364
McConahay, J.B., 564
McCord, W.M., 317
McDaniel, P.A., 285
McDowell, S., 286, 845
McGee, D.P., 49
McKee, J.B., 752
McLemore, S.D., 214
McLenore, D.S., 413
McMillan, J.H., 846
McPherson, J.M., 149
Mead, M., 10
Meier, A., 663, 663, 690
Melish, I.H., 287
Melvin, B.L., 29
Meyers, E.D., 848
Mhatia, O.L.E., 310
Michel, A., 11
Middleton, R., 459
Mieme, A.W., 612

244

Rainwater, L., 515
Rakowska-Harmstone, T., 1020
Ramsey, 264
Ransford, H.E., 289
Record, J.C., 759
Record, W., 290
Redekop, C., 122
Reed, J.S., 720, 721, 854
Reed, R.J., 760
Reid, I., 855
Reid, J.S., 255
Reitzes, D.C., 172
Renaud, A., 1032
Rent, G.S., 856
Rex, J., 33, 123, 124, 125,
    167, 980, 1007, 1008, 1009
Rhodes, L., 126
Rich, P., 981
Richmond, A.H., 13, 152, 160
Riedesel, P.L., 516
Rinder, I.D., 153
Rodgers, I.D., 153
Rogers, C.A., 928
Rohrer, W.C., 247
Romero, P.W., 338
Roof, W.C., 629, 761
Rose, A.M., 256, 346, 517,
    895
Rose, A.N., 762
Rose, P.I., 34, 218, 219
Rosenthal, E., 257
Rosenthal, R., 329
Rossi, P.H., 14, 53
Rothman, J., 154, 763
Rothstein, D., 143
Roucek, J.S., 127, 155, 220,
    221, 222, 668, 857, 1021
Rousseve, R.J., 693
Rubin, I., 824
Rudwick, E.M., 722
Ruiz, R.E., 1036
Ryan, W., 518

Saloutow, T., 248
Saltman, J.Z., 669

Samuels, F., 382, 383
Sampson, W.A., 555
Sanow, M.L., 858
Sarna, J.D., 86
Savage, M., 982
Scanzoni, J.H., 291
Schaden, E., 1047
Schaefer, R.T., 223, 1010
Schermerhorn, R.A., 128, 131,
    144, 168, 859
Schoen, R., 129, 422
Schoffield, J.U., 860
Schubert, F.N., 646
Schuman, H., 35, 467
Schusky, E.L., 393
Schwartz, H.G., 1066
Schlemmer, L., 983
Searles, R., 694
Seigel, A.I., 544
Senn, M., 258
Shepperson, G., 339
Sherman, C.B., 259, 260
Shibutanu, T., 130
Shin, E.H., 764
Shuval, J.T., 919
Shreiner, S.C. 695
Siegel, A.E., 556
Siegel, P.M., 309
Silverman, I., 799
Simmons, O.G., 423
Simpson, G.E., 224
Singh, B.K., 225
Sithole, N., 910
Sizemore, B.A., 800
Skeen, J.T., 545
Slavin, R.E., 861
Sly, D.F., 606
Smith, A.L., 546
Smith, C.U., 696, 765
Smythe, H.H., 1067
Sodhi, K.S., 15
Sorensen, A.B., 594
Sorkin, A.L., 394, 395
Sowell, T., 595, 766
Spain, D., 630

SUBJECT INDEX